OWN YOUR
FINANCIAL FREEDOM

OWN YOUR FINANCIAL FREEDOM

Money, women,
marriage and divorce

Andrea Kennedy

Marshall Cavendish
Editions

© 2014 Marshall Cavendish International (Asia) Private Limited
Text © 2014 Andrea Kennedy

Published by Marshall Cavendish Business
An imprint of Marshall Cavendish International
1 New Industrial Road, Singapore 536196

Other Marshall Cavendish Offices:
Marshall Cavendish Corporation. 99 White Plains Road, Tarrytown NY 10591-9001, USA • Marshall Cavendish International (Thailand) Co Ltd. 253 Asoke, 12th Flr, Sukhumvit 21 Road, Klongtoey Nua, Wattana, Bangkok 10110, Thailand • Marshall Cavendish (Malaysia) Sdn Bhd, Times Subang, Lot 46, Subang Hi-Tech Industrial Park, Batu Tiga, 40000 Shah Alam, Selangor Darul Ehsan, Malaysia.

Marshall Cavendish is a trademark of Times Publishing Limited

National Library Board Singapore Cataloguing in Publication Data
Kennedy, Andrea,
Own your financial freedom : money, women, marriage and divorce / Andrea Kennedy. – Singapore: Marshall Cavendish Editions, [2013]
pages cm
ISBN : 978-981-4484-00-8

1. Women – Finance, Personal. 2. Divorced women – Finance, Personal.
3. Financial security. 3. Investments. I. Title.

HG179
332.024008653 — dc23   OCN 861855401

Printed by Fabulous Printers Pte Ltd.

DEDICATION

*I would like to dedicate this book to
my mother, my sister and my daughter.*

ACKNOWLEDGEMENTS

I would like to acknowledge the following people for their patience, support and feedback in the writing of this book: J.R. Wu, Shelly Maneth, Jain R. Brown, Philippa Marriott, Leilani Ponzi, Dr. Susan Mistler, Janice Ngeow LLB, Mitchell Presnick, Dane Chamorro, Leigh Talmage Perez, Alexandra Morse, K. Fun Loh, Elaine Fong and David Steinglass.

I would also like to acknowledge my two children Stefan and Elena Chamorro for their patience and understanding while I wrote.

Finally, I would like to thank my tireless and extremely patient editor Katharine Carpenter and all the staff at Marshall Cavendish who have made this book possible.

CONTENTS

INTRODUCTION

IT'S YOUR MONEY, HONEY!

Back in late March 2008, a week or so after the investment bank Bear Stearns had collapsed, I had lunch in Hong Kong with one of the region's then leading pundits. An economist by training, he holds a PhD and has been in this region for decades. He is widely quoted by the local media and sought after by private banking institutions for his insights.

Now that Bear Stearns was ostensibly bankrupt, I asked him, "What happens next?" I asked this question because the markets were still acting erratic to say the least. Rents in Hong Kong had gone up 50 to 100% in a year but property prices were now plummeting. He smiled and reassured me with these exact words, "There is nothing to worry about. The markets have cleared. Now is as good a time as any to invest."

I found this comment ironic, given that *nine months prior* I was told to consider selling all but my most reliable investments.

What prompted me to sell was a breakfast conversation with a woman who was a long-time individual investor. Out of nowhere she asked me how much I had invested in the markets. I told her and she said, "The stock market will go down by 50% so you might want to take some money off the table." On the date of our conversation, the Dow Jones Industrial Average, the major US stock market index, was at 13,907.

I asked her why she was so concerned and she replied that she felt there had been too much easy money, and the markets had just run too far and too fast. She also added, "Honestly, I went to a home showing last week and I was sitting there with the local waitress from my diner, who was looking to buy the same home as me. I discreetly asked her how she could afford such an expensive property. This waitress told me the banks were 'givin' loans to everyone'."

Well, that was the nail in the coffin, so to speak. This woman left the showing, went home and began rearranging her stock, bond and cash positions over the next several months. As someone who had invested in financial and property markets for 40 years, she intuitively knew something was very wrong. She had no idea of the degree of financial chaos that was about to ensue but she suspected a banking crisis of some sort was not far off.

At the market bottom in 2008, the Dow Jones Industrial Average was at 6,626 (a crash of 50% as predicted!). By the end of 2008, her broker called her to let her know that she was only down 7%. The rest of the known world was in a panic and had lost somewhere in the range of 30 to 70% of their investments.

So, you are probably wondering who this woman is. You may be thinking that she worked on Wall Street or for a hedge fund. Or maybe she has some black belt in finance or some high-profile academic background that qualified her to know how fast and how hard the markets might fall. Or maybe she is a mathematical savant? Wrong, wrong, wrong, wrong and wrong.

She is my mother. My mother is a high-school graduate who was so afraid of maths that she had to be taught the subject by my father at age 22 (Chicago public schools for you). She then went on to teach herself more about financial markets, tax and accounting issues than anyone else I have ever met in my life.

My mother was named one of Chicago's top independent investors in the 1980s by Merrill Lynch. She has stared down market crashes, referring to them as "a sale at Saks Fifth Avenue", and bought when others were fearful. There has been much trial and error over the years, but my mother stuck to what worked for her, learnt from her mistakes and created a small fortune for their retirement.

I feel very fortunate to have been raised in this home as I was lucky to have a simple idea conveyed to me from a very young age, namely "It's Your Money, Honey". I was taught I didn't need a PhD or an MBA to invest my own money.

In our household, we unabashedly discussed managing and investing money. My father was an entrepreneur and my mother was the bookkeeper, billing manager, accountant and investment adviser. I realise that my life experience with money, particularly as a woman, is different to that of many people. And having the chance to help people develop the money management and investment skills my parents taught me is what brought me to practise financial planning.

I have encountered a variety of clients over the years with a myriad of different financial concerns. Some of these situations can be resolved through better planning and budgeting and others still through a more mature perspective on how to invest for the long term.

However, as I crossed the Rubicon into my forties, I realised that a growing number of clients were clearly dealing with more than the usual financial difficulties that needed a bit of tinkering to set right. Increasingly, clients faced some significant life change such as divorce, job loss or death of a life partner. So not only were they having to make decisions that could affect their immediate and long-term financial security, they were having to do so under a chronic cloud of emotional duress.

Divorcees struggle uniquely with money management issues before, during and after divorce. In fact, I've come to the conclusion that so much energy is spent on the emotions of the divorce (the grieving, the anger and the drama of dealing with ex-husbands, etc.) that finances go on the back burner, often for years. And yet even when finances are front and centre, the reality is that many people have never had the opportunity to develop the habits of successful money managers and individual investors.

Therefore, I have laid out a three-phase approach to guide anyone who is suddenly required to take over all aspects of money management from budgeting to cash flow management to long-term investing. These phases are Entitlement, Ownership and Empowerment. Each phase will guide you through a different stage of money management and touch on the psychological, legal and financial aspects of creating long-term financial stability.

Within these phases, I will allude to the Golden Rules of creating long-term financial stability. These Golden Rules are listed below.

MONEY MANAGEMENT RULES FOR LONG-TERM FINANCIAL STABILITY

Golden Rule One: Conquer the Zoo in You—You must be able to control your own mind to be able to control your own money.

Golden Rule Two: Savings Nirvana—You must get to a place of consistent, stable positive savings every month in order to adequately build a significant base of assets.

Golden Rule Three: Excess Debt Is for Dummies—There's good and bad credit; know the difference.

Golden Rule Four: Real Returns for the Real World—Face the reality of inflation head on.

Golden Rule Five: Tailored Plans Not Hand-me Downs—Tailor a savings and investment plan for you and you alone.

Golden Rule Six: Buy the Sale!—The price you pay for any investment matters, so develop the habits you need to spot a sale among different asset classes.

Golden Rule Seven: KISS—**Keep Investing Simple Sister!** Only invest in what you can understand and avoid complex financial strategies or investment vehicles.

Golden Rule Eight: Keep Investing Expenses Low—Make money for yourself, not the finance industry.

Golden Rule Nine: Commit to a Strategy—Know thyself and choose an investment strategy that aligns with your needs and temperament.

Golden Rule Ten: Slow and Steady Wins the Race—Investing is not a sport for adrenaline junkies.

SECTION 1
ENTITLEMENT

If you are reading this book, there's a good chance you are contemplating or initiating the process of divorce. Or possibly your spouse has admitted to having an affair or served you with divorce papers and you are not sure what to do next. If you have been served divorce papers, you will need to look into hiring a lawyer sooner rather than later in order to understand your legal rights and protect your financial assets. Do realise, however, that your lawyer (and your financial planner) can only help you embrace your legal rights and protect you financially in as much as you can help yourself.

What stops most women from fully embracing their legal and financial rights is fear. Sometimes that fear is based on a lack of information or understanding of how to proceed in the divorce. Fear can also be rooted in more long-standing psychological issues that have been with you longer than you have been married.

While you may feel anger and a myriad of other emotions, it's fear that leads to paralysis or self-destructive behaviour, which benefits no one during the divorce process. Fear can affect unequivocally your ability to get help, make sound rational decisions and gain access to the information you need to protect yourself in a divorce.

So if you have fears, they need to be acknowledged and faced before we dive into the details of your finances. You have to understand how you as an individual react to fear, and then arm yourself with the information you need to embrace your legal and financial rights. Consequently, Chapter 1 deals with the fear of being divorced and unrealistic expectations around money while Chapter 2 addresses the information gap you may be facing that is preventing you from handling your immediate financial and legal issues.

CHAPTER 1

FROM HOPELESSNESS TO HEALTHY ENTITLEMENT

> The most common way people give up their
> power is by thinking they don't have any.
> —*Alice Walker*

There is always a straw that breaks the camel's back in divorce. It can be as simple as a "final slight", a moment of disrespect that was the culmination of so many unhappy years of marriage or as dramatic as a husband deeply deceiving or abusing his wife to the point of endangering her health and welfare.

While most women initiate divorce, some women are on the receiving end of a divorce. Women being served divorce papers often feel ambushed and shocked because the perception of their marriage changes so dramatically and irreparably. Their deepest insecurities rise to the surface and they may feel a perceived loss of face within their peer groups and families, which lead to feelings of shame or failure.

Women initiating divorce are generally in a more proactive place because they have already taken the first step. But very often, by the time a woman chooses to divorce, she is drained of energy from years of struggling with an unhappy marriage. Humans, by nature, do not like dramatic change and this is why most people tolerate an unhappy marriage until they are pushed to a point of emotional depletion, and the only choice left is to divorce.

Regardless of who is asking for the divorce, people go through the same stages of mourning that are experienced with the death of a spouse: shock, anger, grief and then acceptance. It is completely normal and expected that you will feel each of these emotions. What is important, however, is that you get through these stages not paralysed with fear but, instead, with a sense of Healthy Entitlement.

HEALTHY ENTITLEMENT

Healthy Entitlement is a mindset. It has nothing to do with who has asked for the divorce and why. Rather it has everything to do with your level of self-esteem, namely how you gauge your value as an individual and your contributions within a marriage.

When you approach divorce in a mindset of Healthy Entitlement, you

- know you deserve to be treated with respect
- approach divorce in the here and now
- know you can only control your own actions (and reactions)
- have a realistic sense of your contributions within the marriage (For the record, being a full-time mother is a contribution!)

- have an understanding of your legal rights within your jurisdiction, or territory
- have a sense of what you own in terms of property and assets
- are not using the divorce platform for revenge, tempting as that may be

Healthy Entitlement, however, is easier to write about than to feel. With the onset of divorce, healthy self-esteem can give way to deep-seated insecurities, and this is where fear takes control. These fears can interfere with your perceptions around entitlement, or what you feel you deserve financially and legally.

This leads me to the first rule of money management: **How you control your own thoughts, or how they control you, is the most important aspect of successfully handling the divorce process and your money thereafter.** Someone who can tame their fears and self-doubt can achieve Healthy Entitlement more easily than someone who lets their fears overwhelm their thoughts.

As already mentioned, getting to a state of Healthy Entitlement is easier said than done because a lack of information and a flood of emotions, such as the numbing feeling of shock or betrayal, fear of being on your own and unrealistic monetary expectations, all cloud the ability to think analytically. To better understand where your head might be at, you need to understand how we are wired as humans to react to fear and stress.

HOW FEAR AND STRESS AFFECT OUR DECISIONS

For even the most euphoric divorcees—the ones literally grabbing their children and fleeing out the front door—divorce can provoke anxiety. On top of anxiety, separating from a significant other can also bring all your fears of abandonment and the unknown to the surface.

How people react, or act out, is wide and varied and depends entirely on their emotional state. When confronted with the prospect of divorce, some people act out aggressively against their spouses through revenge spending or "back at you" affairs. Many other women go into denial, passively self-abusing with alcohol or eating disorders, while others drop out of circulation altogether. None of these are useful coping mechanisms when divorcing. You need energy, health and strength, not to mention focus.

Why we react in these ways is brilliantly chronicled in the book *Mind over Money* by psychologists Brad and Ted Klontz PhD. The Klontzes note in the chapter "The Zoo in You" that our ability to process our fears analytically and rationally is often at odds with how nature has wired our brains to react to fear. To summarise: How our brains have developed over millions of years in order to survive in the wild does not help us make cogent, rational decisions under duress in the 21st century.

As the Klontzes note, the oldest and most developed parts of our brain are the limbic system and the cerebellum (or, if you will, our monkey and lizard brains). And not the analytical "scientific" brain we engage regularly to make "rational" decisions. In normal circumstances, our analytical brain works together with these older "wild" brains to navigate us through our more subtle, empirical and complex human world.

However, when confronted with situations that bring on fearful feelings, where we have not been taught the appropriate coping skills, nature's more simplistic defence mechanisms kick in and our inner zoo takes charge. These animal brains are stronger and faster than our analytical brain and they go into defence mechanism mode by using their own circuitry to bypass our analytical brain altogether.

These defence mechanisms, namely fighting, freezing up and fleeing, evolved to help us react to physical danger. For example, if you meet a tiger in the jungle, you run or if you encounter a large slithering snake, you freeze. However helpful these defence mechanisms might be in the jungle, they do not help us cope with the complexity of divorce or long-term financial decisions. Instead, these mechanisms have us react to many issues around divorce in ways that are short term and counterproductive. I've seen women giving up their homes, their rights to future income and so on in the face of fear.

We must therefore train ourselves to over-ride these knee-jerk "wild reactions" to feelings of fear that hold us captive to negative thought or, worse, keep us in a permanent state of denial. Recognising how you react to fear and stress is half the battle to conquering it and regaining control of your longer-term decision-making abilities.

RECOGNISING HOW YOU REACT TO FEAR

Although this book is about creating optimal awareness to make good financial decisions, you first need to recognise how you react to fear so that you can leave your fears behind and move towards a place of Healthy Entitlement.

When you react to fear in an unproductive way, a certain pattern of thought reoccurs often enough to create a self-fulfilling prophecy and then a prism, or mind-trap, through which you see everything. These mind-traps interfere with a woman's ability to help herself and, as a result, lead to unfavourable divorce settlements and/or ongoing financial difficulties post-divorce. I call them mind-traps because with the right self-awareness, you can free yourself from them.

Learned Helplessness

Helplessness means that people give up trying to improve their situation, even if the opportunity to do so is present. Learned Helplessness takes this concept one step further, meaning that over time people feel they cannot change their situation for the better because they have past, repeated experiences of failure. As a result, these people perceive themselves as victims and their inaction perpetuates a cycle of defeat and victimhood.

"Feeling powerless" is the feeling most associated with helplessness. It usually stems from a number of previous life experiences, not just the marital relationship, and can afflict anyone of any status. I've known very wealthy divorcees who were kept so financially in the dark that they had no idea if they owned the flat in which they were residing—and they felt too powerless to even ask!

Feeling helpless sometimes stems from a fear of being left by your husband, a will-he-or-won't-he-leave-me feeling. This is more common after children are born, when there is poor communication and/or if financial dependency on him has tilted the power in the marriage far out of balance.

The financially dependent woman is often unaware of her and her husband's overall financial situation because she has always left the investing to her spouse. Or, in other cases, she manages the bills but is not empowered to control household spending.

The one common factor among women who feel helpless is that they are not involved in the family finances as much as they should be. Some of these women may even be the main breadwinners but have left the investments and money management to their husbands.

Generally speaking, women who suffer from helplessness tend to retreat into denial or flee the situation when confronted with divorce. Part of this is a natural response to coping with shock but if she retreats too much for too long, she can short-change herself in the divorce process. Furthermore, instead of getting help to find the way forward, she tries to handle it alone until it is too late.

In some cases though, the helpless woman doesn't seem powerless at all. She acts out, using provocation as a means to get attention, through aggressive behaviour (shopping sprees, heavy drinking, flagrant affairs, etc.) as if to dare the end of the marriage. And in many cases, her husband may respond in kind.

A person lacking the self-control or the necessary self-awareness to resolve her marital problems productively is not a powerful person who understands her entitlements within a marriage. Instead she is more like a helpless person acting out because her lack of power makes her feel fearful.

Take the case of Aisah who worked at the same company as her expatriate husband. Shortly after the birth of their second child, he began running up credit card bills which they had trouble paying. As the sole breadwinner during her maternity leave, he felt that he could run up his credit cards as much as he liked, regardless of the family debt load.

What was really going on was that he was having an affair with a co-worker. Aisah felt a sense of deep shame and embarrassment when she learnt of the affair. She moved out of their flat and into government housing, taking the two children with her. She did not expect or feel entitled to the home they owned; she just wanted to leave, or flee, as fast as she could to get away from her husband. Her husband's new girlfriend moved into the marital flat and he provided little or no support to his children but continued to run up debt under a joint account. Aisah quit her well-paid job and took a salary demotion to join another company so that she did not have to see her husband at work every day. At the same time, she took her children out of their school and moved them to a more affordable one.

I spoke to Aisah on behalf of a client of mine who encouraged her to seek legal and financial opinions. Aisah said to me on a number of occasions, "I knew something like this might happen" and "My parents always said I was lucky to marry at all." Aisah clearly feared confronting her husband and had shame issues around money and wealth.

Aisah's helplessness and feelings of shame betrayed what was best for her and her children as well as allowed her husband to walk off with more than his share of the assets and renege on child support. Aisah's lack of willingness to confront her situation head-on and seek help meant her financial situation continued to deteriorate, along with her self-esteem.

While you may feel ashamed about the subject of divorce, you will feel more ashamed and do more damage to yourself in the long run if you do not reach a point of Healthy Entitlement— knowing what you need and what is legally yours. It is about coming to terms with the reality of your situation and being as prepared as you can to enable you to move forwards and embrace a new vision of your life post-divorce.

Below are common thoughts that fall within the realm of Learned Helplessness:

- I have been lucky to have been married at all.
- I need others to approve of me.
- I felt something like this (divorce, betrayal, etc.) might happen.
- I am not good enough.

- I am ashamed and cannot talk to anyone about this.
- Good things only happen to other people/clever people/ beautiful people.
- My parents think I was lucky to have found someone who wanted to marry me in the first place.
- I am afraid of what my husband will do if …
- I am afraid or ashamed of what people will think.

The helpless woman needs to change radically her belief system about money, herself and the possibilities in life. If you are experiencing Learned Helplessness, you must make a conscious decision in a step-by-step manner to move away from the fears that restrain you and get yourself onto the road that leads to entitlement, ownership and empowerment over your life's affairs.

Unhealthy Entitlement

On the other end of the spectrum from Learned Helplessness is Unhealthy Entitlement (UE), or the world of "could have beens", "should have beens" and "would have beens". A woman experiencing UE issues has usually been in the marriage for a number of years and hoped for progress only to feel somehow disappointed in the end, regardless of who is divorcing whom.

A woman trapped in a UE mindset most likely entered her marriage assuming it would turn out very differently. Often this is the result of unrealistic expectations centred around the kind of person she married and what she expected her husband was going to bring to the table, financially, socially or a combination of the two.

The UE woman is often fixated on getting a return on her "investment" in the marriage beyond what is possible or realistic. This leaves her frozen and unable to move on to a new and improved vision of her own life. Let me illustrate this using the following two examples.

In the first case, Angela called me in distress when her husband asked for a divorce. A mother of one, she was distraught as she had envisaged her life as the wife of a banker turning out rather differently than it had. Despite a history of mixed feelings and second thoughts during her marriage, she had stuck with the relationship, quitting her job and moving with him from place to place as he tried to establish himself professionally.

I could tell that Angela was in a state of shock. Her conversation looped away from concrete problem-solving steps and back to comments such as "I thought marrying a banker was the smart thing to do" and "He had so many opportunities that he never took advantage of."

Nonetheless, Angela insisted that she felt comforted because her husband had been cordial and had "promised to do right by them". Regardless, I asked her to touch base with at least two lawyers immediately to determine what jurisdiction would most favour her situation and how best to proceed legally.

Shortly thereafter, another acquaintance, Priya, told me that she had decided to leave her husband after years of verbal abuse as she felt the abuse would eventually turn physical. On top of this, he was an alcoholic and would not seek treatment for his problems.

To make matters worse, he was so controlling that he had engaged every top divorce lawyer in town to block her chances of finding good legal representation. When I asked her about her finances, she knew every account and asset down to the last cent but told me, "I just want to get divorced, take my kids, return to Hong Kong and go back to work."

Now, as Priya had initiated the divorce, you may think that she was in a "better place" than Angela. Truth be told, unless you have lived with an abusive alcoholic, you probably wouldn't be able to begin to comprehend the living hell she had been through during her marriage. There is nothing more damaging to a woman's self-esteem than living with a violent and abusive drunk while trying to shelter and take care of three small children.

However, what Priya had in her corner was a sense of Healthy Entitlement: (a) prioritisation of purpose, i.e. to protect herself and her children, (b) clarity of a plan, namely to relocate to a place where she had some support and (c) a comprehensive list of what she and her husband owned together.

Over the next several months, Angela remained in a mental fog with the help of anti-depressants. She made a few phone calls, though in her words, half-heartedly and found herself mulling the past while mired in indecision and inertia. Predictably, the next call I received from Angela found her in a state of panic. Her husband had started to take large sums out of one of their joint bank accounts.

Of course he was, no one was there to stop him.

Angela had not taken the initiative to protect herself in any way during the previous six months because she had been caught up in what "should have been". She had not come to terms with what she needed for herself and her child nor was she aware of what she was legally entitled to as she had not taken up any offers of help.

Priya, on the other hand, had gone to great lengths to find and secure legal representation. As she had reached out for help, her lawyer was able to help protect the bulk of the assets until the divorce proceedings were over. At the very least, Priya knew that she deserved a life free of fear and abuse. The dream of marriage with that particular man may have died but she already had a new vision of a better future in place.

Common thoughts in the realm of Unhealthy Entitlement include:

- I expect to have the things my friends have.
- I expect a large settlement/significant maintenance.
- If he made more money, I would be happier because I would be able to ask for more in the settlement.
- My friends all married financially successful men or men who have well-paid jobs (and I didn't).

- I expected him to make more money.
- I want him to get a better job to support my lifestyle.
- I thought that marrying a foreigner/banker/doctor would give me happiness/a different lifestyle than I had growing up.

Some women may feel that the concept of Unhealthy Entitlement smacks of giving up more than what they feel they are entitled to. This is not what this is suggesting. What you feel you are entitled to though has to make sense within the realm of what you own, what is earned, what your husband can realistically pay and/or what you would be awarded based on the laws of your jurisdiction.

Nearly every woman has moments of Learned Helplessness or Unhealthy Entitlement at the end of her marriage—it is only natural when faced with fear and regrets. What is not natural is becoming a prisoner to either of these ways of thinking.

Recognising Outdated Thought Patterns

As noted above in the sections on Learned Helplessness and Unhealthy Entitlement, much of what we think does not begin at the start of marriage. How our beliefs about ourselves and the world around us evolve have been formulated over a long period of time.

The third mind-trap—Outdated Thought Patterns—speaks to the warnings and advice that have been passed down to you since childhood. These thought patterns are wedged firmly into your psyche because you have heard them so often that you do not regard them as "opinion" but as "the truth".

Here are some examples of Outdated Thought Patterns:

- Don't ever invest in the stock market, you'll never make money.
- Don't trust men, they all cheat and lie.
- If you do not go to a good college, you won't be successful.
- Women don't make good investors.

Okay, I can dispel these views as fast as I typed them out. The world is full of examples of successful stock market investors, honest men, college dropouts who are billionaires and exceptional women investors. However, the person with an over-reliance on Outdated Thought Patterns will have a very difficult time believing any other reality. And when a person has believed someone else's opinions for a long time, they leave little time to form their own opinions.

While the advice and experiences of others can be helpful, they can also be destructive and self-limiting. Yet when under stress, many people turn to these thought patterns, which contain beliefs about what we were told the world is like, not how it actually is, and then play these "old comfort tapes" in their heads.[1]

Let me give you an example. I was advising a working single mother who, mid-divorce, insisted on renting accommodation

---

1 Outdated Thought Patterns and old comfort tapes are similar concepts to the "generational tapes" introduced by the Klontzes in *Mind over Money*.

instead of keeping her home even though she could afford to do so. I remember asking her why she had chosen to sell and move back into rented accommodation. She replied, "My mother says single women do not own homes."

At first, I was shocked that anyone would believe such a comment but then I realised there was a reason why my client's mother felt this way. The home was mortgaged and what her mother feared was not home ownership, but debt. This is because when her mother was young, forty years ago, single women couldn't even get an appointment with a banker, let alone a mortgage.

Regardless of her healthy financial position, my client actually believed that she did not have the right to own her own home because she was single. Her mother had spoken throughout her life with such powerful conviction about what women could and could not do financially that these beliefs had become embedded in my client's mind as "the truth".

The impact of parental experience is powerful everywhere, but even more so in Asia because of the tradition of filial piety (the virtue of respect for your parents and ancestors). Most parents have only the best intentions at heart for their children but almost everyone has heard outdated advice from well-meaning relatives.

To begin clearing your mind of Outdated Thought Patterns is to ask yourself if what you think is based on your own experience or on the past successes and failures of others. Don't end up viewing the world through the prism of another generation. And as we will see in chapters 7 to 10, when it comes to creating a financial plan and investing your money, it has to be a plan that works for you given your circumstances, which may well be different to those of your parents.

So, as part of your march towards Healthy Entitlement, you need to revisit how embedded the opinions of other authority figures are in your mind, and how these influence your decision-making. Reflect on when the advice of others has served you well, and when it has not. Then filter out what advice does and doesn't advance your long-term financial well-being.

HOW MUCH ENERGY SHOULD YOU EXERT?

Every divorcee has her work cut out for her in terms of taking care of herself, her family and her financial health. And this will need to be done while going through a cycle of grief, fear and/or anger. Now that you know what Healthy Entitlement does and does not look like, consider how much energy you want to throw at things you cannot control or change.

The reality is that you cannot control what your soon-to-be ex does and says any more, or at least not for much longer, except in some cases through a court order. There is little you can do if he lies or tells half-truths or makes promises that he cannot keep, thus disappointing you or your children. So why spend a lot of time trying to control things that you now have little or no control over?

Now consider how much time and energy you should devote to constructive action every day. As you will see later, money and time have a unique relationship. The longer you delay confronting the real issues that you can exert some control over, including fears about finances, the more worries you will have down the road.

As one perceptive client said, "It's one of the worst experiences you can go through, but do not let your divorce define the rest of your life." Start today trying to visualise what a positive and productive life can look like after your divorce. Even if you can only devote one hour a day to productively moving forward, do so. Be assured that once you feel a sense of Healthy Entitlement around your divorce, these feelings will begin to flow into every corner of your life.

I would recommend seeing a therapist if you feel stuck and unable to move forward without professional help. Some low-cost options are listed in "Resources" on pages 369–376.

CHAPTER 2

DOS AND DON'TS IN THE LEAD-UP TO DIVORCE

PLAN YOUR WAY TO HEALTHY ENTITLEMENT

The road to divorce begins with preparation. In order to understand what you are entitled to, you need to be familiar with the law in your jurisdiction and know what assets you own as a couple (referred to as the "matrimonial pot" by lawyers). As the legal aspect of divorce and how much you are entitled to in the financial settlement are covered in Appendix 1, this chapter will focus on the monetary issues that need to be addressed as quickly and as early as possible in the divorce process.

Money issues take centre stage in divorce for very practical reasons. You should fight for what you believe you are entitled to, but you can work towards a state of Healthy Entitlement faster by taking a realistic approach to claiming assets and/or requesting monthly maintenance and child support. All too often, money becomes the platform through which a couple acts out power issues and other underlying causes of their marital problems. Such fighting can make divorce vengeful and scarring as it provokes emotions that waste time, money and energy.

While reading through this chapter, keep reminding yourself that you have a choice as to how you behave and what you act upon or react to during the process. As you will see in later chapters, financial security often has less to do with your settlement and more to do with how you end up managing your post-divorce finances.

HAVING PLAN A: KNOWLEDGE IS POWER

People working towards Healthy Entitlement take the necessary actions to protect themselves even before the divorce papers are formally filed. In addition, if you get organised and know what you want from your divorce, your lawyer will be able to act more effectively and efficiently.

THE DOS AND DON'TS

The dos and don'ts below cover information that your lawyer will need. Do be aware, however, that the information needs of your lawyer may vary depending on your location. Nevertheless, the checklist is fairly comprehensive and has been broken down into five easy-to-follow stages. If you are in the early stages of divorce and are uncertain as to what beneficial steps you should be taking, following this checklist is a good start.

If you have been presented with divorce papers, go straight to Stage II. Start interviewing lawyers and ensure that they take the necessary actions to protect your interests. Then read "Divorce—The Legal Procedure" in Appendix 1.

Taking Action

One of the first of many issues that your lawyer will be responsible for during the divorce process is taking precautions to ensure that your interests are protected until the final settlement is reached. These precautions may include but are not limited to the following:

- protecting bank accounts to ensure neither party drains the accounts

- ensuring that your husband does not cut off any credit cards that you need to have access to

- receiving monthly maintenance payments until the proceedings are finalised, if necessary

- ensuring any financial obligations continue to be paid, such as mortgage payments, school fees and so on

PRE-DIVORCE DOS

STAGE I

Lay a Foundation of Privacy and Estimate Your Needs

Many women worry about "getting cut off" or not having access to money to even begin divorce proceedings. This stage is about trying to re-establish yourself independently BEFORE you get divorced, as much as that is possible, and estimating your financial needs during and after your divorce.

- Women who are solely dependent on their spouses for access to credit or money should set aside "fighting funds", i.e. cash and valuables that are stored in a safe deposit box or with trusted relatives. Your lawyer, once you hire one, will tell you that you will need to declare these assets.

- If you have no means for fighting funds, you can borrow money from friends or family or apply for legal aid to hire a lawyer. In most developed countries, a lawyer can make a request through the courts that your household be maintained financially (the bills continue to get paid) until a settlement is reached.

- Be discreet and set up a private email account that only you and your lawyer will know about.

- Get a PO box or an alternative mailing address to your home address so that private mail from banks and/or lawyers can be sent there.

- Add up your usual monthly expenses. This is your budget. It should cover rent/mortgage, school fees, insurance if applicable, food and other necessities. You should have a range in mind for a monthly budget when you meet with your lawyer.

- Open a bank account in your own name and establish credit by getting a credit card in your own name too, independent of your spouse, if possible.

- Get a feel for what is in the matrimonial pot as it will be reviewed to settle your divorce. List out your assets or the things you own: bank accounts, insurance policies, brokerage accounts, trusts, property, pensions, expensive art or jewellery and so on. If there is a will, much of this will be listed in it if it is up to date. So get a copy of the will as this can be a good starting list of the assets that are owned.

- Make note as well of what is owed, jointly and individually. Whatever you owe are your liabilities. Liabilities include mortgages, personal loans, loans tied to companies or partnerships, credit card debt, etc.
- If you are unsure how to meet your expected financial needs after divorce, meet with a certified financial planner (CFP). Lawyers can only help navigate you to a settlement; a CFP can show you what your finances can look like 15 to 20 years down the road.

A note on hiding assets: You will be told to declare all your assets by your lawyer. If you have to go in front of a judge and hidden assets are found, the judge will not view this favourably and will very likely penalise you with the fees it took to find those assets. While people do hide assets, it is getting harder and harder to do so because bank secrecy laws are weakening and money trails are getting easier to track.

Stage II
Interview and Retain Legal Representation

You will have a professional relationship with your lawyer. Therefore, you will need to understand the scope of their services and what role you will play in your own divorce proceedings. The more organised you are and the more you know what you want from your divorce, the more effective and efficient your lawyer can be.

- Interview as many lawyers as necessary until you find a suitable lawyer whose style and personality matches your own. Find someone with whom you can speak openly, who meets your needs and who you feel may be able to persuade your spouse IF you plan to settle out of court. A word of caution: If there is not a lot of money involved, partners of large firms will often pass you off to an associate who may be less experienced.

- When you find a lawyer with whom you are comfortable, engage the lawyer by paying a retainer to establish the relationship so that your spouse cannot engage the same firm. Paying a retainer is generally a requirement of most firms and worth doing to get the lawyer you want. It is worth mentioning that both you and your spouse cannot be represented by the same lawyer or firm as it's considered a conflict of interest.

- Make sure that you ask your lawyer about their fees and how the divorce can be handled efficiently, as well as how legal fees can balloon. You will be shocked at how quickly the costs can spiral out of control. As a rule of thumb, however, the more amicable the proceedings and the less discovery involved, the cheaper the divorce.

- The local "shark" can be useful to force a quick agreement if they can get the job done the most efficiently.

- Depending on what stage of the divorce you are at, have your lawyer do what is necessary to protect any asset upon which you might have a claim.

If you feel you cannot afford a lawyer, a list of legal aid and community centre support is given in "Resources" on pages 369–376.

STAGE III
Information Gathering for Discovery

Discovery is the process by which your lawyer proves what you both actually own. This information will also serve as a paper trail that will justify your lifestyle and your spouse's earning history as well as act as a means to track any odd financial behaviour. At the outset, only provide copies of what your lawyer requests as lawyers charge by the hour and you don't want to give them unnecessary paperwork.

- Find all the documentation you can on sources of income (salary, bonuses, commission payments, dividend income from investments or partnerships). This could include business contracts, salary contracts and tax returns.

- Find documentation on all assets (titles to properties, bank records, pension records, life insurance, shareholder documents that represent company ownership, trust documents, etc.) and liabilities (loan agreements, mortgages, credit card statements). If this information is kept on a computer, download it or get a technician to copy the hard drive. If the computer is password protected by your husband, don't do anything until you have spoken to your lawyer as there are legal issues that you need to be made aware of.

- Take a formal inventory of all items of value that you own, including jewellery, art, furniture, cars, boats, wine collections, etc.
- If you suspect a mistress or a second family is being supported, you can try to track transfers or payments to these third parties through bank accounts and credit card charges. Illegitimate children and mistresses rarely, if ever, take precedence over the wife and legitimate children in a divorce settlement.

For the most controlling of spouses, clients have had to make copies of keys, go to the local land registry to confirm that they owned the home in which they resided and even rummage through the rubbish to uncover some of this information. Get creative but be wary of doing anything illegal.

Stage IV
Insurance and Pensions

If you are dependent on your spouse, it is likely that you are covered for medical insurance and are listed as a beneficiary on his life insurance policy and in a will if there is one. How insurance is handled through the transition and post-divorce phase is crucial if you remain financially dependent on your spouse, if you or your children have special health needs and/ or do not have access to a universal healthcare system.

- Go through all of your insurance policies (medical, life and others) and make sure you are aware of all the policies that involve you and your children and how you benefit from them. (If you know your benefits before you get divorced, you can then try to fight to have similar benefits post-divorce.)

- Make sure you understand what life insurance policies (term, whole life, annuities, endowment, etc.) exist and who the beneficiaries are. As part of the settlement, if you receive maintenance, try to remain as the **irrevocable beneficiary** of a life insurance policy on your ex whereby you are the policyholder and make the payments (out of your maintenance) to ensure the policy remains in force. For more on this, refer to "Inflation and Insurance: Safeguarding Your Payments" in Appendix 1.

- You should also check to see the provisions of any pension to which he is entitled.

Stage V
Gathering Hard-to-Come-by Information

The most common means of sheltering income and assets are trusts, offshore companies (companies established in the British Virgin Islands (BVI) or other tax havens) and family businesses. These financial entities would have to be uncovered under the discovery phase (*see* Stage III) of your divorce. Trying to unravel these more complex financial entities often involves a longer discovery phase and the hiring of specialists, both of which can add to the expense of your divorce.

Here are some of the most common financial vehicles used to shelter assets and how specialists try to determine if they exist and their value:

Trusts. If you have married into a wealthy family, there is a very good chance that part of your spouse's income is derived from a trust and that any assets are held under a family trust. While you may not be able to win any portion of the assets in a trust, the tactic here is that you have established some standard lifestyle throughout your marriage which you can document through monthly bank and credit card statements. Your lawyer can make the case that you are accustomed to a particular lifestyle and intend to be maintained as such post-divorce.

Family Businesses. Similar to trusts, with most family businesses, it is hard to untangle the assets of just one family member, so lawyers often will hire accountants to help assess the value of these entities. You need to consult your lawyer as to what would be the best strategy here and be aware of the costs that go into the discovery process in terms of hiring specialists. In the past, courts loathed having businesses sold to settle divorce claims. This, however, is changing.

Offshore Companies. With BVI and other tax-haven-based companies, it is nearly impossible to find out what is held under a BVI company and who the owner is. However, laws are rapidly changing in regard to tax havens and account secrecy. If your spouse is sheltering income in a BVI company, the best way to track the flow of funds is to look through onshore bank records. The money to establish a BVI company would have to have come from a normal onshore bank account, and there are likely subsequent flows in and out to a normal onshore account.

Safe Deposit Boxes. Keeping a safe deposit box is a very simple way to hide assets, most notably cash, condo keys, insurance policies and smaller items such as watches, gold coins, diamonds and jewellery. You would have to locate the key or some record of a safe deposit box to know that one exists.

If you are the one holding the majority of assets, then you may be advised to use trusts and offshore companies to protect your assets, particularly those acquired before marriage. Be aware that you generally will need to disclose these in the proceedings. Of course, many people get away with sheltering assets, however, you should appreciate how hiding assets may look if they are found and your case goes in front of a judge.

Preparing for divorce as much as possible by working through this Do checklist will help you feel organised, empowered and in control so that you can manage not only the divorce process but also your lawyers. If you have been served the divorce papers, then these steps will bring you closer to Healthy Entitlement as being organised should allow you to conserve your energy, your time and your money during your divorce proceedings.

While the Dos list is mostly action-oriented, the Don'ts list revolves more around behaviour and mindset recommendations. Going through the motions of getting yourself organised will keep your mind focused.

PRE-DIVORCE DON'TS

You, Your Family and Your Home

- Don't sell the marital home until it is clear who benefits from the sale in your divorce.
- Don't leave your home unless you or your children are faced with physical abuse. Stand your ground and get your spouse to rent alternative accommodation. This is doubly true if you have children and are the primary caregiver. It doesn't matter who is seeking the divorce.
- Don't disrupt your children's activities or schoolwork. It's your divorce, not theirs.
- Don't take your children out of their school in preparation for some worst-case scenario that may never happen.
- Don't overuse or abuse drugs or alcohol. You need to sleep, eat well, exercise and keep your mind strong and clear. Good health is necessary for good money management.

Your Lawyer

- Don't use your lawyer as a psychologist or financial planner. Lawyers are not qualified to do either and will charge by the hour just to listen.
- Don't expect your lawyer to read your mind. Make up your mind as to what you want out of the divorce and how you want your lawyer to proceed once you've read "Divorce—The Legal Procedure" in Appendix 1.

Your Money Behaviour

- Don't begin to exhibit extremely frugal, uncharacteristic or exorbitant spending patterns. Keep your spending as "per the norm" as this establishes a normal budget and spending pattern for your family.
- Many women are told not to get a job, even if one is available, as it will affect their monthly maintenance settlement. The idea behind this is that you may be able to receive some (or more) maintenance if you are not employed and thus completely financially dependent. This is a tricky issue and should be considered on a case-by-case basis. If you find yourself in this predicament, here are some questions that you should ask yourself:
  - » Can your husband financially afford to maintain two homes and two lifestyles in the way you are both accustomed? If not, do you want to pass up the chance to work and create some means to maintain your

lifestyle should the settlement end up being less than you want or expect?

» Do you want to forego an opportunity for independence?

» Is working part-time an option until a settlement is reached?

Many judges, if your divorce goes to court, will look at your work history and education anyway and whether you are able to work. They often factor in your ability to work, age, time out of the workforce, the needs of your children and so forth when making an assumption of your earning capacity in the final settlement decision.

The Kuok's Divorce and Settlement Assumptions

• Don't compare your divorce with someone else's divorce. Every divorce is different and there is no guarantee that you will get a divorce settlement as good (or as bad) as that person's. Focus on what you can control by going through the Pre-Divorce Dos checklist.

• Don't go into your divorce assuming that there will be a 50/50 split. The court looks at many factors such as direct and indirect contributions, earning capacities of the parties and so on.

• Don't assume that it will feel "fair". Very rarely do both parties leave the divorce proceedings feeling the settlement was fair.

- Don't assume you have the rights to assets acquired prior to marriage. It is important that you seek legal advice on this issue as it is jurisdiction dependent.
- Don't consider what your girlfriends think to be actual legal advice. This is why you hire a lawyer.
- Don't get revenge for revenge's sake. Use your divorce to get what you are entitled to and move on.
- Don't rely on the rumour mill. When it comes to your settlement, prepare for the worst and hope for the best.

A BRIEF POINT ABOUT DISCRETION—IT MATTERS

In addition to having a plan, wise divorcees know that discretion matters. You will never be able to control what others think, not for very long at least, but you can control your own actions. So if the possibility of divorce is on the cards or if the process has begun, keep it between you, your lawyer and only your most trusted confidantes.

The best confidantes can add value if they know the divorce process and can be quietly supportive. Discretion can give you an upper hand and some dignity through the process while a lack of discretion can torpedo your ability to get a proper settlement.

Take the case of Carina, an acquaintance, who told her entire social set she wanted a divorce before she broke the news to her spouse. Talking it out gave Carina courage but her spouse became suspicious about the change in her behaviour. His insecurity led him to put his own plans in motion, namely hiding the assets of his advertising agency in an offshore account.

Once their divorce became public, it became a real-life soap opera among their friends. Carina believed the grapevine assurances from people who said things like "I told your spouse to do right by you and he said he would." As if such self-important busybodies could actually sway a settlement! Unfortunately, Carina believed they could.

So instead of planning and preparing for her divorce, Carina relied on gossip to get a feel for everything from the process to the settlement. Her friends had large settlements, so why wouldn't she? In the end, Carina received no division of assets and now lives from maintenance cheque to maintenance cheque.

These "tribes" on either side can muddy the waters and confuse the couple divorcing, making settlement all the more difficult. So once you decide to divorce, keep it as private as possible. Don't make it a drama du jour among your social set.

Remember Healthy Entitlement is not about rumours, innuendo or emotions. It is about facing difficult situations with the right intent and the right information. The more energy you spend learning about your assets, the legal process and the sources of income you can rely on in the future, the closer you will get to a place of Healthy Entitlement.

SECTION 2
OWNERSHIP

The first two chapters covered the concept of Healthy Entitlement and coming to grips with what you would receive in the settlement. The next three chapters will focus on your relationship to money, namely how you spend it and what you think it can or cannot do for you and your family. This is about owning your financial decisions, because how you manage your settlement is now entirely up to you.

The challenges that you will face in what I refer to as "Phase II" are often the greatest. Immediately after divorce, many women feel a newfound sense of freedom or even euphoria. Such feelings may stem from the fact that you have been awarded a large settlement or you feel liberated and able to get on with life now that emotional scars are healing. Interestingly, this phase happens to coincide with a time when money is most poorly spent as divorcees seek to reinvent their lives.

So before putting any plans for reinvention into gear, you will need to first put your day-to-day budget in order. By doing this, ideally, you can create positive monthly cash flow or a budget that will allow you to live off your lump sum settlement as far as this is possible. Creating a realistic budget that you can live off is essential, otherwise you will find yourself lurching from month to month or year to year wondering how you are going to make ends meet. Budgeting will enable you to begin to lay a realistic foundation for long-term financial security while you are adjusting to your new status post-divorce.

In order to achieve the above, you will have to own your own decisions about money. You will also need to communicate to and involve anyone, i.e. your children, extended family and sometimes even friends, who needs to hear and understand about how you will be handling your money from now on.

CHAPTER 3

THE ART OF
CONSCIOUS SPENDING

No problem can be solved from the same
level of consciousness that created it.
—*Albert Einstein*

SHORT-TERM SELF-CONTROL = LONG-TERM FINANCIAL STABILITY

While money means different things to different people, such as freedom, love, happiness and status, it means "financial security" to most divorcees. Most women genuinely want to feel financially self-sufficient and able to provide for themselves. Thus it is understandable if women facing or going through divorce have nightmares about running out of money or depending on others for handouts.

Long-term financial stability is a rational concern, and to address it you need to take a rational approach to your day-to-day fiscal management. This will put you in control of financial decisions in the short term so that you have financial stability in the long term.

Ideally, prior to divorce, you would have prepared a set budget for living off based on a monthly income assumption. Realistically though, most people need to develop not only new spending habits but also **a new relationship with money** in the wake of divorce. This is because old spending habits and expectations around the availability of money may not fit the new budget.

To prepare you to be the fiscal manager, or chief financial officer (CFO), of your household, this chapter will cover:

- household cash flow and balance sheet
- strategies to develop a pattern of "conscious spending"
- how to determine your savings ratio
- wants versus needs
- the necessity of emergency money
- why you need Plan B
- eliminating credit card debt

How much money you feel you need in order to be happy may vary from person to person. However, your ability for self-control will truly be your greatest asset in creating financial security in the long run.

TAP INTO YOUR INNER MRS WATANABE: HOW TO BE THE CFO OF YOUR HOME

Economists put forth a number of reasons as to how Japan, after living through nearly 20 years of recession, can still have one of the world's wealthiest middle classes. It is an economic phenomenon of sorts. The government is a basket case and the banks still seem dysfunctional but the households are cashed up despite stagnating wages and depressed asset values.

Experts say Japanese households are still cash rich due to the Japanese currency, the yen, which has remained strong over the years, thwarting the impact of inflation. Some say it is Japan's "tradition of saving". Others say it's the sense of "shared sacrifice" as a nation so the middle class has not got richer, but it has not become poorer either.

While there is truth in these presumptions, after having lived in Japan for five years, I can tell you that one of the most important reasons for Japan's fiscal stability is Japanese housewives. Namely, in your average Japanese household, the wife manages the money. She takes her spouse's salary, puts savings and investment aside first, gives her spouse an allowance and uses the rest to pay bills and the mortgage and for household management.

Many Japanese women keep a ledger called a *kakeibo* to record all monthly expenditure. The kakeibo enables them to record items daily, weekly, monthly and annually. The value of the kakeibo is that it forces a daily ritual on the housewife to keep track of every yen.

In addition to the kakeibo, the Japanese have traditionally had an aversion to using credit cards for daily needs so Japan is, as yet, a largely cash-driven society. Most bills are paid online through direct transfers, then the remainder of the money is invested for future needs including education and retirement. These daily habits develop over time into conscious spending patterns.

REINTERPRETING THE FRUGALITY MYTH

Paying in cash and eschewing credit cards are often habits that outsiders misinterpret as Japanese frugality. Yes, World War II, two atomic bombs and the ensuing poverty left a deep psychological scar on Japan for decades but modern Japanese are notorious consumers.

It's not that they do not like to spend, it's that they do not like to waste anything. Your average Japanese family buys exactly what it needs at the supermarket and is not in the habit of throwing away food. Petrol prices are high so people use the extremely efficient public transportation system instead of always driving their own cars. Even well-to-do families have been known to use old bath water to do laundry in order to save on utility bills.[1]

Many Japanese are actually "intentional spenders". They will save to spend money on what they perceive has value and reflects their hobbies or ambitions, whether it be the perfect plate of sushi, English lessons for their children, ski gear or a trip to Paris. It may not be what you would perceive as value but there is a common sense of what one does and does not blow precious savings on in Japan.

This confluence of cultural fiscal tradition—strong budget planning, adherence to value seeking and disregard of waste—has made Japanese housewives, of a certain generation, possibly the greatest amateur fiscal managers in the world. By living below their means through conscious spending, they have preserved wealth through nearly 20 years of recession and massive financial market instability.

---

1 Hiroko Tabuchi, "When Consumers Cut Back: An Object Lesson from Japan," *New York Times*, 21 February 2009.

So to excel at household fiscal management, you need to tap into your inner Mrs Watanabe and practise conscious spending. By doing so, you will begin to develop the habits needed to build financial stability going forward, as well as master basic money management skills that you can then pass on to your children.

Good Habit #1: Own Your Cash Flow

Many divorcees want to discuss investing, setting up a business or buying property without taking a good hard look at how much money they spend every month. What comes into your bank account and then goes out is called cash flow. If you have negative cash flow, you are spending more than you get every month. If you have positive cash flow, you are building savings.

Cash flow is the starting point for all financial planning. You cannot ignore your cash flow situation and create a stable financial foundation. The reason why financial planners focus on cash flow is that it is impossible to set financial goals and determine how to invest until you know exactly what money you will *consistently* have at the end of every month.

The reason you have to "own your cash flow" is because you will be the only one determining how you will spend money. The goal is to have money left over at the end of the month to invest for retirement, buy or pay off a home, invest in a business and have peace of mind later in life.

If you have received a lump sum payout in a divorce, the goal is to preserve the lump sum as long as possible. I will discuss strategies and examples of how to do this in chapters 8 to 11. The bottom line, however, is to live a lifestyle that is within your means and doesn't drain away your lump sum settlement.

Here are six common problem scenarios around cash flow management that people run into:

1. You are running a deficit (in other words, more money is going out than coming in) on a regular basis.
2. Your income only just covers your expenses, and in an emergency you need to borrow off friends or family or tap into credit cards. And such emergency moments happen more than once a year.
3. You have sufficient cash that you earn or get from maintenance but you are not really saving anything consciously, and are not sure where the money goes.
4. You have received a large lump sum but it is sitting around in a bank being eaten away by inflation and you don't know how long it will last.
5. You have received "enough" in your settlement but you are worried that it will not last or cover the things that you need, and these worries keep you up at night.
6. You are asset rich (generally property) but cash poor.

Worrying will get you nowhere and hope is not a strategy. If you are experiencing any of the issues above, then you need to begin with a review of your spending patterns. **Your first step to becoming a fiscal manager is to own your cash flow, stabilise it and adhere to a cash budget.**

Cash budgets force conscious spending habits onto a household. This entails putting away credit and debit cards for three months and understanding where your money actually goes. Do this by taking out exactly what you need at the beginning of each week and make it last until the following week without using any plastic (credit or debit). This process will show you over the course of a few weeks where you can cut back.

Good Habit #2: Budget to Live Below Your Means and Bolster Your Savings Ratio

For some, this may be the first time in your life that you are faced with the task of budgeting while for others it will be old hat. Whether you are starting with $1,000[2] or $10,000,000, the process of gaining control over your cash flow is essential for the purposes of investing and preserving whatever wealth you do have.

Putting together a budget is simple—you just tally all your fixed costs and variable costs throughout the month. Fixed costs are things that generally do not go up or down dramatically in price from month to month, such as rent or mortgage payments, school fees and tax savings. In contrast, variable costs are costs that can change frequently, such as extracurricular activities, shopping, car repairs, entertainment, etc. Be conservative and

---

2   Unless otherwise stated, the currency used throughout the book is the US dollar (US$).

factor in for emergencies, for example, your car needing repairs, then take an average of your variable costs and add it to your fixed monthly expenses.

Once you have your total expenses for the month, subtract it from your total monthly income. Your income is everything that comes into your bank account: salary, maintenance payments, interest payments, dividends and so on. Once you subtract income from your expenses, you either have a positive figure (savings) or a negative one (deficit).

Income	$
Income from Yoga	2,500
Child Support	2,000
Maintenance	3,500
TOTAL	8,000
Expenditure	$
Food and Clothing	1,000
Mortgage	1,000
Transport	300
Entertainment	400
School Fees	1,000
Extracurricular Activities	300
Helper	400
Utilities	200
Tax Savings	400
TOTAL	5,000
Savings/Deficit	3,000

If you have a positive number, like we do above, divide that number by your total monthly income, i.e. 3,000 (savings)÷8,000 (income), and find the answer. This answer will tell you what per cent of your income you are saving, in this case 3,000÷8,000=37.5%. This is called your savings ratio.

The savings ratio is more important than the total amount you earn as income every month because it shows how efficient a saver you are on the income you receive. This means if you receive more income, you will likely save the same amount. If you have a deficit every month, then you need to go through all of your spending and see where you can cut back.

The core of financial security is here—how much you save versus what you spend. The higher this ratio goes, the greater your discipline and ability for long-term financial security. This is often called "living below your means" and is practised by millionaires and billionaires all over the world. The best example of this is Warren Buffett who, as one of the richest men on the planet, still lives in his first home in Omaha, Nebraska. According to *The Millionaire Next Door*, nearly all serious accumulators of wealth live below their means and save or invest nearly 30 to 40% of their income over decades.

What per cent you should be saving can vary with age and needs. However, as a rule of thumb, habitual savers target at least 20% or more of their total income. In Asia, among an older generation, this number is often significantly higher, over 30%. Women who do not receive maintenance but who are instead expected to live off lump sum payments, however large, should learn how to live off the interest from their investments, if possible. The trick here is to keep the lump sum intact as long as possible as you can "make money off your money" through investing.

In either case, if you spend more than you make or cannot live off the interest from your lump sum, you really should try to find ways to tighten your budget and earn more.

The best way to demonstrate good and bad cash flow positions is by example. Julia and Sumita are two divorcees who live in the same city and have one child each, yet they have greatly different incomes and expenditures. Julia is a dentist and Sumita is a yoga instructor.

Julia

Income	$
Income as Dentist	15,000
Child Support	3,500
Total	18,500
Expenditure	**$**
Food and Clothing	3,000
Mortgage	3,500
Transport, Petrol	1,500
Entertainment, Clubs, Travel	2,000
Car Loan	1,500
School Fees	2,000
Extracurricular Activities	500

Helper	750
Utilities	500
Tax Savings	2,000
TOTAL	17,250
Savings/Deficit	1,250

Sumita (shown earlier)

Income	$
Income from Yoga	2,500
Child Support	2,000
Maintenance	3,500
TOTAL	8,000
Expenditure	**$**
Food and Clothing	1,000
Mortgage	1,000
Transport	300
Entertainment	400
School Fees	1,000
Extracurricular Activities	300
Helper	400
Utilities	200
Tax Savings	400
TOTAL	5,000
Savings/Deficit	3,000

Based on appearances, namely job title, residential address and superficial items like holiday destinations, a designer wardrobe and a luxury car, there is no doubt that Julia would appear "wealthier". However, if you take one look at Julia's budget, you will see that she is just about making it from one month to the next based on her spending habits, saving well below 10% of her income.

Sumita, on the other hand, has less than half the income that Julia does every month and yet saves over 35% of her income every month. (In some months, she is able to save 40% or more through disciplined money management.) By living below her means and through conscious spending, Sumita has become an excellent fiscal manager of her own household.

CONSCIOUS SPENDING IN PRACTICE

Sumita's divorce left her with a small lump sum, part of which she used to buy a small flat near her parents while the rest was put aside for emergency savings. She gave up her car for public transport as she felt the cost of petrol, parking and maintenance were unnecessary. Her daughter went to a quasi-private school and the daily cost of clothing, food and "keeping up appearances" was lower than it would have been in a different neighbourhood.

On top of this, Sumita did good value-seeking homework on schools when she bought in a "second-tier" location. She noted that the parents were more vigilant and ambitious about their children's education because they *were not* in the wealthiest neighbourhood. This "need to achieve" resulted in her daughter's school turning out top scores on standardised exams citywide several years in a row.

In contrast, when I went through Julia's monthly expenses with her, she was amazed at how much money she actually spent. At one point, she was regularly running a deficit during half the year and relying on a partnership bonus to pay down some of her bills.

We discussed several ways she could reign in her spending and it came down to looking at entertainment, travel expenses, food and clothing expenses and possibly selling or downgrading her car. As the cutting back entailed some lifestyle changes that Julia was not comfortable with, I told her about Sumita. Julia wondered how Sumita was able to save so much with half the income that she had. Below are some of Sumita's conscious spending tactics:

1. **Investments First.** Every month when she gets her salary and the support payments, she takes 16%, or $1,000, and puts it into a savings and investment account to which there is no easy access or credit card attached.

2. **Needs before Wants.** She takes out exactly what she needs each week.

3. **Save for Wants.** Any leftover money at the end of the week is kept in a "fun" drawer where it is put aside to supplement entertainment, birthdays, gifts and other nice-to-have but non-essential expenditures.
   (*Note:* It is better to deposit the money into a bank account than have it lying around at home where it could easily be misplaced or stolen.)

4. **Rewards for Good Behaviour!** Sumita celebrates her ability to save and her self-control by strategically splurging on herself every now and then.

5. **Minimal Credit.** Sumita has one credit card that she only uses in absolute emergencies.

6. **Emergency Money Is a Must.** Sumita has built up a six-month emergency savings account (*see* Good Habit #5). This means that her credit card is the absolute last resort in an emergency.

7. **Make Money on Your Money.** Every savings account that Sumita has is earning interest in some way, and every investment is earning a dividend. In other words, Sumita is making money on her money.

8. **Make Banks Work for You.** Sumita has never allowed herself to be charged fees by banks nor has she ever paid credit card interest. She has chosen the lowest cost accounts by examining all the fees and understanding the penalties involved for overdrafts, etc.

These habits have made Sumita deeply conscious of how she spends money. In her previous job in advertising, she used to go out after work with her colleagues but came to realise that although it was good for a laugh, it was not benefitting her materially or spiritually. Thus, she replaced an after-work pub-crawling lifestyle with one that gives her peace, practising and now teaching yoga.

Sumita used to rationalise that the stress of her previous job gave her an excuse to spend money on non-necessities. Then she realised that those habits—regular dining out, weekly spas, weekend junkets and shopping sprees—ate into the time she had with her daughter and drained far too much from her bank account. So she redirected all that otherwise wasted energy and money. She learnt how to maximise her income and eliminate or minimise every single expense item that was unnecessary.

Good Habit #3: Value Your Net Worth over Your Possessions—Build Your Balance Sheet

The reason why you want to save more than you spend is to build your balance sheet. Earlier we discussed putting together a list of assets (the things we own) and liabilities (the things we owe). This list is your balance sheet. Your net worth is your assets minus your liabilities. By adding savings (and not debt) every month, you are strengthening your financial position and your balance sheet, not to mention your long-term financial security.

Going back to Sumita, after 10 years of being single, she has saved and invested "more than she would have imagined in a lifetime". She began investing slowly in the stock market in dividend-paying stocks and, even with the stock market crash in 2008, her balance sheet is good for a 40-year-old woman. This is what her balance sheet looks like:

Assets		Liabilities	
Cash	60,000	Mortgage	200,000
Retirement Account	120,000		
Brokerage Account	50,000		
College Savings	40,000		
Property Value	800,000		
TOTAL	1,070,000		200,000
Net Worth	870,000		

Sumita understands the difference between her net worth and her possessions. She has actively saved and paid down her debt in lieu of spending on non-necessities. Her main prized possession is not a handbag or a pair of shoes but her property, which also happens to be an asset.

For anyone struggling with budgeting and saving, try going on a cash-only budget and pay down your credit cards. Then, at first, try saving 15% of your monthly incomings and budgeting with what you have left for three months. Once you are in a savings groove, set a goal for yourself, such as saving 20% for three months in a row.

If you run into difficulty, start to employ Sumita's conscious spending techniques. You will be surprised at how differently you may look at your spending habits if you simply put your savings away first and try to manage on the money you have left over for the month. And no cheating with credit cards!

Good Habit #4: Understanding Wants versus Needs

Discussing wants versus needs is always a tricky subject because it can sound very judgmental. A person who is focused on creating financial security should only be judgmental about their own spending. I'm sure Julia and Sumita would have very different interpretations of their wants and needs.

Many of these feelings stem from what your relationship to money is, something that was established when you were a child. It is important to understand your own relationship to money as it controls your perception of what is a want and what is a need. And this can be the difference between financial security and financial ruin.

I have a friend, Angelica, who had nearly $4 million in her account after her divorce. She had never had so much money at her disposal before, and she felt wealthy and very independent. She was going to finally start the swimwear business that her ex-husband had refused to fund while they were still married.

Four years later, Angelica was down to her last $500,000. I was shocked when she told me this. She was finally seeking advice as to how to invest what was left and "make it last longer". When we started going over where the money had gone, it became obvious that Angelica has been confusing her wants versus her needs.

Angelica felt she needed to start a business immediately upon getting a divorce to make money. She also needed holidays away from her children as she needed a break from single parenthood. Angelica felt she needed ongoing cosmetic treatments in order to feel young, restock her wardrobe with more youthful clothing and circulate at all the trendiest hot spots. It was really a *Vogue* magazine approach to post-divorce rejuvenation.

It is normal for divorcees to splash out and treat themselves, particularly if they felt ignored or resented throughout marriage. No one would argue with a bit of pampering. However, it is a different thing altogether when the need to constantly spend to "feel good again" becomes an ingrained habit irrespective of affordability or budget constraints.

When we sat down to discuss her needs, Angelica started to reveal more about why she spent money the way she did. She felt one way to regain face after her spouse left her for another woman was to look youthful and be fun-loving, thus the cosmetic treatments, travel/shopping sprees and nightclubbing. She also wanted respect, and by saying she was a business owner she thought she would get this respect, regardless of whether the business was actually profitable.

As Angelica reflected over the past four years, she concluded that all this effort at reinvention had actually been very stressful for her. She had taken on far too much too soon and had burnt through a lot of money on a fledgling business that had not been well planned. And while this flurry of activity had at first felt exciting, it was not earning her the respect she so wanted.

Indeed, as the money began to run low, the anxiety it provoked took a toll on her ability to appear youthful and be fun-loving. She actually was having no fun at all. And pretending that all is well when, in reality, you cannot sleep at night due to money concerns is both physically and emotionally painful.

After some soul-searching, she realised that her relationship to money was distorted, and that it was truly difficult to buy both youth and respect. What ultimately gave Angelica greatest peace of mind? She finally became her own CFO. She put together a reasonable budget, practised conscious spending, got a part-time job to supplement her expenses and closed her failing business.

After changing her relationship to money, Angelica also felt the need to be involved in more meaningful activities. She started giving of herself and spent time and money on interests that she enjoyed far more than hitting the local hot spots. She signed up for volunteer work twice a month, took up tango dancing and formed an informal home-based wine tasting club.

These initiatives gave Angelica structure and introduced her to communities of like-minded people, some younger, some older, thus enabling her to create a genuine support network. Instead of trying to create a false image, she started living a life that reflected who she was and with that she regained control.

So what is a want versus a need? Suze Orman said it best on *Oprah*. Fill in the blanks: I _____ to eat food every day to survive. I _____ a new pair of Jimmy Choos. It's not brain surgery. One may make you feel good momentarily but you need the other to stay alive. (If you don't know which is which, please go straight to Chapter 5.)

I can make this easy and say that the only necessities really are food, shelter, clothing, clean water, good health and, in the case of children, education. For working women, I would also include any reasonable expenditure that will help you advance in your career or your business *if* that business is a profitable growing business.

"Wants" is just about everything else. In other words, the things, however large or small, that make you feel good or better about yourself temporarily: frequent travel, regular spa pampering, multiple club memberships, cosmetic treatments, shopping binges, budget-blowing dining experiences and any type of "keeping up" or "bragging rights" spending.

Having said this, it is important to recognise and visualise the things that enrich your life and boost your senses. Everyone is different and for one person this may be travel, for another an investment in further education or perhaps a sport or a collection hobby. These things that enrich you, however, have to be enjoyed within the realm of what is possible given the state of your finances. Let's take the travellers among you, for example. Are you travelling or are you escaping? Can't one or two trips be just as fulfilling as six?

People who struggle with their spending, as covered in Chapter 5, may need professional intervention, be it a financial planner or a psychologist. However, the vast majority who struggle with wants versus needs just need to rethink what they value and how they spend (or waste) money.

Consider the amount of time you spend feeling not good about what you cannot have and, instead, focus on what is attainable and how to supplement what you do have. Consider who you spend time with and how they earn and value money. Resolving your feelings over wants versus needs can be done through some honest soul-searching and by developing new habits that grow, instead of drain, your wealth.

If you can afford the wants, indulge by all means. No one has the right to judge you. However, if your wants are destroying your budget, then you need to get a reality check or you will feel forever stressed and in a financial hole.

Good Habit #5: Have Emergency Savings

Once your budget is in order and you are able to start saving regularly, the first and most important item to save is emergency money. Emergency money is three to six months' worth of expenses that sits untouched and is inaccessible in cash and/ or short-term time deposits that are renewed upon maturity as this money is only to be used for emergencies. If you do not have a regular income or if you are worried about your ex-spouse's long-term job prospects, aim for six months of emergency savings.

TIME DEPOSITS

A time deposit (also referred to as a term deposit or a certificate of deposit) is a cash deposit commitment, usually over a short term (from one week to one year), for which you receive a small return. The longer the term of the deposit, generally the more interest you will receive. Time deposit investments carry penalties for early withdrawals so this is not the place for your emergency money, except over very short terms. Rather, time deposits are an investment option for cash that can roll around collecting interest for several months or longer—an ideal place to keep cash away from the impulsive spender!

How we all define emergencies is different, but if you have read Good Habit #4, you will know that emergencies do not entail anything under the "wants" section. So no emergency spending on Botox treatments, keeping up with your neighbours or joining clubs you cannot otherwise afford.

The reason why emergency savings are so important for divorcees is that you do not have the same backup that a two-income household can draw on in the event of job loss, long-term illness or disability. Even if you have friends and family that you can lean on for extra cash, it does not strengthen your ability as a fiscal manager, and there's no guarantee that one loan from a loved one will lead to another.

Emergency money is especially key if you are relying on maintenance. While the job market is robust in Asia at the time of writing, the underlying strength of the global economies is tenuous at best. It was only 15 years ago that Asia was coming out of its worst financial crisis, then there was an Internet bust followed by the severe acute respiratory syndrome (SARS) scare. To assume that things like this can never happen again is foolhardy.

No one's ex-spouse is irreplaceable in the job market today, and if he runs a business, no one can predict if that business can survive a severe downturn. I have lost count of the number of bankers and financiers who made a fortune in a short period of time, only to lose their jobs in the 2008 crisis. Many of these men now have shaky prospects at best and need to live off their savings for far longer than they ever imagined.

If you have no emergency savings, then allocate that money immediately or put a savings plan into place to ensure you can cover at least six months' worth of expenses. Having emergency savings comes before spending any money other than what is necessary. If that means you cut back on fun for six months or a year, so be it. You will find yourself worrying less and in a better place once your emergency savings are in place.

Good Habit #6: Develop and Own Plan B

Having Plan B is not the same as having emergency savings. The best planners in the world have a backup plan, or Plan B. Plan B often entails a major lifestyle change and/or possibly a move to another country in the event that your current living arrangement runs into major trouble. This trouble can come in the form of:

- skyrocketing inflation
- loss of maintenance or child support

- loss of job
- an inability to enforce the support payments that you should be getting
- children having a medical condition that requires special schooling
- loss of some major form of support that alters your current lifestyle

Never expect your ex-spouse to be as prepared as you would like him to be in an emergency. And never expect him to keep you up to date on any financial problems he is facing. *You will almost certainly be the last to know.* And, as a result, you may feel blind-sided or ambushed all over again.

Take the case of Belinda who had been divorced from her spouse for three years. She did everything right, including practising conscious spending, keeping emergency savings and retraining herself to go back into the workforce so she could have a part-time job. What she was not prepared for was her ex-spouse's business to fold and for him to declare bankruptcy.

While Belinda was able to continue to live in the city thanks to her emergency savings, inflation continued to severely eat into her income. Now with his job loss, her ex was unable to pay maintenance as, unlike Belinda, he had not put away any emergency savings.

We discussed the following options:

1. moving back to her place of birth and living with her parents in order to conserve costs
2. moving to a less expensive locale within the area
3. moving to a less expensive area and finding a full-time job

None of these was ideal. Option one meant needing to look for another job, her children changing schools and the family having to share a home with her parents, something that she had not done for years. The second option meant living with even greater scarcity than the family had become accustomed to. And the third option would have reduced significantly the time she would have had with her children *assuming* that she could find a job that paid as much as she needed.

In the end, Belinda chose to move back in with her parents. This was the one choice that allowed her to sleep at night so it was the right choice for her. What could have been different is if she had actually discussed and had a Plan B to start with. This way she and her family would have been more psychologically prepared for the upheaval when it came.

Good Habit #7: Eliminate Credit Card Debt

If this book had been written 20 years ago, I would not have had to even broach the subject of credit card debt in Asia. Back then, very few people in Asia had more than one credit card, and even fewer were likely to use them for daily expenses.

Fast-forward to today—credit card usage as well as personal loan debt have skyrocketed. Singaporeans are the largest users of plastic in Asia, with 3.3 cards per person, while Hong Kong and Taiwan residents carry 2.7 cards on average per person. People in Hong Kong have the largest balances and the highest number of late payments.[3]

Credit cards are possibly the worst fiscal management tool known to man as they are notorious for high interest rates and excessive fees. When you do not pay off your credit card every month, the unpaid balance gets added onto future charges, resulting in you paying much more in the end.

Take, as an example, a $1,000 balance at 18.9%. If you pay off the minimum of $40 monthly, it will take you almost three years to pay off your debt (assuming that nothing else is charged in the meantime). You will have incurred nearly $280 in interest payments. Honestly, you may as well just stand over a stove and burn your cash outright.

The rule of thumb is that you should use your credit card for the "float", meaning you pay off your credit card debt every month and never carry over a balance. This way you incur no interest charges but you have the convenience of the card.

If you are deep into credit card debt, you need to resolve this before you put any other investment plans into place. Try to consolidate your debt on the card that pays the lowest interest or through a personal loan with a bank and stick to a payment schedule. Stop buying anything other than necessities.

---

3 *Business Times*, "S'poreans own the most credit cards in the region", 13 April 2012.

If you need assistance in consolidating your debt, credit counselling centres are listed at the back of the book. If you cannot control your impulse buying habits, find a therapist. Addictive shopping and out-of-control comfort spending are emotional disorders that often need professional treatment.

Good Habit #8: Make Your Bank Work for You

This is a very simple good habit. Look at all your accounts: Are you being charged fees? Are they letting you earn interest? Look at what fees you are being charged and the minimum balances. If these seem exorbitant or even unnecessary, find another bank.

Depending on the city you are in, there may be big or small differences between the banks. I personally look for low or no fees for simple accounts, such as savings and checking accounts, and the opportunity to earn interest wherever possible. I also look for good service and happy bank employees because they are likely to have better management in general.

Do not get sucked into buying insurance or structured products (more on this later in Chapter 10) as part of your quest to earn money from your bank. Just find the best value for the money that is sitting around in checking or savings accounts, and avoid "lock-in" periods as these stop you from getting to your cash without incurring penalties. Banks are notorious for their fees and for attempting to lock in your money, so make sure your bank is working for you, and not the other way around.

ADVANCED FISCAL MANAGEMENT QUESTIONS

Once you start practising conscious spending and your budget and balance sheet are in reasonable shape, there are additional tactics that you can employ to assess if there are other expenses you can eliminate. Here are some standard budget questions that I ask clients, and ones that you should ask yourself:

Place of Residence/Property

- Are you living in the most cost-effective location as possible if it is not your home country?
- Does your mortgage or rent account for more than 30% of your income? If so, does relocating make sense in order to keep your expenses intact, either to a cheaper location within your city or a new destination altogether?
- Are you holding onto a holiday home that doesn't earn a good return or that you either do not visit or cannot comfortably afford?

Health Insurance

- Are you buying health insurance when you can make do with a nationalised healthcare system?

Transportation

- Do you absolutely need a car or can you use public transport? In other words, does having a car allow you to save time and money in other areas of your life?
- If you absolutely need a car, are you considering buying a new car or a second-hand car? A word of warning: Never buy a new car, find a gently used second-hand car. Next to whole life insurance policies, new cars are the world's worst use of money disguised as an investment; a new car loses around 25% of its value as soon as it is driven out of the showroom.

Children's Education

- Is private education a "must have" or a "best to have" option? What are the alternatives?
- If you are paying for private education, can you afford to spend now on private education and save enough for your child(ren)'s university/college education in the future? Or are you sacrificing college savings or, worse yet, your own retirement savings for private education?

Career

- Do you genuinely like your job and does it give you career advancement prospects? If not, have you considered retraining for a different career?

- Do you deserve a pay raise and, if so, have you asked for one?
- Are you running a business and is it profitable? Does it provide you with enough income to make it really worth the time you spend on it?
- Is your business growing? (*Note:* If you have been in business for a year and you are not covering expenses, you need to sit down and do a business plan, otherwise it's a hobby, not a business.)

Others

- Are you lending money or paying for others when you really cannot afford to do so? If so, why?
- Are you taking full advantage of tax deductions and/or any aid available to single parent households?

There are many more questions that you can use to assess how you are spending money and if it makes sense for your situation. You can never go wrong if you employ conscious spending techniques and really think about wants versus needs to ensure you are maximising your monthly income.

CONCLUSION

The eight habits outlined in this chapter highlight the habits of individuals who want to own their day-to-day financial decisions in order to create the building blocks of financial security. As soon as you begin to practise the art of conscious spending, you will become aware of how, why and where you are spending money and why it is necessary to plan for emergencies. And once you are on top of all your spending decisions, you'll be able to own your budget and increase your ability to build your balance sheet over time.

CHAPTER 4

TALKING TO FAMILY ABOUT MONEY

The first generation plants the tree, the next generation sits in the shade.
—A Chinese Proverb

By now, you should have an idea of what your cash flow looks like as well as the basic tools, budget and balance sheet to help you "own your money". As a result of your own analysis, it is highly likely that you need to change how money is spent in your household. These changes could be either large or small.

Unless you have no extended family or children, involve your family in any discussions regarding how you plan to readjust your budget/monthly expenditure if the changes will impact them in any way. How much information you share is at your discretion. This way, it won't be only you "owning" your budget or your balance sheet but your family as well.

This chapter will cover:

- how to speak constructively with your parents about finances
- money myths you may have grown up with

- how to discuss wants and needs with children
- how to not be perceived as a hypocrite by your children with regard to money and spending

PREPARING FOR MONEY TALKS

As stated earlier, money means different things to different people and the same is true for your family members. This is why the topic of money can bring to the fore very strong emotional feelings for many, and it's why poor communication around money can lead to anger, resentment, fights and ruined relationships. As best put by Olivia Mellan in *Money Harmony*, "You're not just fighting about the money; you're fighting about what money means."

Understand Everyone's Relationship to Money

For most divorcees, money means both freedom and security. Children tend to view money as freedom or the freedom to buy things their friends have. For our parents, it can mean many things, including power over the behaviour of others. Therefore "what money means to you" can occasionally run up against what it means to others.

One point of contention may be that of shared sacrifice or an expectation that, no matter your financial situation, you are expected to contribute money to extended family. As a single parent, this can be a problem because you may not be in a place to support or help anyone other than yourself and your children for a while. So your need to build or maintain your personal financial security might lead to arguments with siblings over how best to support elders or others in need.

Another point of contention may be that of control in some Asian communities. Some father–daughter relationships revolve around fathers controlling their daughters' behaviour through access to money and/or access to work outside the home. This leaves these daughters dependent on their husbands in marriage and then once again on their fathers after divorce.

Lastly, if you feel that discussing money with your children is a "problem", it's more likely your hang-up than theirs. Even though most kids are just building their relationship with money, they take their cues from you. Children are as capable as adults (sometimes more so) of putting aside selfishness for the sake of family harmony as long as they perceive equitable treatment for all.

Set Simple Goals to Start With

Now that you are psychologically prepped for dealing with family members, the next step is to determine some basic financial goals for yourself and/or your household. For now, let's keep it simple. Take a few minutes to define some basic savings goals and possible investment priorities such as:

- I want to be out of debt in one year.
- We need to establish emergency savings.
- We want to set up a fund to accumulate a down payment for a property.
- We want to raise enough money to fund a small business.

The reason why goals, as we will cover more thoroughly in Chapter 6, are important is that it's sometimes unclear to family members why you are going to save money that they may feel can be "shared" or used for alternative purposes. By establishing such goals, you will feel well-organised and have the necessary information at your disposal when you sit down and explain your perspective on how money should be earned, saved and invested for the future.

TALKING TO PARENTS (AND EXTENDED FAMILY) ABOUT MONEY

It may be that you and your parents are involved with each other financially in some way. Examples of such involvement include:

- supporting elderly parents
- contributing regularly to your parents' financial welfare
- moving in with your parents (or they with you) to help you manage through your divorce

In Asia, there is often a sense of "what's yours is mine" among family members, in some cultures more so than others. However, as we have just discussed, it is important to set individual goals for yourself when you are divorced because (1) you will likely outlive your parents and (2) unless there is complete transparency, you have no idea what assets OR debts your family members have. Anecdotally speaking, it seems that children are aware of their parents' assets, but not necessarily their debts.

Family Discussions—Open the Kimono

The easiest way to have money discussions with anyone you care for, or are dependent on, is to be transparent. In other words, everyone needs to "open the kimono". This is necessary if you are supporting elderly parents, physically or financially, in any way and it should apply to all family contributions, including those from siblings. Sharing some of the skills in your new financial toolbox, i.e. savings ratios and budgets, is a good starting point when discussing financial matters. Even more so if you need to make major changes to your monthly budget that will affect how much you can contribute in future or how you can no longer be as hands-on looking after your parents because you need to go back to work. By using these skills, you can show family members your new budgets, discuss your financial goals and find the most equitable way forward for the family as a whole.

These discussions have to come from the right place, meaning with everyone's interests, including yours, at heart. If you have family members who do not want to discuss money openly, or if money matters have never been transparent, try to "Be the Adult" but use your discretion. The budget and balance sheet tools that were covered in Chapter 3 are the best means to educate your family members as they create a neutral platform for constructive conversation.

Here's an example of why kimono opening is so important. In the case of Mylihn, her elderly parents moved in with her after her divorce because her mother had physical challenges. Mylihn's two brothers and their wives worked full-time, leaving Mylihn to do much of the hands-on work with her parents. As she was unable to work full-time or advance in her career at all as a result, Mylihn was dependent on both her ex-husband and her brothers who pitched in financially every month to support their elderly parents.

While Mylihn's family was not wealthy, Mylihn received opaque assurances from her mother that "she would not have to worry about the future". No one really discussed money except for the monthly cash flow, in other words, how much was needed monthly to manage and support Mylihn and her parents. Everyone's balance sheet was still hidden under the kimono, so to speak.

What Mylihn did not plan for, and what her mother did not know, was that her father had used the family home asset, better known as the equity in the home, to take out personal loans that had not been paid back. When her father passed away, these secret loans came out into the open through a process called probate. Because you have to pay off such loans before you are able to inherit any money, the estate shrunk considerably from over S$1 million to just over S$500,000.

In addition, Mylihn's parents forgot to change their wills to compensate Mylihn for her sacrifice. Traditionally, like in many Asian cultures, sons generally contribute more financially to help their ageing parents than daughters, so Mylihn's parents, like many

Chinese parents, left more of their estate to their sons than their daughter. It was an honest oversight that they did not change their wills to compensate Mylihn; in many cases, there are no wills whatsoever. So now Mylihn is dependent on the goodwill of her brothers (and their wives) to sustain herself into old age.

The lesson here is that there is nothing at all wrong with taking care of your parents regardless of their financial situation, or yours. However, if you are making financial sacrifices by not working, or by using what would be your retirement savings to help them, you need to be fully aware of the risks involved. And to know the risks, you need to get everyone to open the kimono and be aware of what the overall family balance sheet is and even broach the subject of a will.

It is important to note that many families do not even have wills because of superstitious beliefs around planning for death. If there is no will, most estate distribution laws divide up the assets of the deceased equitably among surviving children with little regard to who has contributed or sacrificed along the way. Therefore, it is all the more important that these matters are discussed openly.

The major advantage of multi-generation living, whether you and your children move back in with your parents or your parents move in with you, is that grandparents can be present in the lives of their grandchildren and vice versa. The major disadvantage, however, is if there is disagreement regarding the financial contribution that each party makes. That is why it is extremely important to have a discussion about the family budget at the onset to see where you can help and how you can start saving long term for your family.

At the end of the day, talking to family members about money can be anywhere on the continuum of very easy to extremely difficult. If your parents have good money management and investing skills, and they are good teachers, you can learn a lot from them. If, however, they lack this "toolbox", you may need to get the discussion going. Just keep in mind that this is a process, so be patient.

My Parents Won't Talk to Me about Money

It may be that you are faced with parents who simply are uncomfortable talking about money or have extremely unhelpful views towards money. This is where you need to remember what Healthy Entitlement is. You are entitled to plan for your financial future.

You may well have to assert what you need and want for yourself and your children. It can be scary at first but it's empowering in the long run. On this point, I'd like to acknowledge two common money myths that run in families where money issues are not discussed with women.

MONEY MYTH I: WOMEN WHO UNDERSTAND MONEY DON'T FIND HUSBANDS

If you divorce, it might be that your family hopes or encourages you to remarry. I can appreciate, having seen it, how an uneducated mother can behave in the face of an ever more independent daughter who is suddenly talking savings ratios and cash flow. The response from an insecure mother may be, "If you become so educated about money, no one will ever marry you."

As outdated as this thinking is, it's not unheard of in some communities in Asia. Going back to Chapter 1, and those generational tapes, if this is what your mother thinks, nothing is going to change this belief. Ever.

She has probably spent a lot of time in the company of women who think the same. So it's community pressure talking, pressure to force you to "fall into line" and not be different, even if being different means being financially secure.

If faced with such pressure, you need to acknowledge that while this is their opinion, it is their opinion only. Just ask yourself this: Do you really believe it is better for you to be ignorant about money matters? It is *never* a positive thing to be uneducated about money matters.

Money Myth II: It Is Unattractive to Discuss Money

You don't need to live in Asia to hear women say, "It's unattractive to discuss money." I hear people say this within my peer group as much as I hear it from an older generation. I concede that there is a time and place to discuss money (and politics!), regardless of your gender. And that talking up what you own or have is uncouth wherever you are in the world.

However, it is not unattractive to know your budget and your balance sheet nor is it unattractive to be actively involved in investing and managing your own money. In fact, I'd say it is a problem if you don't.

Yet people who think of themselves as "the chattering classes", aka "the ladies who lunch" aka "the country club set", often state with distorted pride that "My husband manages the money, I just spend it" or, my favourite non sequitur, "It's just money".

Like the uneducated mother mentioned above, most of these women do not have a clue about investing so they disparage anyone who does. They also find comfort and camaraderie among women who are equally unaware. Ironically, or call it karma, it is exactly this type of person who gets ambushed in a divorce or a financial crisis and is forced into a huge lifestyle change.

In addition to your own welfare, you have to think about the generational mindset you are passing down to your children. What kind of message do you want to pass on to them? "Be dumb and do well" or "Play dumb and do well"? Couldn't there be a better message such as "Don't be dumb, know your budget and your balance sheet, keep it to yourself and do well"?

HOW TO TALK TO CHILDREN ABOUT MONEY

Your own parents may have discussed money matters with you as a child but many others may not have enjoyed this privilege.

So here is another "toolbox" to help you talk about money with your children. Embrace this opportunity positively as it is a chance to begin a tradition of financial education with your children.

If you need to change how money is used in your household based on your analysis, your children will need to "own" the budget as much as you. Recall the concept of relationship to money. Your relationship to money is most likely about financial security but for most children it is about "freedom" or "access", the ability to do the things their peers are doing. These are opposing needs to yours so you need to find a way to educate them about the long-term value of saving and investing money while not disparaging how they feel when family needs conflict with their wants.

Although there are a lot of money discussions worth having, for the sake of this chapter, I will focus on how to create a conscious spending household in order to conserve financial resources for future needs.

It's Not What You Say, It's What You Do

Any parent should know that children of any age will pay far more attention to what you do than what you say. Children know what hypocrisy is before they can even say the word. Therefore, if you need to adjust how money is spent, you need to align your behaviour with your words.

If you need to cut back on wants, for example, but only cut back on what your children want, this will be perceived as hypocritical and drive a wedge between you and your children. They will be less likely to cooperate and will very likely lose respect for you.

Take the following example. A couple that I counselled prior to divorce always struggled to balance their household budget. As a result, the couple, Tabitha and Bill, ended up divorcing over money issues. Obviously, the divorce did not solve budgeting for either of them. In fact, it made matters worse.

As they were both proud people and resentful of their diminished financial status, they both turned to credit cards and spending sprees, which neither could afford. Bill took his new girlfriend on exotic holidays and leased an unnecessarily expensive apartment for himself while Tabitha, though more frugal, indulged herself beyond what she could afford.

One day, Tabitha's rent went unpaid and continued to be unpaid. Finally, the landlord rang both Tabitha and Bill demanding the full rental payment that had gone in arrears. Because it was Bill's responsibility to still cover Tabitha's rent, Tabitha hadn't felt the need to have emergency savings. Then Tabitha found out that Bill hadn't been paying her rent for months because he had lost his job months earlier!

All the while, their children had been perceiving an ersatz life of plenty when, in fact, their father had gone into a debt spiral and their mother had no emergency savings. As their father and mother had both spent money they didn't have, they were now forced to sit down and tell their children that they no longer had a home—possibly the one consistent factor in the children's lives—because neither parent could afford the rent.

While you may have zero sympathy for two grown adults who find themselves in such a situation, can you imagine how confusing this would be for a child? Ultimately, it has to be your responsibility, and yours alone, to own and control what you can. Having emergency funds is money management 101, as we learnt in Chapter 3.

It is neither easy nor fun to be The Adult in such a situation but you have to be when children are involved. And while the above story is an extreme example, it's not altogether unusual for parents to indulge themselves at the expense of their children once they are divorced. Parents do this because they are trying to buy happiness for themselves.

This brings us to our second lesson for children of all ages. If *your* relationship to money is that "money buys you happiness", then that is what your children will learn. And here's the problem with this belief: It is has been proven, time and again, that over a certain threshold money doesn't make people happier.[1] In fact, there are studies that show that too much money makes you unable to genuinely enjoy anything anymore.

Furthermore, it is also true that stockpiling money does not ensure long-term happiness but how you use money does.

---

1   www.scientificamerican.com/article.cfm?id=can-money-buy-happiness

Studies have shown that people who spend money on others are generally happier than people who spend money only on themselves. In nearly every country in the world, people who give to charity are happier than people who do not, according to the "World Giving Index 2010" conducted by Gallup.[2]

This is not to say that you need to donate all your savings to charity in order to be happy. It simply highlights that people who use money to enable themselves or other people to accomplish something special are happier than the general population.

So before you start to talk about money, perhaps one of the first questions you can ask your children is "What makes you happy?" In the conversations that I have had with children of all ages, here are some of the common things they will say when asked this question:

- doing X with a friend
- friends/friendship
- doing X sport
- hanging out with a friend
- spending time with mummy or daddy doing X
- reading
- watching my favourite TV show
- playing at the park/going to the beach/swimming
- playing tag
- listening to music/singing/dancing

2   www.csmonitor.com/Commentary/Editorial-Board-Blog/2010/0910/Gallup-poll-Degree-of-one-s-charity-depends-on-happiness-more-than-wealth

- eating my favourite food
- talking on Facebook/twittering
- painting or drawing
- Lego/Pokémon
- playing with my dog/cat/hamster/rabbit
- playing X box, Wii, video games

Do you see a pattern here? Most children do not say, "I am happy only when I do something that involves a lot of money." Things that *do* involve spending a lot of money include:
- going shopping for designer clothing
- fine dining
- club memberships
- spa treatments
- going on trips
- having a private jet or a 5,000-plus sq ft home
- travelling
- buying a brand new car

So, first off, do not confuse what makes you happy as "doing something for the family" because children aren't stupid and they won't buy it. They know it's for you. Second, it does not take much money for children to feel happy *if* they are living in a happy home. No matter how large or small your home, creating a happy home environment is something anyone can make happen with the right attitude.

Have Monthly Family Discussions

As stated repeatedly in this chapter, if you need to make changes to how money is spent in your household, everyone needs to be informed. Even if your little ones don't completely understand everything at this point, don't leave them out. If your children have reached a point in their lives where they have a clearer concept of money, they may not be happy at the prospect of "everyone" having something that they do not have or no longer having easy access to money following your divorce. However, if you open the kimono, you will help them understand why you need to make these changes and, consequently, get them to "own" the family budget as well.

This isn't an easy thing to do, especially as you do not want to scare your children or make them anxious. Below is a step-by-step guide of how you can structure your first major discussion about money and your new family budget. Remember to go slowly and be as gentle (and patient) as possible.

1. Explain that the discussions are private and will happen regularly.

2. Then say something along the lines of "I am now the money manager of our household and I have to make some hard decisions as to how we use money so that we continue to feel financially secure."

3. Share a major family financial goal that you have set and explain why. For example, "We need to save for an emergency fund. An emergency fund is when you are able

to pay for all your bills for three months in the event that something serious and unexpected happens. It will take us XX months to save this amount of money."

4. Then tell them that, starting from today, the family is living on a new budget which is $X per week.

5. After you have stated the fixed weekly budget, emphasise that the family is going to have to cut back on, or stop, spending money on certain things. For example, "As part of our new budget, we will all have to make some sacrifices. For instance, I am going to stop eating out twice a week/getting my nails done."

6. Let them know that you are the boss and that there won't be any free handouts. Say something like "When I lay down a rule about money, we stick to it. For example, you will receive money/an allowance when you earn it. Here is a list of chores I expect you to do as part of this family, and here are other things you can do to earn your allowance."

7. Conclude with something positive such as "Let's learn how to earn, save and spend money as a family."

How you talk to children of different ages about money matters greatly. Consequently, I've broken down the age groups into the following: (1) eight and below and (2) eight and above. And like anything in life, how you say something and the tone you use is as important as what you say.

TALKING TO YOUNG CHILDREN UNDER EIGHT

While I firmly believe in providing an allowance, I do not believe in just giving children money whenever they ask for it. By and large, my children loathe asking me for money because I always ask in a gentle tone, "What have you done to earn this?" Yes, they get annoyed with me but they don't love me any less. By reinforcing that money comes at a price, you have the best chance of influencing their mindset before they reach the I-want-what-everyone-else-has stage of their lives. You can also motivate them positively with small rewards.

So imagine this scenario: Someone in your child's class has a new toy—an expensive one—and you know you cannot buy it but your child begs and begs. When you tell your child that it isn't in the family budget this month, your child looks either sullen or sad or starts to ask why all the other children have something and they don't.

First, give them a hug. Then, as hard as it is to say "it's not in the family budget" the first time, you must start saying no to things you cannot afford. They will gradually start to understand that the family budget is taking priority over what they want. Frustrated as they may seem, you can help your child in the long run by having them experience delayed gratification. And lots of hugs never hurt anyone.

If you really want to buy the toy for your child, but money is tight, then tell them to make a list for their birthday or some other celebration when gift giving is normal. The goal here is to demonstrate that money doesn't just fall from the sky or out of mummy's pocket on demand. And by learning that money is earned, you will be positively motivating them to set their own savings goals.

Next, consider giving a small allowance for a specific activity that they can do on a regular basis. If they are too young, or if it is not possible to give them money, then a special dinner treat, gold stars or setting up a sticker chart, for instance, are all meaningful and great incentives to children of this age group. The lesson here is that they can "earn" these rewards by helping you regularly.

If you can afford even the smallest allowance, give them three cups—one for saving, one for spending and one for donations. Let them choose how they want to allocate the money. In effect, this is what you are doing in real life so you are helping them understand what you do with money by having them imitate how you are managing the family finances.

Some people use the "family economy" concept whereby you actually set up a bank (in the form of an old shoe box), establish a bank ledger and create cheques for your children to write and cash. This concept is okay but unnecessary for the overburdened mum. It's better to get your child a real account at a real bank and show them what a real bank is all about. What's most important here is that they learn that money does not "come out of a machine" for free.

TALKING TO CHILDREN OVER EIGHT

The strategies that you can employ with younger children still apply to this age group. However, it is important to realise that this is the age at which children really begin to be sensitive to what their peers have, and if material goods are all they obsess over, it can impact their sense of happiness. In Asia, as most schools require uniforms, their envy will play out less in terms of clothing and more in terms of new technology, holidays abroad, expensive sporting gear, tickets to expensive concerts and other accoutrement.

Fortunately, while they may be more stubborn at this age, they will have built up their intellectual capacity which will enable you to talk to them in earnest about wants versus needs (as in Chapter 3). It may take a while for them to realise that you are serious about sticking to the family budget but their mindset will change if they see you also putting your needs before your wants. To bring this point home, you could also show them your household budget, and perhaps what the savings are intended for, i.e. a college/university fund and/or your retirement.

Even though you may have to play bad cop, let them know that you genuinely understand how they feel and that you would like certain items for yourself or a nice holiday but that those things are wants, not needs. You need food, shelter, clothes, etc., but no one really needs the latest designer trainers, a new iPhone or a trip to Phuket.

Technology brings about its own issues because it is at the forefront of your children's social lives. The problem with indulging in technology all the time is that nothing is new for long, so nothing feels special for very long. This feeds a very bad cycle of buying-makes-me-happy materialism that is so hard to break.

As a guideline, here are my rules for technology:

1. When you do invest in technology, explain that this is the only purchase that you will be making for the next three to five years. In other words, "Take care of it, make it last and don't ask me for new technology next year."

2. Apart from mobile phones, make sure that whatever you buy is a shared benefit to the family. This way everyone "owns" it and it's both a joint benefit as well as a responsibility.

3. Go out of your way to express disgust when you come across extremely over-priced items or about the waste of buying a new product every year. This sets a tone for what you are not going to spend the family's money on, and you will find that your children will mimic you after a while.

4. Instead of technology purchases that trap children in a virtual world, consider setting aside money for experiences that are special and can be shared as a family, for instance going to a concert or the theatre. Show the benefit of saving money that would otherwise be spent on technology, i.e. one iPhone buys two plane tickets or a year's worth of tennis lessons.

Any time a child of this age is adamant about what they want, encourage them to start doing chores around the house to earn this money. Set up a schedule and have them work for what they want. If earning money from you, or around the neighbourhood, is not possible, then spend time discussing that you know how they feel but you can only spend on "what we need" for now. End of conversation.

The bottom line is that you need to help them nurture a healthy relationship to money, even in these large Asian cities where rapacious consumption spending is the norm. If you spend and say yes out of guilt, spend to help them "keep up" or say no without any feeling or discussion or hug, they can easily develop a dysfunctional relationship to money. Extreme indulgence is as bad as extreme rejection without logic or explanation.

For those who are in a position of maximum thriftiness, do what you can to occasionally splurge on birthdays and holidays. This is important because while your children will be making do with day-to-day sacrifices, you can demonstrate that all this discipline yields reward at special times. By instilling these healthy-relationship-to-money thoughts and practices in your children, you will give them a gift that will last a lifetime.

Fun without Money

No matter the age of your children, it would benefit your family to come up with a list of activities that simply do not involve much money (or technology!). These activities can be as simple as everyone taking a walk after dinner together, having a movie night with popcorn, stretching out or dancing to your favourite music, cooking your family meals together, going to museums or the beach, going for hikes, using community centres or YMCAs for activities, doing charity work together, riding bikes and/or rollerblading in the park, practising tai chi or yoga ... the list could be endless!

The more creative you get, the more creative your children will be when it comes to earning money, understanding how to own their own financial decisions and having fun without it.

CONCLUSION

How our families have handled money and how we talk to those we are closest to about money leave a deep and lasting impression. No matter how your family may have talked about and/or handled money, you have the opportunity to change this dialogue forever and for the better. You are not only entitled to personal financial stability, you also have the ability to own decisions and communicate the spirit of financial ownership to your children.

CHAPTER 5

MONEY DISORDERS = SELF-SABOTAGE

As we've noted, savings and positive monthly cash flow are necessary to create wealth and long-term financial stability. And as you will learn in subsequent chapters, the sooner you begin to strategically invest, the better you can combat the detrimental effects inflation has on savings.

However, there will be a subset of readers who, up to this point, still find themselves unable to save or invest regularly and consistently. Or for those of you who have a lump sum settlement of sorts, you may as yet find it challenging to live within a reasonable budget. If you fall into this group, then this chapter is for you. You need to examine more closely why you don't have a positive cash flow or why you cannot live within a reasonable budget that allows you to stretch your settlement and do whatever it takes to turn things around.

If you are spending money as consciously as possible and still struggling, you may need to re-enter the workforce to supplement your maintenance or lump sum settlement. Even if you cannot do this right away because you are taking care of infants or small children, think about how you can supplement your income. Think about what skills you have to offer and/ or research an area or industry in which you can retrain and develop a career over time.

Many divorced women have found opportunities working from home doing part-time jobs or even starting small businesses. While I do not recommend starting a business until your cash situation is stable, there has been a boon in single parent households developing niche workplace opportunities for themselves.

If, however, everything other than savings and long-term investment seems like a priority, or the idea of paying down debt is constantly on the back burner, and you face one financial crisis after another, then there is a chance you are practising financial self-sabotage. Wanting financial stability on the one hand but feeling you cannot control where the money goes and cannot make plans to help yourself speaks of a significant mental block or a money disorder.

BAD HABIT OR MONEY DISORDER?

Money disorders are bad money habits in extremis that rarely begin with divorce, but instead are exacerbated by it. Most money disorders are born from a dysfunctional relationship to money due to those generational beliefs we spoke of earlier or esteem-related problems where money is used to compete or make the person feel better.

The difference between a bad habit and a disorder is acknowledgement. If you recognise you have a bad habit and can break it, then find your adult willpower and do so. Try using some of the lessons taught in Chapter 3 such as putting aside savings first and living within your means for the rest of the month or hiding any credit cards for a few months and see what you can live without. If you are prone to saying or thinking, "I don't know where the money goes", then use credit or borrow to spend on wants, there's an obvious disconnect between what you say and what you do.

Just as smokers and drinkers find comfort in people with similar addictions, someone with a spending problem may seek out like-minded saboteurs with similar destructive thought patterns. While these addictive relationships may give you temporary comfort or camaraderie, they are helping you cheat yourself out of a better financial future.

Although we discussed a few disorders, namely Learned Helplessness and Unhealthy Entitlement, at the beginning of this book, the disorders discussed below are the ones that will hurt you the most after your divorce. This is because they impact your ability to either spend consciously and/or invest productively.

Financial Victim

Do you need to lean on others for freebies and favours, even though you could afford to pay for something yourself or pay full price if you cut back on non-necessities? Are you always "in financial trouble" or often say, "I try so hard and cannot make ends meet", despite having ample income or a comfortable lifestyle relative to others? Do you not like being told what to do, even if it is for your own financial betterment? In other words, are you prone to ask for advice and not take it?

If the answer is yes to any of the above questions, you may be playing the role of Financial Victim. And while you may be playing it well, you will probably not be able to play it forever. There is a good chance that you are covering up impulse spending or other bad financial habits, then pleading poverty or cash flow problems. You may be rationalising purchases that make you feel good but that also put you in a financial hole.

The problem with the Financial Victim is that eventually the people you lean on "get it" and try to wean you off by no longer granting you financial favours. Playing the Victim only works in the short term because people become resentful towards what appears to be a narcissistic approach to money management, namely it's all about you.

Your ex-spouse may also be playing this role. In this case, you will have to take responsibility and be wary if he is the type of victim who enjoys manipulating others. He may well make repeated attempts to dodge his legally binding maintenance or child support payments. If he does, you need to nip this in the bud before the problem escalates. If he can afford to make his payments, you should get a court order as some jurisdictions will then have the payments deducted directly from his salary.

Reality Check: Most people with this money disorder have been papering over sadness or pain through their spending for a very long time. Or their issues are more sociopathic in that they get their high by manipulating and cheating others.

If you are a Financial Victim, you are very likely alienating friends and family, possibly for good. Go back to Chapter 3 and adopt the steps of conscious spending. Conscious spending is one means of financial salvation for the Financial Victim. Find your true financial footing without the freebies.

Make the payments you need to make honestly, with no one-upmanship over friends and colleagues. Pay back loans that you owe to others. And apologise if you have leaned on people too hard for too long.

The building blocks of self-esteem don't come from spending money on non-necessities for "sugar highs" or from petty wins over money but by financially enabling yourself to the fullest through discipline and willpower.

Bragging Rights

The bragging rights mindset often rears its ugly head long before divorce is in the air. I have noticed that women who have held fairly high-flying jobs but leave these positions to become full-time mothers often find the transition very hard. Where at one time the rewards, both monetary and public recognition (i.e. having a title, etc.), came from their work, some of these women struggle with the lack of esteem and recognition that go along with full-time motherhood. Consequently, there can be transference of fulfilment; what came with professional competence and is not found in being a mother is transferred to more material and superficial things. For instance, being able to brag about your latest, greatest luxury holiday raises your profile among peers in lieu of your work.

Fast-forward to divorce. If while you were married, you were accustomed to doing activities that gave you bragging rights among your social group, a significant change in lifestyle can come as a shock. This is because your self-worth has become partly rooted in exercising those bragging rights. It becomes a problem when dining at the newest restaurant, staying at the latest boutique hotel or buying that latest fashion item leads you to indulge beyond what you can now afford, destroying your balance sheet as a result.

Think about when the bragging rights habit started, and why it has become so pivotal to who you feel you are. Are you using bragging rights to feel better about how you really feel? Are your bragging rights more important than more real and sustainable accomplishments that have evaded you up to now? If you are a super competitive person, it may be worth exploring healthier ways to act out your competitive drive.

Reality Check: As a mother, I experienced a low when I quit work to be with my children. Their infant years were wrought with financial difficulties and personally were among the least fulfilling years I can remember. And yes, society makes this worse by undervaluing the role of motherhood and making you feel guilty for not loving every nappy change, every bath and every burping session.

That said, it was only a phase in my life, and the time I put in with my children when they were little has paid back hundredfold because they are loving, well-adjusted young adults. I work less hard now as a parent because of that and years of financial discipline have paid off handsomely. I have had time to rebuild a career (and write a book!), get involved with charitable causes and engage a close circle of friends. All of this has provided me more enjoyment and self-respect than anything I have ever bought.

For the divorcee, this reality check is doubly important. Drowning in debt or living from hand to mouth for the sake of appearances has never garnered anyone sustainable self-respect. Find a way to set up a savings plan (*see* "Conscious Spending in Practice" in Chapter 3) and then reward yourself, only after you have set aside savings. Find some little luxuries that you can indulge in more often without needing to splash out to feel good about yourself. Take out your competitive zeal in a healthier way through mastering a sport, an art or some other activity. Or get a job that lets you have the bragging rights you want.

Keeping Up with the Kuoks

> Never keep up with the Joneses.
> Drag them down to your level. It's cheaper.
> —*Quentin Crisp*

Divorce leads to a blow in self-esteem for most people, and it can hit doubly hard when you cannot maintain your social circle's level of spending. A close cousin to Bragging Rights, Keeping Uppers are faced with a mix of shame and envy when faced with cutting back in front of friends and often continue spending in order to maintain face. This all leads to ugly balance sheets.

Keeping Uppers are notoriously easy to take advantage of by people who have money or are in positions of power. Wealthy people can single out Keeper Uppers from miles away. These frenemies, if you will, lord it over the Keeper Upper. Maybe they'll guilt you into spending money on their charity drive or, conversely, bargain hard on a service you are offering in the hope that your need to curry favour overcomes your common sense.

As an example, a girlfriend who ran an interior design studio very much wanted to maintain a Who's Who client list as part of bolstering her image post-divorce. As it turned out, these clients whom she wanted so dearly to keep were the very clients who haggled the most over price and the least appreciative of her efforts.

The need to keep up or run with the right crowd can really do damage to your purse in more ways than one. The sooner you start saying no to such friends, just like your children, the faster you will garner respect for your financial boundaries.

Here are some scenarios in which you should start to assert yourself:

1. You have gone out for dinner with girlfriends who are aware of your precarious financial state. Everyone is drinking except for you but when the bill comes, you are expected to split it equally and pay towards their drinks. Tell them you love their company but don't want to pay for their drinks. If they don't like it, they are the ones being inconsiderate, not you. Also, reconsider if going out with them really is the best way to spend your time.

2. You have the chance to go on a trip with a wealthier girlfriend. She insists on going 5 star but you can only afford 3 star or less. Tell her that you really want to go but have a budget of $X. If she wants to go 5 star and readily offers to pay the extra to upgrade you to 5 star, TAKE THE OFFER, with thanks of course.

   Write her a heartfelt letter when you return (not an email but a handwritten letter that you post), make her dinner or buy her a bouquet of flowers. Friends with money do not make friends without money blow their tiny budgets; they find a way to compromise. And put your ego, or pride, to one side; true friends share what they have willingly.

If your friend isn't willing to compromise, then you need to ask yourself whether she really is a true friend.

3. You run a small business and your wealthier friends want favours. Say, "I do pro bono work for charities. As someone who is financially successful, I am sure you can understand my priorities." If they beg, say, "Are you going through some sort of financial difficulty? Would you like to talk about it?" No one who lords it about as wealthy would admit to this for fear of the rumour mill.

Reality Check: Be honest as your true friends will understand. You can tell people that you have a retirement plan in the works and have committed yourself to saving and investing regularly, and these are now your priorities. Your best friends will respect your financial boundaries and support your desire for financial stability. If people do not respect your needs and desires, they might be the friends you want but are they the friends you need?

Denial and Rationalising

It is pretty common to go through denial during the different stages of divorce. Denial helps protect us psychologically by blunting the trauma that divorce can inflict on our psyche. Some people, however, continue to deny any needed changes through super optimistic thinking, even when their balance sheet is screaming for adjustments. These people can be referred to as Denial and Rationalisers (D&Rs).

Denial of financial problems or an unwillingness to plan for the future leads D&Rs to financially destructive behaviour. I've seen insolvent, or broke, D&Rs rationalise luxury travel and the need to buy non-necessities because "they are on sale". I've seen D&Rs rationalise spending emergency money on spa memberships.

By prolonging the acknowledgement of needed budgetary adjustments, D&Rs never develop conscious spending habits and they never come to terms with the changes they may need to make to right their financial ship. Nor do they practise the self-control needed to reign in impulse buying. The result is that this all-abundance-all-the-time thinking usually devolves into plain old wishful thinking, an empty bank account and mounds of credit card debt.

People who have the D&R personality often have dependency issues. These dependency issues lead them to put off planning and positive action because they spend inordinate amounts of time trapped in emotional battles with the same people (ex-spouse, family members, etc.) without resolution. As a result, they can come off as clinging to false hope and ignoring reality.

D&Rs only tend to face reality when they hit rock bottom financially speaking, which is often bankruptcy or some significant loss of income. They then either face up to it all or become Financial Victims due to their inability to face reality.

I once knew a woman, let's call her Susan, who had the traits of a person trapped in a classic D&R emotional struggle. She liked that "people talked about her". She felt that life was like advertising: "It's better that they say something about you—good or bad—than nothing at all."

After five years of being divorced, Susan went from having some savings and a decent settlement to being in significant debt. People talked for sure but for all the wrong reasons. They were saying that Susan, who ran around espousing "how grand life is", seemed unstable. This need for constant reassurance and attention from others is a telltale sign of dependency.

Do you feel the need to tell people how wonderful your life is? At the same time, do you have chronic credit card debt or cash flow problems that just won't go away? Do you often make plans and cannot follow them through? Do you prefer to run away from problems? And is all of this exhausting? Answering yes to any or all of these questions is a telltale sign of a D&R.

Reality Check: There is a difference between hoping for the best and planning for the worst, aka being realistically optimistic, and "just believing it will all work out". What you are likely searching for is peace of mind, so admit that first and start living honestly with yourself.

Put together your balance sheet and cash flow statements. Spend consciously with the money you have. Commit only to what you know you can do and put everything else on hold. If the truth is too painful to recognise on your own, please go and see a therapist who can help guide you from a place of denial to a place of reality.

Scarcity Mindset

The opposite of people in an all-abundance-all-the-time mindset are people who believe the world is a pie of a certain size, and it can never grow larger. So what they have today is what they will always have, and there will never be any more. They feel adversity is around every corner and that there is no "breathing room" to take on opportunities or make educated investment choices.

They believe that for everyone who wins, there must be a loser. Thus, they hold extreme risk-averse views and shy away from the means to create wealth, such as through new job opportunities or sound investments. This is not about feeling "bearish" (a term used when people think an asset will go down in price) or being a "conservative" investor (someone who prefers low risk investments). Scarcity-minded individuals are chronically afraid and constricted, and this stress eats into their creativity and energy.

Fundamentally, these people do not trust themselves, or their own judgement, so they do nothing. This constant feeling of scarcity is often the result of experiencing financial trauma or having a trauma passed down from a previous generation— remember the old generational tapes playing and warning us to never trust anyone.

It's like a mother who had a bad visit to the dentist when she was young. Because of her bad childhood experience, she doesn't take her own child to a dentist until the child's teeth are rotting. Now the child will relive the adult trauma when they have to sit in a dentist's chair for hours getting root canals. This is how trauma is passed down from generation to generation and never solved.

Reality Check: Hoarding is for squirrels, not for humans. Going through life in fear and stressed out with little hope will make you physically sick. Finish this book and if you are still overwhelmed by what to do next to create a more stable financial future, go and see a therapist to help you work through your negative thought patterns and redirect your energy into positive means.

CONCLUSION

As I have stated in chapters 3 and 4, financial security has a lot to do with developing consistent, healthy habits towards spending and investing. It is also about understanding what you are entitled to and owning your financial decisions on a day-to-day basis. Most of the time, you can do this without any professional intervention of any kind as long as you have the discipline or can develop it.

If, however, you feel unable to develop such habits or unable to chart a realistic course for your financial future, seek a certified financial planner (CFP) to help bring clarity to your financial situation. If you cannot stick to the financial planner's suggestions to help you budget and save, then you may want to try therapy or counselling.

SECTION 3

EMPOWERMENT

Empowerment is such an overused word, particularly in books addressing women, that it can sometimes lose its true meaning so let me define what empowerment means in the context of financial planning and investing: Empowerment speaks to informed choices which, in turn, lead to improved investment opportunities. Empowered investors understand that there are risks when investing but they also understand the options that allow them to mitigate, but not eliminate, these risks. Empowered investors learn how to make money off their money as opposed to hoarding it in cash or relying only on advisers who may not always have their best interests at heart.

As part of your divorce settlement, you will have all or a combination of the following:

- a lump sum settlement, some of which is likely cash
- ongoing maintenance and/or child support
- legacy investments such as property, pensions or investment plans and portfolios

Therefore, any money for investment will come from your monthly cash flow, your current assets in the case of a lump sum cash settlement or from the proceeds of a property sale or the like.

These final chapters will demonstrate why people invest their money in different assets to meet future financial goals. They will give you a prism through which you can view actual retirement planning, different asset classes and the finance industry as a whole so you can choose how best to invest your settlement or the monthly cash flow that you currently have in order to meet specific financial goals.

CHAPTER 6

TIME, GOAL SETTING AND RETIREMENT PLANNING

Actual goal setting and strategic investment planning are the least appreciated and most disregarded parts of investing, most egregiously by a hyper sales-oriented financial services industry. As a result, beginner investors either err in being too tactical or in having no real long-term goal or plan.

Tactically oriented investors want to dive into investing by focusing on one-off investment ideas, such as "I need a couple of good stock picks or funds" or "I want to get in on gold when it falls 10%." This is the equivalent of saying you will plan a three-week holiday but then only choose which spa treatments you want. Alternatively, clients who are unaware of how to properly do long-term investment planning often have me look at their portfolios and ask, "How am I doing?" Well, how you are doing is relative to a lot of things, namely what did you expect from your portfolio? What return did you want and need from these investments?

Often, beginner investors invest because they know they should and because everyone else is doing so, but they haven't really thought about what they are trying to accomplish and why. Therefore, you need to understand why investing is a good idea and then establish financial goals that suit your unique situation *before* you invest a dollar. So, instead of investing just for the sake of investing, let's first understand why investing your money at all is a good idea in the long term.

HOW TIME CAN CREATE OR DESTROY WEALTH

As noted earlier, there is a special relationship between time and money, which is why the sooner you embrace Healthy Entitlement and Ownership, the better off you'll be. Many people fear investing but the key to understanding why you should invest money as opposed to just keeping it in a bank is best explained using the Time Value of Money concept. This is the most important economic concept that you didn't learn at school.

You need to think Time Value of Money whenever you hear someone say, "The cheque is in the post." The Time Value of Money simply means that money earned, received or saved today is worth more today than it will be tomorrow. This is because of two opposing forces at work: (1) the ability of money you have in your hand to give you a return, meaning it is invested in a way that generates even more money for you, and (2) the force of inflation, which slowly destroys the value of uninvested cash savings simply sitting in a bank.

THE BEAUTY OF COMPOUNDING AND THE PERILS OF INFLATION

While leaving all your money in the bank may seem a safe strategy, your savings will face the ravaging effects of inflation if you choose not to invest it and earn a return. Therefore, to combat inflation and make money "work for you", investors often seek out returns and invest beyond the safety of a bank account.

Returns and Compounding Returns: The Money Creator

The two main "money-making" components of most investments are:

1. the capital gain (the difference between the price you pay for something and the price you sell it for) and
2. the income (cash flow) you earn off your asset while you hold it

A return is based on the total money you gain (or lose) on an investment. If, for example, you buy a home outright for $100,000 and sell it a year later for $120,000, your capital gain will be $20,000. If, over that year, you were paid a rental income (after any expenses) of $10,000, that would be considered your income. So, your total gain would be $10,000+$20,000=$30,000. Your total return for that year would be $30,000÷$100,000, or 30%.

You can only get a capital gain if you invest in something that someone else eventually pays more for. The investment doesn't have to be in property, it can be any type of investment including stock in a company ("stock"), a piece of art and so on. If no one pays more for your investment, then you incur a capital loss when you sell it.

Income in the example above is the money you make on the home while you own it, regardless of its price or perceived value, which will fluctuate over a long period of time. If you have cash in a savings account, the income would be the interest that the bank pays you. If you lend money to someone and expect to be paid back in full, then the income would be the interest or the extra money you get paid for lending the money to that person in the first place. These capital-gaining, income-producing "things" are referred to as assets. Ideally, your assets give you income and capital gains over time to produce a larger total return in the end.

COMPOUNDED RETURNS

Let's say that you took the $10,000 rental income from the example above and put it into a savings account the following year that paid an annual interest rate of 4%, compounded quarterly. This means that each quarter the bank will pay into your savings account 1% on the account balance, steadily growing your balance and giving you more money each quarter, as you can see on the next page.

	Q1	Q2	Q3	Q4
Money at start of period	$10,000	$10,100	$10,201	$10,303
Money you make	$100	$101	$102	$103
Balance	$10,100	$10,201	$10,303	$10,406

In this case, your compounded return is 4.06%, not just 4%. As your money compounds, the investment base, or balance, of your money grows, and it grows faster the longer your money stays invested, even if you do not add another dollar to the pile. If this money were left in this account compounding at the same rate, you would have a balance of $22,167 in 20 years.

If interest in the example above were paid daily, as opposed to just every three months, your money would grow even faster. Your compounded return would be 4.08% for one year and, in 20 years, your balance would be $22,254. It is important to realise and remember that for compounded returns, **it's not just what interest rate you are paid, it is how often you are paid.**

This is what my 13-year-old son calls "the snowball effect" of invested money that compounds. Basically, you roll a small snowball and keep rolling it so that it picks up more snow. The longer you roll it around, the bigger the snowball in the end. Therefore, if you start investing and receiving compounded returns when you are 30 years of age, you can earn a much larger return than if you just begin investing at 40 or 50, all other things being equal.

THE RULE OF 72

The Rule of 72 is a classic rule of compounding for beginner investors that illustrates how quickly you can double the money you invest depending on your return. The rule goes like this: If you divide the interest you receive on any investment by 72, you will know how many years it will take to double your money.

Compounded interest earned per annum	Number of years to double your money
1%	72
2%	36
3%	24
4%	18
5%	14.4
6%	12
7%	10.2
8%	9

If you are able to earn 4% on an investment annually, it will take you 18 years to double your money. If you are able and willing to take on more risk to earn 7% per year, it will take you slightly more than 10 years to double your money and so on. Hopefully you are beginning to see the positive linkages with time and money!

Consolidated Spreadsheet—Margaret's Assets and Returns

The most useful way of looking at your total assets and the income you earn off those assets is to prepare a balance sheet and track or estimate the income you earn each year. Having a consolidated spreadsheet of all your assets and their returns is one way of getting an overview of what you hold and spotting the opportunities to improve your income position. Here is an example of the asset portion of a balance sheet that tracked returns over just one year:

Margaret's Assets						Income	Capital Gains	Total Return
	1.27	1.00	0.16	1.22				
	CAD	SGD	HKD	USD				
Cash Accounts								
Bank - HK			500,000			0	0	0%
Bank – SG		20,000				0	0	0%
Subtotal					100,000			
Investment Accounts								
Investment Account #1				125,000		2,375	5,000	6%
Investment Account #2				55,000		825	3,000	7%
Subtotal					192,100			
Property								
Canadian Property	500,000					0	25,000	6%
Hong Kong Property			15,000,000			0	250,000	2%
Subtotal					3,035,000			
TOTAL ASSETS SGD	635,000	20,000	2,480,000	219,600	3,354,600	2,623	81,510	2.5%

Margaret's assets are very typical of many female investors. Margaret is a Singaporean living in Hong Kong, who has substantial assets, however, she is earning very little income from her asset base every year. Most of her gains are *on paper*, meaning that the gains we can see under "Capital Gains" is the value of her properties as they rise in price. I have italicised "on paper" because all capital gains look great on paper, but that gain is not realised until you sell the asset and pocket the cash. If the property market began to trend downwards, these "gains on paper" would begin to shrink, or even turn negative.

What Margaret needs to do is understand how to create more cash income streams from her current assets as she is only returning 2.5% per year on her overall assets, and only 0.08% is real cash income. Capital gains are fine and necessary over the long term, but since all assets go through cycles of rising and falling in price over time, it's the income you earn from your assets that can make a huge difference to your financial stability. We will discuss how to earn more income in later chapters. Here, I am simply presenting an overview of one investor's overall assets and returns.

Inflation—The Money Destroyer

As I have said, whereas time works for you with compounding, it has completely the opposite effect with inflation if you are not investing your savings. Inflation, like termites boring through wood, eats away at your purchasing power so as the necessities of life such as food and housing rise in price, you need to pay more just to keep up with inflation. Inflation has been particularly debilitating to savers of late as the cost of items like food, rent and medical care has soared globally.

In the realm of divorce, what may seem like a lot of money at the point of settlement can become severely diminished when the cost of life's necessities rises over time if you are earning no income and not receiving a return on your money. It's a bit like watching an ice cube melt, except it is your pile of money shrinking in size from the heat of inflation.

But I Want to Keep My Money in the Bank!

When talking about investing, you need to address how you feel (or fear) about taking risk. We are all scared of losing what we have—this is natural. But however damaging a downturn in financial or property markets is, more damaging over the long run is the effect of inflation when all your money is parked in a bank savings account with little or no interest being paid, which is the reality we face today. That said, I do appreciate how unnerving investing is and how complex and unhelpful the financial industry as a whole has become.

For the insistent saver, who does not want to take on any risk investing for return, you need a different plan, and that would be "How do I combat future inflation?" This is largely done by saving more, earning more and spending less.

Below is a table that demonstrates two comparative situations in which the individuals have different approaches to saving and investing. Preema wants to invest her money for long-term return while Katherine is afraid of investing so she decides to leave all her money in the bank. Both women want to retire in Hong Kong.

Let's assume that inflation is running at 3% per year, which is actually a modest projection based on the last five years in Asia. They each start with a retirement savings "pot" of HK$2 million. Preema invests and gets 4.5% real return (after inflation) over 15 years. Katherine does not get a return because her money is sitting in a bank account so she essentially "loses" 3% a year in purchasing power due to inflation. The respective columns represent each woman's real return at the end of each of the 15 years.

End of Year	Preema	Katherine
1	2,090,000	1,940,000
2	2,184,050	1,881,800
3	2,282,332	1,825,346
4	2,385,037	1,770,586
5	2,492,363	1,717,468
6	2,604,520	1,665,944
7	2,721,723	1,615,965
8	2,844,201	1,567,486
9	2,972,190	1,520,462
10	3,105,938	1,474,848
11	3,245,706	1,430,602
12	3,391,762	1,387,684
13	3,544,392	1,346,054
14	3,703,889	1,305,672
Year 15 Total Real Return	3,870,564	1,266,502

Whereas Preema has almost doubled her money (72÷4.5=16) over 15 years, Katherine would need to save almost HK$49,000 a year just to "stay even" after inflation. If this is hard to believe, think about what a home might have cost you 15 years ago and what it would cost you today. There is no way that the same amount of money 10 or 20 years ago will buy you the same bundle of goods and services today. Inflation is real and its effects on our standard of living are not going away any time soon. Yes, your money is melting!

We will go through bouts of deflation and disinflation, or declining prices, and we will have years like 2008 again when most of the world's assets essentially "go on sale". Personally, I look forward to sales like the one we had in 2008. In the long run though, inflation is persistent and it's the worst enemy of a retiree or someone living on a fixed income such as maintenance. So, if you do not want to invest your money beyond a bank savings account, you must find ways to strategise for the inflation you will most certainly face in the future through either earning more income or spending less money.

BRAHMA VERSUS SHIVA

If you know Hindu mythology, think of compounding returns as Brahma the Creator and inflation as Shiva the Destroyer. These concepts are important to understand, particularly for divorcees who may be tempted to leave all their money just in cash but, by doing so, will earn no money on their money.

We will revisit these concepts as we get into the nitty-gritty of investing. The longer you wait to begin earning a return or "money on your money", the more you may feel the need to take greater risks later in life to make up for lost time or beat inflation—the money destroyer. This is a trap that many people 40 years of age and above fall into as their retirement horizon nears and they realise they have nowhere near the funds they need for a comfortable retirement. For the predominantly risk-averse single woman household, it is imperative to enjoy the benefits of compounded returns, however large or small, as soon as practicable.

Real Returns versus Nominal Returns

In the example above, I mentioned Preema's after inflation, or "adjusted for inflation", return. This is called a real return, not a nominal return. Nominal return is what you see touted in most marketing for financial products which is why these products so often seem too good to be true. Nominal returns do not factor in inflation. Ironically, we live in a world obsessed with nominal return and there's not nearly enough discussion about real returns.

A real return is what it says it is—it's the return you will have to live with! Real return factors in your purchasing power. So if your investment adviser says he can get you a return of 8%, you need to ask, "Is this the nominal or the real return?" It's almost always a nominal return. If inflation is 3%, then your real return on that 8% is just 4.85%.[1] Although not precisely

---

1 For more guidance on how to reach the calculation here using a financial calculator, please refer to "Using a Financial Calculator" in Appendix 3.

accurate, if you subtract the rate of inflation from the nominal return, you will get a ballpark figure for your real return.

When you are planning how to live off a divorce settlement or a retirement sum, you should always think in real rates of return. Nominal returns sound more comforting, but real returns are the most realistic and by using them you will be able to parse through more clearly the information given to you by the financial industry. Most importantly, by using real returns, you can ensure you do not fall short when planning for something as significant as retirement.

Home Currency

In respect to returns, the other thing you must keep in mind is currency. You need to think of your "home currency". I've noted of late that many financial advisers in Hong Kong and Singapore are pushing clients to look at US$ returns. Just like you need to think in real returns, you need to see returns in the currency in which you intend to deploy any investment.

That means that if you are investing in a retirement portfolio and you will be living and retiring in Singapore, then you need to see a Singapore dollar return. If you are a Canadian living in Hong Kong and building your Canadian retirement nest egg in order to retire in Canada, then you need to see returns in Canadian dollars and so on. Returns can look better in one currency than another at times so make sure you see your returns in a currency that is meaningful to you.

Risk and Return—Long-term Investing Basics

The general rule of thumb for risk and return is as follows: the greater the risk, the greater the return; the lower the risk, the lower the return. For example, over the last 40 years, you would have been able to make more money on your money if you had invested in an equity index fund (stocks) or property in most Asian cities compared to leaving your money sitting in a bank. But you would have also needed to have weathered some stomach-churning market ups and downs as well as a few financial crises through the years.

As I have noted, if you do not want to risk any loss at any time, then expect 0% return, or negative return, if you consider how inflation imperils your purchasing power over time, as shown in the above example with Katherine's money. Here is a graph showing investments that are called "asset classes", such as stocks, bonds etc., and their historical risk-and-return profile.

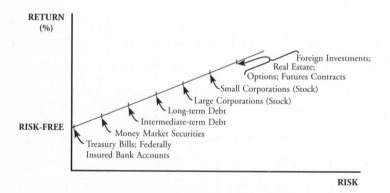

Source: http://fycs.ifas.ufl.edu/younginvestor/module3/mod3sec1-3.shtml

This may be a US-centric chart but the point is simple: As you take on more risk, you can generally expect greater returns over the long term. Keeping your money in a bank account is less risky than buying a property or stock in a company but you get very little return for very little risk. In fact, in today's low interest rate environment, you will get less than 0.5% return for most bank deposits or time deposits in Asia's major financial hubs.[2]

Raising the Red Flag

There is also no such thing as high return, low risk investing. And it is here that I want to briefly mention two financial fraud red flags. Anyone who tries to sell you a concept such as high return for low risk is likely peddling some sort of financial fraud. There's almost no such thing as a risk-free, high-reward investment, at least not one that is legal.

Furthermore, if someone tries to sell you a "consistent positive returns every year" type of concept, without any "down" or "loss" years, you need to sit back and wonder how that is possible. Despite what the financial media attempt to convey, there are very few financial geniuses out there managing other people's money. You can probably count the world's truly great investors on one hand. If there really were a way to invest year after year without any loss, it wouldn't be a big secret for long and everyone would be practising it.

You just need to look at UK retirees who put all their money into "high return, no risk" Icelandic savings accounts, only to

---

2   For more on this, read "A Word on Risk and Return" in Appendix 2.

see these accounts all but evaporate when Icelandic banks failed during the 2008 financial crisis. Or you may have heard of Bernie Madoff who bilked retirees and charities out of billions of dollars on the promise of "consistent year-on-year returns". Madoff didn't have a "bad year" until it was uncovered that he was a fraud who had fooled the likes of small and large institutional investors.

Divorcees can be particularly vulnerable, getting sucked into the idea of "risk free" or "consistent returns year on year" because these promises sound tempting to the financially fearful. Fraudulent behaviour can go on for a long time in an "easy money" environment, as we have now, in which there is plentiful lending and economic times seem good. It is often only when there is yet another financial crisis that fraud finally becomes apparent. You must consider carefully any proposition that raises either or both of these two well-known risk-and-return red flags.

GOAL SETTING: GETTING STARTED

Now that you know why you should invest, and with your balance sheet firmly in hand and cash flow under control, you need to ask yourself what you are investing for. What is the goal of this investment? When do you need to meet this goal? What will you be using the money for once you have reached your goal(s)? Based on all these questions, what return do you need? And in what currency?

If you are new to investing your money, set yourself two goals to start with: one long-term and one short-term goal. The reason why goals are broken down into short term and long term is that these goals have different time horizons. Time horizon is the final concept you need to be familiar with before you invest that first dollar. Your time horizon is your investment finishing line; it's when you will need to begin to draw down and use the money you have been investing.

Because your time horizons differ in length, you may end up using different savings or investment strategies to reach different goals. A short-term goal is something that can be accomplished within three months to two years. Examples of short-term goals include paying down debt, saving enough for a home down payment or establishing an emergency fund. Your only investing strategy for short-term goals may be to find a good interest bearing savings account as you need access to this money sooner rather than later.

A long-term goal is something that takes longer to achieve, even though you may start investing or saving for it immediately. Examples of longer-term goals include debt-free home ownership or building a retirement nest egg. College savings would also fall under long-term goals if your children are under the age of 11. Remember this however: Do not even start to think about college funds for your children until your retirement savings are well underway. No one is going to give you a scholarship to fund your retirement.

Your goals can be wide and varied, but the three goals every single woman should have before all others are as follows:

carrying very little credit card debt (or cease depending on credit cards entirely, save using the monthly interest-free float), ample emergency savings and a retirement fund that you can live off once you are no longer earning an income (or receiving maintenance). Ideally, the latter goal should include owning a home or residing in a property that you can call your own without fear of eviction.

Intent: The Mindset to Meet Your Financial Goals

Goal setting helps people focus their plans, but you must remain flexible and allow for some degree of change. There is an old Chinese proverb that states, "As long as the direction is correct, the goal need not be too specific."

As the proverb goes, it really speaks about intent. In other words, your intentions to achieve your goals should be honest, true and within the realm of possibility. It doesn't matter if you end up finding a better way of investing than originally planned or if instead of using money set aside to fund someone's college education, you end up sending yourself back to school to upgrade your skills. The point is that the discipline you develop through strong money management skills, such as cash flow management, when combined with the correct intention will lead you in the right direction.

As you may have sensed while reading this, I cannot emphasise enough the importance of retirement planning. Most people start far too late in life trying to understand how they will live off and invest their retirement savings. For someone who has experienced divorce, if you plan for nothing else, start thinking about how to provide for yourself when you are no longer working or receiving an income, such as maintenance.

EXAMPLE OF SETTING A FINANCIAL GOAL: RETIREMENT SCENARIO PLANNING

For some women, retirement begins with divorce. In other words, you may be forced to live off whatever your settlement is, without the means of a significant career comeback. For other women, retirement begins in their sixties or later if they intend to work through to a specific retirement age.

Some divorcees will plan to remarry and, particularly in Asia, many women will plan on living with their children in old age. Of course it's great to assume it will work out that way, and a lot of the time it does. However, for the sake of good planning, it is always wise to consider how you will live if, for any reason, you must support yourself. On this point, while it would be wonderful to depend on pensions from governments or corporations, it is best to plan as if those resources are simply a supplement to your income and not your entire means of support.

There are four basic questions that you have to ask yourself when planning for retirement:

1. Where will I be living?
2. When does retirement officially begin? In other words, at what age will you no longer make an income or receive a significant income in the form of maintenance from your ex-spouse?
3. How much income will I need every year to support myself?
4. What will my lifestyle be (i.e. active or more sedentary)?

Of all the questions above, "where" and "when" are the most important because they will most likely answer the "how much will I need" question.

Regarding "where", being near family is what everyone wants but consider the cost of living near family if you cannot live with them. Understanding the cost of simple needs such as medical care and food, not just now, but in the future, is imperative because of the persistence of inflation.

This is especially true in Asia's large cities, most notably Hong Kong where the peg to the dollar has caused huge inflation in property and imported goods. Singapore, as an island, has also experienced significant rises in food prices over the last several years because much of what we eat is imported from other countries. Therefore, it helps to consider which other locations you could retire to if you needed to stretch your retirement savings.

"When" is important because it specifies what finance people call your time horizon. How long can you invest your money before you need to begin to draw down on your savings and use them to support yourself? You might still remain invested but you will need to look at drawing down some of your nest egg every year to ensure cash flow.

The last question pertaining to retirement planning—"what"—can be answered in degrees of necessity and luxury. It would be wonderful to have enough money to choose your lifestyle. If you do enough forward planning, you can be in a position to make choices and not have them hoisted upon you due to a lack of savings.

In order to become familiar with the retirement planning process, let's look at two scenarios: a divorcee with maintenance and a divorcee with only a lump sum settlement.

How Much Do I Need For Retirement? Maria's Story

Let's take the case of Maria, a 40-year-old divorced mother of one boy aged 10. They reside in Singapore where her son attends United World College of South East Asia. Maria does not have any debt and already has S$80,000 set aside in an emergency fund which would easily cover six months of expenses.

On the one hand, she would like to live with her son's family in old age but, on the other hand, she knows it is wise to plan to live independently. Maria wants to build a retirement fund for herself because she would like to be self-sufficient after she retires.

As of today, Maria works full time earning around S$3,000 as an administrative assistant. She will receive maintenance of

S$5,000 and child support of around S$3,000 until her son graduates from college or university. Maria has no retirement assets right now so there is no balance sheet but her monthly cash flow looks like this:

Income	$
Income as Admin Asst.	3,000
Child Support	3,000
Maintenance	5,000
TOTAL	11,000
Expenditure	$
Food and Clothing	2,000
Rent	2,500
Travel, Transport, Petrol	500
Entertainment, Clubs	500
School Fees	paid by ex-husband
Extracurricular Activities	500
Helper	500
Utilities	300
Tax Savings	500
TOTAL	7,300
Savings/Deficit	3,700

Maria would like to retire in Singapore, but because the cost of living is so high, she is considering Bali as an alternative. By carrying out scenario-planning exercises for Maria, in which we assume she retires at 62 as well as receives maintenance from her ex-husband up until she is 62 (he should pay maintenance as long as he is making an income but we are making conservative assumptions here), we will be able to compare the cost of retiring in Bali with that of Singapore.

Maria does not have any retirement savings, aside from a small amount in her Singapore mandatory retirement account, so we are beginning at zero. (Remember that her emergency money is to be kept separate from this investment exercise.) Maria is assuming that she can return to Singapore for any major medical care as she is a Permanent Resident and can utilise her provident fund insurance scheme.

The point of this is to find out how much Maria needs to save and invest every month if she would like to meet her retirement goal. We also need to find out what her return needs to be on her investment(s).

BALI RETIREMENT PLANNING

The reasons why Maria has chosen Bali as an option, in addition to the low cost of living, are that she enjoys Bali's casual lifestyle, she has an interest in the arts and she likes that she can have help around the house at a very low cost. The downside is the accessibility to medical care so she would need insurance to evacuate her to Singapore in the event of an emergency or a serious or life-threatening illness.

Maria is currently living on S$7,300 a month while working and supporting her son. Maria has estimated that if she retires in Singapore, she would need only S$5,000 a month to support just herself. In Bali, however, Maria believes that her monthly outlay would be S$1,750, including rent. Given that Bali is only 35% of the cost of living in Singapore, Bali looks like a very attractive option.

It is important to note that both of these figures—S$5,000 for Singapore and S$1,750 for Bali—are "today's dollars" because we have not accounted for inflation from now up until her actual time of retirement. So when we work out the calculations, these figures will increase because more money will be needed each month to buy the same goods and services in the future due to the effects of inflation.

The calculations for Maria are based around these assumptions:
- She will retire at 62 years of age.
- She will live to 90 years of age.
- Her ex-husband will no longer support her once she reaches 62.

From now until retirement, these are the assumptions:
- Maria will invest S$2,000 per month.
- Maria will get an average 5% real return over the years before retirement and only a 2% real return after retirement.
- Inflation will run at 2% before and after retirement.

Since Maria will be investing a set amount every month, she is "dollar cost averaging" into her investments, or "dripping" her money into her investments, in lieu of buying a lot of equity or bonds all at once. The advantage of dollar cost averaging your investment is that you do not have to worry about timing the market for highs and lows. While you may invest some at market highs, no doubt you will catch the market when it is low as well, and this will smooth out your returns over time.

Maria will dollar cost average into a portfolio of investments that are projected to give her a 5% real return over 22 years. So is investing S$2,000 a month enough? Is her 5% real return enough to retire on? Let's calculate and see.[3]

The S$1,750 that Maria needs today to live in Bali every month will need to be S$2,705 in 22 years' time when she plans to retire. In other words, she will need S$2,705 a month to buy the same goods she can buy today with S$1,750. This is the effect of inflation.

As you might imagine, that $2,705, or $32,465 a year, will also have to increase slightly every year to account for inflation until she is 90. Consequently, we have calculated that she needs to begin retirement at 62 with S$704,714 in savings.

These savings will remain invested but Maria will start to draw down on her investment every year after retirement. Nevertheless, her nest egg will continue to compound and she will continue to earn money on her money during retirement,

---

3   For more guidance on how to reach the calculations here using a financial calculator, please refer to "Using a Financial Calculator" in Appendix 3.

even though the rate of compounding will slowly diminish over time as there becomes less of a nest egg.

So if all goes as planned and Maria achieves 5% in real return per year over 22 years, she will have S$958,708 in her nest egg. In fact, she could save a little less, or take on a little less risk, and still meet her retirement savings goal.

For the sake of comparison, if Maria wanted no investment risk and deposited S$2,000 a month for 22 years into her bank account, earning 0% interest, she would only save S$528,000. This is a good enough amount but not enough to achieve her retirement goal.

So what have we learnt from this exercise? Maria has time on her side and while she has to take on some risk, it's not as much as previously thought; she could invest at 4% instead of 5%, take on less risk and still achieve a modest retirement nest egg. Alternatively, she could stick with the original plan and invest at 5%, thus building up larger than needed retirement savings.

SINGAPORE RETIREMENT PLANNING

Now let's compare using the same strategy of investing S$2,000 a month, and different cost of living assumptions, to see what Maria's financial prospects would be if she were to retire in Singapore. Maria said she could live on S$5,000 per month in today's money but in 22 years' time, she would need S$7,730 per month.

So the question here is how long will her S$958,708 nest egg last from the start of retirement given the higher living expenses of Singapore? Unfortunately, that amount would last her only 11.5 years. This means that at the age of 73 Maria would need to resort to some other support to care for herself.

If Maria were set on staying in Singapore, she could certainly try to invest more every month and build up a larger nest egg—she has the extra savings to do so. Perhaps she could work past the age of 62 or cut back and try to live on less each month after retirement.

Through these comparisons, Maria is able to do some forward planning for her future.

Lump Sum Only Settlements

If you have received a lump sum settlement and are not effectively making an income, you are for all intents and purposes retired. And, just like a retiree, you should do your best to live off the interest or income earned from investing the lump sum, and preserve the capital (the lump sum) for as long as you can.

It is obvious why you should preserve this nest egg. If you can live off the income or interest from your nest egg, you will not need to touch your lump sum, thus preserving it for emergencies or as your estate.

For some divorcees, this option is entirely possible while for others it isn't because the lump sums they were granted in their settlements are not large enough to live off. Divorcees who fall into the second category will need to either return to the workplace in order to supplement their lump sum settlements or move to a location where it is possible for them to stretch their money further. Or they can do both.

Whatever the case, if you are granted capital, or a cash payment, in your divorce, try to preserve the capital as best you can. You should set yourself the goal of finding ways to make money off, at the very least, some of your lump sum payment through wise investing regardless of which assets (property to rent, stocks, bonds, time deposits) you choose.

ALICIA'S STORY

Let's take 56-year-old Alicia who has just divorced her husband of 30 years. They sold their property in Hong Kong in order to reach a divorce settlement with no continuing maintenance. Alicia's settlement came to HK$15,500,000 (around US$2 million).

Anywhere else in the world, this settlement would represent a small fortune. However in Asian hub cities like Singapore and Hong Kong, her settlement will barely cover the cost of a 1,000-square-foot two-bedroomed home. So purchasing a property in Hong Kong would leave her with no money to live on going forward.

That is why the question of "where" Alicia will continue to live is absolutely critical post-divorce. She would love to stay in Hong Kong but she simply cannot afford to do so without returning to the workplace, and she is aware that the chances of this happening are limited because of the length of time that she has been out of the workforce.

Alicia's eldest daughter lives in Australia, so this presents her with another option. She could retire in Australia and invest at least a portion of her money in Australian dollars where she can earn interest on simple time deposits (the interest for which is 4 to 5% in Australia versus almost 0% in Hong Kong at the time of writing).

So let's look at how Alicia can live off her lump sum with something as simple as an investment in a time deposit.

Here is the plan: Alicia will use the equivalent of HK$2.3 million to buy a property near Perth where her daughter lives with her family. She will put aside HK$1.7 million as her emergency money in a simple interest bearing savings account. Next, she will take the balance of HK$11.5 million, convert it into Australian dollars and get AUD$1,635,600. She will then invest this amount at 4.5% in several Australian dollar time deposits. (She will invest in several time deposits to minimise possible risks such as a bank going bankrupt, one bank lowering interest rates but others not and so on.)

By doing so, Alicia will receive interest income of around AUD$73,600 a year. Now we know that inflation will eat into this over time so Alicia will need to learn how to live off AUD$73,600 in the face of inflation or she will have to invest for a higher rate of return in riskier assets. If Alicia can learn to live on AUD$73,600 a year, or AUD$6,133 a month, she will be able to preserve her capital for as long as she wishes (or until interest rates change).

This strategy of capital preservation will allow Alicia to keep her initial capital for the time being without the fear of "running out of money". Depending on how conscientiously Alicia spends her money, she can also continue to build her nest egg even in retirement.

While Alicia's situation is one scenario, not all women will be able to move away from their hometown, and not all women receive lump sums that are large enough for them to live off. If this is your situation, you will need to combine a few or all of the following strategies:

- Minimise expenses to the bare minimum. Consider living with family or at least sharing a space with others by possibly taking in tenants.
- Look for part-time or full-time work to supplement your lump sum. Everyone has value and you are never too old to retrain yourself.
- Find the best ways of making some income off your money, whether you invest in simple time deposits, dividend-paying stocks, bonds or property to rent. Whatever you do, don't let your money sit around in the bank and get ravaged by inflation, have it work for you.

Analysing Your Current Situation and Goal Setting

As shown here and in Chapter 3, regular savings, investment goals and planning are necessities before you dive into investing. By taking these steps, you will have addressed your time horizon, your income or savings, your need for additional cash flow and your future needs, factoring in inflation. Based on that analysis, you should now have an idea of how to begin to make long-term financial plans.

If your situation is uniquely complex or you feel unprepared to analyse your own situation, including the effects of inflation, hire a certified financial planner to do a financial plan for you on a fee basis. This will be an investment of around $1,500 (S$2,000/HK$15,000) or more depending on the complexity of your situation. That's about the cost of an inexpensive holiday or a designer handbag; it's also what some women spend on Botox in a month and club memberships over a year. If you genuinely cannot afford to hire someone, try using a basic online calculator such as http://finance.yahoo.com/calculator/retirement/ret02/ as this may help you derive some basic returns for retirement planning.

Having even a rudimentary plan is the most valuable and most overlooked part of investing. A plan will bring focus to the way you go about earning, valuing and investing money. Driving without a map or diving in without a plan are no-nos.

CONCLUSION

Anyone can learn to manage their own money and make wise financial decisions. The difficult-to-hear news is that most beginner investors are looking for a silver bullet investment practice so that they can skip the planning altogether. However, the habits that you have developed from the first part of this book will put in motion the right habits and right mindset you need to plan and invest going forward.

Now that you've learnt why you should invest and become more interested in developing your own economic security, the more likely you will succeed. Most of all, you must invest to meet your own needs, which may well differ from your peer group or other family members. That is why setting financial goals is so important.

Too often, we find ourselves comparing our situation to another's financially. Comparing yourself to others is really a form of self-abuse, so don't even go there, it's an absolute waste of time. Wherever you are starting, financially speaking, is where you are starting. Your starting position is no doubt better than some people's circumstances but worse than others. As soon as you focus on what you can control, and start charting out financial goals with the right intent, you will begin to make larger strides towards a financially secure future.

CHAPTER 7

ASSETS

As a woman working with women investors, I have noticed two contrasting realities. Women make excellent investors once they develop the habits and the knowledge of how to invest successfully. At the same time, women who don't develop the knowledge to invest confidently are not as honest as men when it comes to admitting what they do or do not know. So, the inexperienced female investor tends to be both distrustful and very passive about advancing her knowledge. Caution and risk management are excellent qualities to embrace when investing but not to the point where your fears or your urge to control cripples you.

Knowing how to manage your money is important but you need to realise that this involves a learning curve. The more honest you can be with yourself about what you do not understand—and ask questions—the more you will learn. The best investors in the world make mistakes, and it's better to make a few small-scale mistakes than to never trust yourself with your own money.

To get you started on the road to investing on your own, this chapter will cover basic asset classes, namely cash, property, equity or stocks and fixed income or bonds, as well as the benefits and shortcomings of investing in each of these major asset classes. All of these assets have the two main money-making components that make up your total return, as covered in Chapter 6:

1. You can sell an asset for a capital gain (the difference between the price you pay for the asset and the price you sell it for).

2. You can make income off your asset while you hold it. This income is measured as your yield. You can use the yield as one way to decide how best to earn income from different assets.

The name of the game when investing is to find ways to create income off most of your assets while you hold them. This is better than leaving all your cash sitting in a bank account or "betting on" a gain in one primary asset, such as property.

The reason why I keep emphasising this point is that **most women I have worked with chose to hold the bulk of their assets in untenanted residential property or in cash, neither of which earns any income!** Of those invested primarily in property, they were focused to an extreme on the potential gain in the value of their asset, and not the possible income, while remaining assets were often held in cash, usually sitting in non-interest bearing checking or savings accounts. This focus only on capital gains or cash hoarding is the biggest investing mistake I see across the board with women and their investments.

So as you read more, you should be asking yourself, "What assets do I own and how much money, after expenses, am I currently making every month or every year from those assets?" If you do not own any assets, you should ask yourself, "How can I own assets that pay me some income while I hold onto them through market ups and downs?"

Wealthy people ask themselves these questions all the time. In fact, most of them don't do much buying and selling, and instead live off the income from their investments. The beauty of investing for income as well is that it's "real cash" that you can use and spend. This "income seekers" mindset is the way forward for those who are seeking long-term economic security and stability.

REAL ASSETS VERSUS FINANCIAL ASSETS

Real assets, as the name implies, are investments in real, tangible goods or property. The most widely held real asset is property, however, real assets include everything from oil to gold to diamonds to art.

Cash, stocks and bonds are financial assets. Stocks and bonds are traded over stock exchanges and through the bond markets. Investors often buy stocks *and* bonds together when they invest because, like waves across an ocean, the perception is that when stocks fall in value, bonds rise in value, and vice versa. Bonds are seen to do well during economic downturns, and stocks generally provide outsized returns during times of economic growth. This pairing of stocks and bonds is what I call a "fear and greed" portfolio—sometimes it works beautifully, other times, not as well.

Diversification and Liquidity

Diversification is like eating a well-balanced meal. If you eat too much of one thing, you are not going to be as healthy as if you eat a greater variety of food. There are benefits to holding both real and financial assets, and it is best to diversify so that you are depending on more than just one asset class for your capital gains and your income.

Regardless of what you ultimately choose to invest in, please keep in mind the word "liquidity". If an asset is liquid, you can sell it quickly for cash. If an asset is illiquid, you can't. Some examples of illiquid assets include property, stamp collections, rare wine, art and even some financial assets such as hedge funds.

Illiquid assets can be good assets, but it can become a problem if you invest in too many of them. If you are at all income insecure or dependent on an erratic ex-spouse for even some of your cash flow, do not over-invest in assets that you cannot easily or quickly sell for cash. This advice applies to *all* investors, not just divorcees.

ASSET CYCLES—THE MOTION OF THE ASSET OCEAN

Asset classes rise and fall, every single one of them. They all go through cycles of popularity and then falls from grace. Investors move from one asset class like bonds to another like stocks and back again over time. When investors are fearful, they tend to move into bonds. When investors feel greedy and optimistic about the economy, stocks and property tend to do better. So like enormous waves crossing the ocean, different assets in different geographies take turns rising in price and then subsequently falling in price, then rising again.

The motion of the ocean is greatly influenced by the world's largest investors, namely institutional investors. These include government pension funds, sovereign wealth funds, banks, insurance companies and the like. There is a misperception that these investors only invest in financial assets; they don't. They invest in everything—stocks, bonds, property, oil, currencies, etc.

Institutional investors' decisions as to how to invest are often influenced by macroeconomic changes such as inflation, job growth, unemployment and even demographic changes. These changes, in turn, can drive large flows of money into or out of different asset classes. Sometimes, this happens so quickly that asset bubbles form. These bubbles may continue to grow but eventually—and inevitably—the bubbles burst and prices drop suddenly, causing many investors to panic and sell.

THE ASSET CLASS OVERVIEW
CASH

The asset nearest and dearest to most women's hearts is cash. It's as liquid an asset as you can get and easy to understand. Almost everyone in the financial industry will tell you to invest all your money at all times because "cash has no value". What this means is that cash earns little or no interest these days and, currency trading aside, cash does not gain in value like other assets such as property.

While cash can die a slow death due to inflation, advisers also want you to invest as much as humanly possible because that's how they make money. As we will explore later, advisers generally charge a fee based on a percentage of your overall assets when you hire them to manage your investments, so if you are holding cash and are not invested, they will lose out. It takes strength sometimes to hold onto more cash than your peers, especially when everyone around you is chasing the investment trend du jour. Cash is also the most important asset you can have when markets melt down, as they did in 2008, so in times of deflation—when prices go down—cash is king.

So how much cash should you hold? Only you can answer this. As I have already explained in Chapter 3, you need three to six months' emergency money on hand. After that, it's said that 85% of your net worth should account for investable assets, including your home. That means 15% of all your net worth should be in cash. So if your net worth comes to $500,000, then at least $75,000 (0.15x500,000) should be held in cash or cash-like investments and the rest invested.

Everyone's situation is different, however. If you need to move within the next year, it might make sense to keep more money on hand to re-establish yourself. If you are dependent on an ex-spouse for support and that income source is not stable, then I would take the above rules of thumb with a grain of salt and adjust the percentages to suit your situation.

Whatever cash you have should be held in an interest bearing savings account, a reliable money market fund or a time deposit at a bank that has some deposit guarantee or deposit insurance.

It is important to note that your cash may only be guaranteed up to a certain amount in the event of a bank going bankrupt. When you deposit money with a bank, you become an unsecured creditor to that bank. As an example, bank depositors in the United States are only guaranteed up to $250,000 per account. This meant that when banks did go bankrupt in 2008, customers with more than $250,000 sitting in a bank account lost some of their money. Every country has different rules and it is important to understand what those rules are before leaving a large sum of money in a bank.

Ultimately, you need to make peace with your cash holdings. Strike a balance between your need to access money and the wear and tear inflation takes on your cash. You need to judge why you are holding onto cash and have a strategy as to why and how you will deploy it for investments. A certain amount of cash on hand is *always* wise, but hoarding is for squirrels, not confident investors!

PROPERTY

Next to cash, property is the most favoured asset among women because it serves as both a home and an investment. There are many ways to invest in property but, for the purpose of this book, I will only discuss private residential property, including condominiums and landed property.

Property can be one of the best investments you can make because it can bring a sense of stability and tends to gain steadily in price over the long term. The downside of property is that, by and large, it is an illiquid investment compared to stocks, bonds and other assets. This means that if you needed to sell your asset and have the cash within 24 hours, it would be nearly impossible to do so.

I Want to Buy a Home

The best way to own a home is to own it outright. If you must finance your home, as many of us do, then realise that you are essentially buying a mortgage payment. It's easy to get caught up in the vanity of home ownership, where some people believe that bigger is better and expensive prime locations are preferred to more reasonable up-and-coming areas. This can lead you to take on a larger mortgage than you can comfortably afford in the worst-case scenario.

It is financially and psychologically more difficult over the long term to be trapped in a property you ultimately cannot afford, especially if it ends up being the only asset to your name. You may well ask, "So how big should my mortgage payment be?" A guideline that answers this question is that a mortgage payment should eat up less than 30% of your gross monthly income. Normally, a bank will only extend a loan, if you are eligible, if the payments remain within this threshold in any case.

If you can secure a loan, be aware that your payments are not fixed payments as all mortgages predominantly are variable in Asia. This means that as interest rates rise, your mortgage payment will as well. Given that we are in an extremely low interest rate environment with mortgages at around 1.5% or less per year, expect and plan for your mortgage payment to rise steadily over the next 20 years as interest rates normalise. Here is a table that shows the change in payment associated with a change in interest rates. If you just follow the first line, you can see that for every $100,000 that you borrow, your mortgage payment rises nearly 6% even if the interest rate moves up only by 0.50%. So a rapid rise in interest rates can seriously put a dent in your cash flow if you are not prepared for it.

INTEREST RATE		4%	4.50%	5%	5.50%	6%	6.50%	7%	7.50%	8%
	100,000	$477.42	$506.69	$536.82	$567.79	$599.55	$632.07	$665.30	$699.21	$733.76
	150,000	$716.12	$760.03	$805.23	$851.68	$899.33	$948.10	$997.95	$1,048.82	$1,100.65
	200,000	$954.83	$1,013.37	$1,073.64	$1,135.58	$1,199.10	$1,264.14	$1,330.60	$1,398.43	$1,467.53
	250,000	$1,193.54	$1,266.71	$1,342.05	$1,419.47	$1,498.88	$1,580.17	$1,663.26	$1,748.04	$1,834.41
	300,000	$1,432.25	$1,520.06	$1,610.46	$1,703.37	$1,798.65	$1,896.20	$1,995.91	$2,097.64	$2,201.29
	350,000	$1,670.95	$1,773.40	$1,878.88	$1,987.26	$2,098.43	$2,212.24	$2,328.56	$2,447.25	$2,568.18
	400,000	$1,909.66	$2,026.74	$2,147.29	$2,271.16	$2,398.20	$2,528.27	$2,661.21	$2796.86	$2,935.06
LOAN AMOUNT	450,000	$2,148.37	$2,280.08	$2,415.70	$2,555.05	$2,697.98	$2,844.31	$2,993.86	$3,146.47	$3,301.94
	500,000	$2,387.08	$2,533.43	$2,684.11	$2,838.95	$2,997.75	$3,160.34	$3,326.51	$3,496.07	$3,668.82
	550,000	$2,625.78	$2,786.77	$2,952.52	$3,122.84	$3,297.53	$3,476.37	$3,659.16	$3,845.68	$4,035.71
	600,000	$2,864.49	$3,040.11	$3,220.93	$3,406.73	$3,597.30	$3,792.41	$3,991.81	$4,195.29	$4,402.59
	650,000	$3,103.20	$3,293.45	$3,489.34	$3,690.63	$3,897.08	$4,108.44	$4,324.47	$4,544.89	$4,769.47
	700,000	$3,341.91	$3,546.80	$3,757.75	$3,974.52	$4,196.85	$4,424.48	$4,657.12	$4,894.50	$5,136.35
	750,000	$3,580.61	$3,800.14	$4,026.16	$4,258.42	$4,496.63	$4,740.51	$4,989.77	$5,244.11	$5,503.23
	800,000	$3,819.32	$4,053.48	$4,294.57	$4,542.31	$4,796.40	$5,056.54	$5,322.42	$5,593.72	$5,870.12
	850,000	$4,058.03	$4,306.83	$4,562.98	$4,826.21	$5,096.18	$5,372.58	$5,655.07	$5,943.32	$6,237.00
	900,000	$4,296.74	$4,560.17	$4,831.39	$5,110.10	$5,395.95	$5,688.61	$5,987.72	$6,292.93	$6,603.88
	950,000	$4,535.45	$4,813.51	$5,099.81	$5,394.00	$5,695.73	$6,004.65	$6,320.37	$6,642.54	$6,970.76
	1,000,000	$4,774.15	$5,066.85	$5,368.22	$5,677.89	$5,995.51	$6,320.68	$6,653.02	$6,992.15	$7,337.65

Source: Yahoo! Finance

OTHER CONSIDERATIONS

There are ongoing outlays associated with home ownership beyond just your mortgage payment, and these expenses can eat into your monthly income significantly. These expenses include taxes, maintenance, insurance and any regular fees or dues. So when taking on a mortgage, adjust your emergency money to take all of these factors into account in your monthly and annual cash flow before you sign on the dotted line.

If you are using maintenance to pay part of your mortgage, you should keep at least four to six months' worth of mortgage payments as part of your savings in addition to your other emergency money. This might seem a lot of cash but the last thing you want is for your ex-spouse to lose his job and, as a result, potentially have your primary source of mortgage payment dry up overnight.

You should also expect to hold onto your property for 10 years when you buy because there are no guarantees regarding how each property cycle will play out. Newly established seller's stamp duties have locked many homeowners in Asia into property for longer than expected. For instance, in Singapore you will essentially be hit with a seller's stamp duty if you sell too soon after you buy your home. Expect governments to continue to intervene as they see fit in an attempt to thwart potential property bubbles.

Post-divorce Property Financing Challenges

The first challenge for a divorcee buying property in Asia if the home is not part of the divorce settlement is being able to afford the down payment and stamp duty. This is the cash that you must outlay to secure a mortgage. At the time of writing, in both Hong Kong and Singapore, the down payment is 20 to 50% while the stamp duty varies but is around 2 to 3% of the home purchase price. Given the sky-high prices of even modest properties in Asia's major cities, this can entail a fairly significant cash outlay.

The next challenge if you can afford the down payment is your eligibility to secure a mortgage. Even if you have a significant lump sum settlement, getting a bank in Asia to extend a loan can be onerous because the bank judges your ability to repay the loan based on several factors, one of which is your current employment and salary.

If you are not employed, it is genuinely a challenge getting a loan extended to you. Of course depending on your settlement, you could ask that your ex-spouse acts as a "guarantor" of your loan, which essentially means that he will pay the mortgage in the event that you can't. For the record, this has been known to happen!

Being a Landlady

Currently, for those of you who have a lot of money or assets, buying an investment property is a great way to create a source of steady income every month. If you can juggle owning two (or more) properties in terms of your cash flow, it's one very good solution for a divorcee looking to supplement her monthly income. To understand if you are making a good investment, and getting a good return for your money compared to other investments, you need to know how to calculate your net rental yield.

For property, a simple way to look at yield is this: If, for example, the rent you earn on your condo is $4,000 a month, your revenue will be $48,000 a year. If annual expenses are $6,000 a year, the net rental income will be $42,000 a year. Given a property cost or value of S$1,000,000, the net rental yield is $42,000÷$1,000,000=4.2%. This is a fairly good yield if you consider that the banks pay almost no interest these days, giving you zero yield for your cash!

As property prices climb, the yield will go down unless you can increase the rent. In the example above, if the flat were sold for $1,500,000, the yield would go down to 2.8% ($42,000÷$1,500,000) if the revenue and expenses remained the same. Generally speaking, steadily falling yields can be one signal that asset prices are peaking.

Leveraging Property to Buy More Property

In this low interest rate environment, it has become popular to take a loan out, or leverage, on the equity in your primary residence to buy an investment property. Equity is the difference between your home's estimated value and the amount you still owe on the mortgage. So, if you currently owe S$250,000 on your mortgage but the value of the home has risen from S$500,000 to S$900,000, your equity on paper would be S$650,000 (S$900,000–S$250,000). But remember that equity can also disappear in a downturn, as mentioned in Chapter 6.

As long as property prices appreciate and the valuation increases, your home equity appears to grow larger, and banks will often lend you money against the equity in your home to buy yet another property. When times are good and tenants are plentiful, living off rental income seems ideal. When the property cycle turns though, over-leveraged property is the first house of cards to collapse. Home valuations tumble, your equity and tenants can disappear and the bank can demand that you pay off more of your outstanding loan. If you do not have the cash to top up your mortgage, you can end up losing your home to the bank.

This is precisely what happened during the Asian financial

crisis, and more recently in the United States. The moral of the story is this: Having a rental property to supplement your monthly cash flow is an excellent way to bring home the income! But being highly leveraged to do so is never a sign of financial genius. So avoid leveraging your primary home for any reason, let alone to buy more property, unless you can ride out a significant long-term downturn without tenants supporting your debt load.

When to Buy: The Property Cycle

Like all assets, property moves in cycles. In the last 40 years, Hong Kong and Singapore have undergone four property cycles. We are currently into our fifth cycle, which began in 2009. The two charts below show the average property values in Singapore and Hong Kong, and you can see the peaks and troughs of each cycle.

Singapore

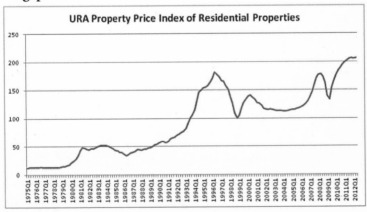

Source: URA

Hong Kong

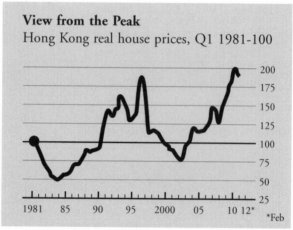

View from the Peak
Hong Kong real house prices, Q1 1981-100

Sources: Thomson Reuters; *The Economist*

Asia's property cycles have been somewhat different each time, but one catalyst has been interest rate changes. Because so much property is bought with leverage, or loans, property prices tend to rise and fall in relation to changes in interest rates. As interest rates rise, loan payments become more expensive. If landlords cannot increase rental prices to match their higher mortgage payments, yields compress, or shrink, and eventually property prices begin to fall.

Price always matters when you buy an asset. So, as logic would dictate, the best time to buy a property, or any asset, is when it is most out of favour, for instance between 1998 and 2003 in much of Asia. This was a time of higher interest rates, 9/11 and then the severe acute respiratory syndrome (SARS) outbreak. That said, if you intend to hold the property for more than 10 years, and would be paying rent otherwise, buying almost always makes more sense if you know you can afford your mortgage payments and tolerate the churn of property markets rising and falling.

Divorce and Property: Mistakes to Avoid

Divorcing couples can obsess over property in all the wrong ways. If you are granted the home as part of the settlement, make sure only your name is legally on the title, and get a copy or proof of this. This is the single most important thing you need to know about home ownership—i.e. that you actually legally own the property.

Second, a home is a place to live and a means of stability. But you have to be able to afford home ownership, otherwise maintaining a property is extremely stressful. Many divorcees cannot afford to maintain their properties given their cash flow situations. Or, as I've seen with rarely visited holiday homes, the property is a big cash drain because there is no income being earned on the asset. So keep what you can comfortably afford and sell, or at least earn income on, anything not regularly occupied.

Then there is the divorcee landlady who believes her investment property must rent for an amount chosen out of thin air—it's what her neighbours got, it's what her family thinks reasonable—then loses out on opportunity after opportunity to secure a good, reliable tenant. You need to have a sense, on average, of what you can command for rent given market demands and the condition of your property. If the property hasn't been renovated for 20 years, which is often the case, expect to get less rental income than your neighbour who has renovated.

Having a home paid off is an extremely desirable asset to have, particularly in retirement. However having your primary home as your only asset, one on which you are betting on a capital gain alone, can put you in a financially precarious position. You need other income in retirement, and if you are divorced and not earning any income, you are ostensibly in retirement. Even for those who can lock in large gains and then downsize to a smaller home, you need to invest your winnings to fund your retirement.

While property is an excellent investment, there is an over-reliance on property as an asset class in Asia and parts of Europe due to a lack of familiarity with other options. Unless you are a master investor in property, and can catch property at consistently low prices, property should be treated as one viable asset class but not the only one for building long-term economic security.

The Pros and Cons of Home Ownership

The advantages of owning residential property are as follows:

- You can live in your asset.

- Property tends to do well in the face of inflation.

- If you are not living in your property, you can rent it out and generate income.

- You can borrow against your property equity.

The downsides of owning property are:

- It is illiquid, which means you cannot easily or quickly convert your property into cash in a time of crisis, personal or otherwise.

- If you have mortgaged your home, you can be at the mercy of rapidly rising interest rates, and thus higher monthly payments, which eat into your cash flow.

- Property is not risk free. While the property market can be more resilient than the stock market, property values can fall significantly. In 2008, property prices in Singapore and Hong Kong fell over 25% in 12 months. During the Asian financial crisis, property prices in Singapore fell over 44.9% from peak to trough and 61% in Hong Kong.[1]

STOCKS AND BONDS

By introducing stocks and bonds, in lieu of just leaving all of your money in cash, you can invest to earn income and potential capital gains. This can help you keep up with the forces of inflation in a way that holding all your money in cash will not. Financial

---

1   Bank for International Settlements, "Property Markets and Financial Stability" in *BIS Papers*, number 64, p. 44. Available at: www.bis.org/publ/bppdf/bispap64h.pdf

assets are much more liquid than property because you can sell them usually within seconds. Therefore, as a means to keep up with inflation, earn some income and enjoy liquidity, financial assets offer all of these benefits over the long term.

I am only going to focus on stocks and bonds here because these are enough to get you started doing some simple investing in financial assets. As an exercise to prepare you for the much feared and misunderstood world of equities and bonds, I'd like to first do a comparison of two imaginary friends. Let's call them Betty and Veronica.

Betty has a part-time job and spends every last dollar travelling the world and eating at celebrity chef restaurants. Betty has no idea what net worth means and she doesn't care because she has four credit cards and relies on occasional handouts from boyfriends and buddies to float her from one fabulous party to the next. She considers herself well connected as her Facebook page is a flood of photo-shopped good times at *DestinAsian* designated hot spots.

Veronica has a steady full-time job and gets promoted regularly. She owns her own home, saves 20% of her income and invests regularly in the markets to fund her retirement plan. Veronica has a substantial positive net worth and her goal is to grow her net worth 10% per year through regular savings and investment gains. She uses credit to travel but pays down her credit card debt monthly. Veronica slowly and quietly expands her personal network through activities she enjoys such as modern dance and book clubs.

Both Betty and Veronica want to start their own businesses and be the CEO of their business. Now, here are two questions for you: If you were only given the above information, who would you loan money to? Whose company would you want to own a piece of? Keep these questions in mind when you think about financial assets because companies, just like you and me, have balance sheets, cash flow statements and even "net worth" that can grow over time.

EQUITIES/STOCKS—THE BASICS

Buying equity, or stocks, simply represents ownership in a company. When you buy stock in a company, you buy shares in a publicly listed company. You will already know many publicly listed companies by name: SingTel, Cheung Kong, Apple, Keppel Corporation, HSBC, UOB, etc. You can also buy stock in a private company like Veronica's or Betty's. It's all ownership and it's all represented through stock ownership.

Remember fear and greed? Stocks tend to be the investment that investors buy when they are confident the economy is going to do well, and thus it is called the greed trade. Stocks, like property, tend to outperform bonds when inflation picks up and the macroeconomic picture looks positive because the investing community perceives businesses will expand and grow.

If your company performs well, eventually your shares appreciate in value. So, for example, if you buy 100 shares of Company A for $5 per share, you will spend $500 for that investment. If the value of Company A rises to $7 a share, your paper gain is $700–$500=$200 and your return will be $200÷$500=40%. Just like property, this is a paper gain until you sell your stock holding and pocket the cash.

You can also earn a dividend (income!) by holding certain dividend-paying stocks. A dividend is a payment generally issued to you based on how many shares you own. This dividend is most often paid as cash quarterly, semi-annually or annually, and many dividends grow over time. The best thing about dividends, if you do not need the cash, is that you can use the dividend payment to buy more stock in the same company. This is referred to as reinvesting the dividend. So, in effect, the company is paying you to buy more of its stock instead of you using your own money.

So the two reasons to invest in equities are to allow the value of your shares to appreciate over the long term and earn steady income. Imagine if Veronica could do the same for her business as she does for herself, growing her income consistently and her net worth by 10% every year. What if she also paid you $1 for every share that you held and promised to grow that dividend payment by 5% every year if you were to remain a shareholder? Who wouldn't want to invest in something stable and growing like that?

Equity Anxiety

Despite the obvious benefits of investing in stocks, after having spoken to many individual investors in Asia, I have come to realise how favoured property is as an asset class and how feared stock is as an asset class. The reasons I have been given as to why this is so are that stock markets are more volatile (bigger swings up and down), stocks seem risky and everyone has a relative who made a bad investment in the stock market, so ever since then, no one in the family buys stocks.

Let me touch on these three issues. First, property markets can fall almost as hard as stock markets, but not usually as fast. This is because property is less liquid compared to investing in financial markets. Financial assets tend to recover faster than property markets, for the same reason. Second, any investment is risky if you are trading for short-term gain and not long-term investment. Trading for short-term gain is known by another name—gambling. Third, you can make a bad investment in anything, but a small mistake in financial assets is easier to correct than a bad illiquid investment.

Property investments do not "go to zero" the way a stock price can if the company you invest in goes bankrupt. That is a realistic comparison. But you can lose your home to foreclosure if it is not paid in full. What really makes financial assets risky for the long-term investor is choosing the wrong investments for the wrong reasons or by trying to trade to beat the market constantly—and stock market cycles will show why.

Stock Market Cycles

The key to making money in any investment is to buy when prices are low, sell when prices are high and earn income while you wait. Stocks are no different. Stock markets, like property markets, go up and down in cycles, and the broader longer-term cycles are called bull and bear markets. You can stay invested through bear markets (downturns) and make money. You can lose money in bull (upward-trending) markets.

There are different types of stock investments, ranging from large blue-chip companies that have a global presence like Procter & Gamble, Coca-Cola and McDonald's to smaller companies. You can also buy shares in sectors such as IT, industrials and transportation. From an international perspective, you have your home market here in Asia but the stock markets are relatively small compared to the United States or other developed markets.

The above groupings move in their own cycles. Defensive stocks are companies that sell consumer staples such as nappies and shampoo and are seen to do well when the economy is not. Growth stocks, which can refer to small- and medium-sized companies and some sectors like IT, do better when the economy picks up. As Asia is still considered an emerging market, the stock markets in this region tend to do well when the US market, which is its biggest trading partner, is doing well.

Here is a chart to show you the traditional pattern of a stock market cycle as the US economy expands or contracts. This cycle runs about 4.5 years at a time.[2]

---

2 Some say that the creation of the Federal Reserve in 1913 made a difference to the length of the cycle. Therefore, Deutsche Bank looked at the period from 1913 to 1982 when the "golden era" started; the average expansion during that time was 55 months and the median 49. Source: www.economist.com/blogs/buttonwood/2011/09/global-economy

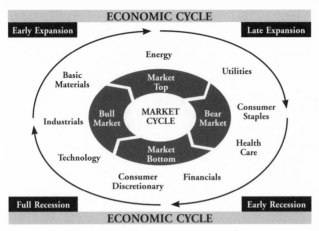

Source: http://static.safehaven.com/authors/ticker/24003_b.png

Because of such cycles, expect your investments to go up and down in price and value. Even Warren Buffett, at the time of writing, was looking at a billion-dollar loss on his investment in IBM.[3] If you are going to invest in stocks for long-term growth and to earn dividends—both good reasons for investing in stocks—you have to learn to ride the ups and downs of the stock market ocean waves.

How to Buy Stocks

Investing in the stock market can be done by picking individual stocks or through investment vehicles such as funds, all of which are traded over the stock exchange. Each investment has its own ticker symbol so SingTel on the Straits Times Index in Singapore is (Z74) and HSBC on the Hang Seng Index in Hong Kong is (005). The prices can be tracked using these ticker symbols

3   www.cnbc.com/id/100657591

on Yahoo! Finance (http://finance.yahoo.com/) or Bloomberg (www.bloomberg.com).

Buying Shares versus a Fund

A share in a company is exactly that; you are taking an ownership stake in a specific company and the price of the company's shares will change daily. A fund is different to a share in that you invest in a basket of companies all through one fund. So instead of investing only in Apple, you might invest in a technology fund or a US stock market fund that has Apple as one of the holdings.

So why would you buy a fund instead of a share? Do you remember what I said earlier about diversification being similar to eating a well-balanced diet in order to be healthy? Think of funds in the same way. A fund is like a sampling platter of stocks. You don't have to commit all of your investment dollars to one company; instead you can spread out your risk and sample many. In addition, a fund doesn't usually ever go to zero but a company can go bankrupt and the shares can become worthless.

Imagine you buy shares in property developer Cheung Kong on Hong Kong's stock exchange, the Hang Seng Index. Then the next day, Cheung Kong is down 1% but the rest of the Hang Seng Index is up 0.5%. Even though Cheung Kong might be a perfectly good long-term investment, it may be having a bad day, a bad week or even a bad year.

While some investors can accept such ups and downs of an individual stock, and they understand that it is part of investing, many cannot. So let's say instead of owning shares in Cheung Kong, you own a fund that follows the total value of all the stocks on the Hang Seng Index. Then instead of being down 1%, you would be up 0.5% because that is what happened on the Hang Seng Index that day.

Do all funds track the market? No, they don't. Although there are hundreds of different types of funds (known as unit trusts or mutual funds), the funds that do track an index, as described above, are known as passive equity index funds and exchange-traded funds (ETFs). Passive index funds and ETFs are very similar. The main difference between the two is that the value of a passive fund, like most funds, is calculated once a day when the market closes while an ETF price can change at any time while the market is open.

So, going back to the example above, by investing in a passive equity index fund (or an ETF), your investment will just track the performance of all the companies that comprise an index. In the above case, the index is Hong Kong's Hang Seng Index, and the companies in that index include China Mobile, HSBC, Cheung Kong and so on. In other words, the fund is passively managed and mirrors the components of a market index. So if you feel positive about economic growth but do not know which specific company to invest in, you can get exposure to many with one passive index fund.

You can find index funds for any index. Here is a list of some of the major indices that you can consider investing in.

Stock	Index
US	Standard & Poor's 500 (S&P)
Singapore	Straits Times
Hong Kong	Hang Seng
Japan	Nikkei

Apart from passive funds, there are also active funds and it is extremely important that you know the distinction between the two. An active fund, as the name implies, is actively managed by a fund manager who is hired to buy and sell the companies in the fund instead of the fund being linked to a specific index, such as the Hang Seng Index, as is the case with a passive fund. An active fund depends entirely on the decisions of the fund manager as to which holdings are invested in and when they are sold.

Passive versus Active Funds

Unlike individual stock investments, *all funds* charge the investor an annual fee to invest. Passive index funds and ETFs have no active trading so they usually have significantly lower fees compared to actively managed funds which have fund managers overseeing the funds. Often the fees for passive index funds and ETFs are below 0.30% whereas the annual management fund fee for active funds can run from 0.75 to 2% or more per annum. The latter fees may seem small but they matter a lot to your ultimate return.

ACTIVE FUNDS—INVESTMENT PORTFOLIO CANCER

Asia has some of the highest actively managed fund fees in the world, and they are money drainers for many reasons. Actively managed funds charge initial fees called loading fees, just for the privilege of being able to buy into these funds, and these fees can run anywhere from 1.5 to 5%. This is a one-time fee *in addition to* the ongoing management fund fees that I mentioned of 0.75 to 2%. This is money that you are giving away regardless of how the fund itself actually performs! And based on the research, you will likely derive marginal value at best from active management in equities.[4]

Forget about that egregious loading fee for a second, and imagine how much a 1% management fund fee alone will drain a $500,000 portfolio over time.

THE TABLE OF DRAIN

Here is the impact of a 1% management fund fee on a $500,000 investment into a fund with no capital gains or income over 10 years:

---

4 Research carried out by AWD Chase de Vere, the advisory firm, showed that in almost every sector the average fund had failed to beat the relevant stock market index over both 5 and 10 years. In some cases, the average fund delivered almost 70% less than its relevant benchmark index. Over a 10-year time frame, in most sectors, more than twice as many active fund managers underperformed when compared with those who beat the market; in some sectors, this fell to just one manager beating the market for every six that didn't. The statistics show that fund managers running emerging market and Japan funds had an ever worse record over 10 years. The average fund underperformed by 11 percentage points in the United States, 16 in Europe, 45 in Asian equities and 68 in emerging markets. (Source: www.telegraph.co.uk/finance/personalfinance/investing/9796561/Active-investment-the-wrong-track.html)

Year	Year End Balance
1	495,000
2	490,050
3	485,149.50
4	480,298
5	475,495
6	470,740
7	466,032.67
8	461,372.34
9	456,758.62
10	452,190.04

If the markets move sideways, and you end up without any real gain to your portfolio over 10 years, you will be left with $452,190, save any dividends paid to you. Paying fees like this is investment portfolio cancer and can severely impact your long-term gains if you do not make the effort to minimise them.

Even better than the low-cost aspect of passive index funds and many ETFs is the fact that they **outperform actively managed funds more often than not.** So as counter-intuitive as it sounds, you are often going to pay less and get more if you use passive index funds to invest in financial markets rather than paying extra for actively managed funds.

Some actively managed funds have their purpose, and many will have their day in the sun. However, for consistent long-term returns in liquid and open stock markets such as Singapore,

Hong Kong and the United States, low-cost passive stock index funds or ETFs often prove to be the best value for money. Ultimately though, I believe it is the psychological benefits that draw investors to passive index funds, namely the feeling that you are following the market and, as a result, you're doing just as well as everyone else.

THE PROS AND CONS OF OWNING STOCKS

The main advantages of owning stocks are as follows:

- Like property, stock market returns tend to keep pace with inflation.

- In Hong Kong and Singapore, you can enjoy tax-free capital gains, meaning no tax on the money you make!

- In Hong Kong and Singapore, you can enjoy tax-free dividends, meaning no tax on the dividend payments you earn!

- You can reinvest your dividends.

- Dividends also can grow, and appreciate, thus giving you extra compounding of interest over time.

- Most stock market investments are easy to sell quickly if you have to do so.

The main disadvantages of owning stocks are as follows:

- Stock market investments are generally more volatile than bond investments.

- You can lose your entire investment if the company you buy shares in goes bankrupt (look at Enron, WorldCom and Lehman Brothers).

- Companies that behave badly issue too many shares and, just like governments printing more money, dilute the value of the shares that are outstanding.

- Dividends are not a sure bet because companies can cut or suspend them at any time.

REITs

I must sneak in a section about REITs as these investments trade over a stock exchange but they are actually an investment in property. REITs stands for "real estate investment trusts" and are required by law to distribute (give back to the shareholders) at least 90% of their taxable income. This rule is very important as most of the profits are paid out as a type of dividend (income!).

REITs typically own and operate income-producing property such as apartments, shopping centres, offices, hotels and warehouses. There are many different types of REIT and some are riskier than others depending on various factors such as what type of property the fund invests in, i.e. retail REITs versus healthcare REITs and so on. REITs are very popular in Asia, particularly among women investors who appreciate getting regular income payments.

REITs trade over stock exchanges and tend to follow the property cycle. When interest rates are heading lower, REITs tend to come into favour. As interest rates rise, REITs can fall hard and fast. Since 2004, REITs have not only been in favour but have also had very good yields, sometimes over 7%. That said, the risk can be substantial, and while REITs have a place in everyone's portfolio, they should be one, but not your only, financial asset investment.

BONDS

With stock market investments your fortune rises and falls with the market or individual company's success whereas a bond is a loan that you make to a company or government. In return, during the term of the loan, you receive a regular interest payment (income!). Then at the end of the term, you receive your money, or capital, back.

Bonds are generally seen as less risky than stock market investments because as a company shareholder, if the company goes bankrupt, you lose your entire investment. Bondholders, on the other hand, are able to stake a claim on the bankrupt company or government to receive at least part of their original capital and/or the interest owed.

Therefore, people who invest in safe bonds are looking primarily for capital preservation, which means that they are making an investment and expecting to get *at least* what they paid into the investment returned back to them (plus a bit of interest income). This is different from stock market investors who primarily want their investment to grow and expect larger returns in the long run but ultimately run the risk of losing some or all of their initial investment.

Despite all the drama around stocks on nightly news channels like CNBC, the bond market is a much larger market. McKinsey

& Company's "Mapping global capital markets 2011" report puts the global bond market size at $157 trillion, or 75% of all financial assets. You can imagine why any kind of bond market bubble might be a problem.

The US bond market represents around 25% of all bonds, at $37 trillion. The size of the US bond market is partly due to the US dollar being the global reserve currency but it is also because the United States has a large financial asset investment base, and as such US pension funds widely hold US treasury bonds. US treasury bonds and the US dollar act as safe havens where investors go to keep their money safe in times of crisis such as in 2008.

As for Asia, outside of Japan, the bond markets are tiny, and the smaller the country the tinier it is. Small bond markets often have small trading volumes and less liquidity, so instead of moving like nice ocean waves, they can move more like ripples across shallow puddles.

Bond Cycles—Interest Rates and Bonds

The big risk around bonds, other than the entity you lend your money to going bankrupt, is interest rates. When interest rates fall, bond prices rise in value. When interest rates rise, bond prices tend to fall. Because of this sensitivity to interest rates, it is generally believed that the longer the term of the bond (the longer the loan), the greater the risk you are taking—this is known as inflation risk.

Remember our friend Betty? Imagine that you will only get 1% on your money if you leave it in the bank. So to earn more money on your money, you decide to lend Betty $10,000 over four years and charge her 3% interest per year. In this case, you are making $300 per year (10,000x0.03=300), or $1,200 in total (300x4 years=1200), as opposed to the $100 per year (10,000x0.01=100), or $400 ($100x4 years=400) in total, if you had left your money in the bank.

As long as Betty keeps paying the interest, this seems like a good deal, doesn't it? Even though you are taking some risk with Betty, you perceive it's worth it to get the extra return. But what happens if interest rates at the bank increase to 3% during the time that you are lending your money to Betty? You would now be taking far more risk leaving your money with Betty than if you had left it in the bank and got the same return.

This is why bonds are sensitive to changes in interest rates going up and down. Many retirees hold bonds as retirement investments because bonds are perceived as low risk. But they do not account for inflation risk—the money destroyer. If you are being paid 2% on your bonds and inflation is 2.5%, then your return is actually negative.

How to Buy Bonds

Just like stocks, you can buy an individual bond, a passively managed bond index fund or actively managed bond funds. Many of the rules pertaining to stocks also apply to active and passive index funds for bonds although you can extract slightly more value for money with an actively managed bond fund as long as the fees that you pay are relatively low, below 1%.

Bond funds trade over most stock exchanges, just like equity funds. These funds pool government or corporate debt holdings and diversify the investor across many types of debt through one fund. There are many types of bonds, just as there are stocks, and bond funds can also be prone to panics and steep declines in value. This is why I advise people to buy individual bonds if they can and hold them to maturity if it is primarily capital preservation they seek, as opposed to buying into bond funds where you can incur capital losses more easily.

Since the bond market is smaller in Asia, most funds in Asia tend to be Pan Asian or global and hold the debt of many countries or companies. These funds almost always pay some income to the investor. The fund itself can trade like a stock or equity fund however, going up and down based on demand for that particular fund.

Investors who do not like the up and down of bond funds, and this includes me, can invest in individual bonds through their local bank or broker.[5] You will then have a direct bond commitment with the company or government to which you are lending. This way, you avoid the volatility of bond funds, hold your investment until it matures and simply collect the interest payments and receive your principal back when the bond matures.

---

5   There may be restrictions in buying bonds due to the large face value of some of the bonds in Asia, which often means that you must loan $250,000 or more at a time.

For individual bonds, it is your yield that matters as long as you hold the bond to maturity. Although there are four different types of yield for bonds, the one that matters to you is the per cent you are paid in income based on the amount you lend. So if you buy a one-year $10,000 bond, you will be lending out $10,000 for a year. If the bond yields 2.5%, you will be paid $250 over the course of that year (10,000x2.5%) in two equal payments of $125 each, one after six months and one at the end of the term when your $10,000 is also returned to you.

If Retirees Buy Bonds, Then They Must Be Risk Free!

Many retirees buy bonds for capital preservation. So does this mean that you can't lose money on bonds? No, it doesn't. If the company or government you lend to goes bankrupt, you will likely only receive a portion of your original investment back. Or if you need to sell your bond to get your initial investment back before maturity, and interest rates have gone up in the meantime, you may well get less for your bond than if interest rates had remained the same or fallen.

The biggest risk as I have already mentioned for bondholders of safe, stable corporate or government bonds is not bankruptcy, it's inflation. You may believe you are preserving your capital but, in reality, the yield is so low that you have a negative return when factoring in Asia's persistently high inflation.

Investors in bond funds also have to be careful when interest rates start to creep up, which tends to happen when inflation takes hold in an economy. It may take a while but interest rate changes will eventually affect the perceived value of bond funds in general. Depending on which fund you have invested in, the fund can fall rather dramatically, shattering your impression of bonds being a safe investment.

Undeniably, bonds are less volatile than stock investments, historically speaking, but they are by no means risk free. They are still investments after all. So if you opt to buy bond funds, stick with short-term or short duration bond funds because interest rates are so low and have only one way to go—up!

Bond Ratings

How do you know which bonds are good bets to ensure your capital is returned and the income paid on time? How do you know whether you should go for a Betty bond or a Veronica bond?

Bonds are rated by credit rating agencies. The highest possible rating is AAA or AA+ and falls to the worst rating of CCC-. Normally, the lower the risk, the safer the investment, and the higher the rating. Bonds with a rating of BBB or above are considered "investment grade". Avoid like the plague anything below the BBB rating as it will be speculative at best. Investment grade bonds simply mean it is highly likely that you will be paid back your capital in addition to your interest payments because the bond is guaranteed by the government issuing the bond or the company is financially strong.

The more stable and secure the company or government, the less it needs to pay to its bondholders because there is demand for its bonds. Right now, AAA and AA+ companies and countries, like Singapore, pay very low yields (1 to 2%) on their debt. The United States also falls into this category as it is the global reserve currency and the US government can issue as much money as it needs to cover its bonds. On the other hand, the less stable the company or government issuing the bond, the higher the yield needs to be in order to attract investors who are willing to lend their money. Some European countries have yields of over 15% on their bonds because investors worry that they will default on their bonds. So a high yield in the bond world is not necessarily a good thing.

Bond Buyer Beware

Despite its "historically low levels of risk", the bond market can be a lot murkier and riskier than it appears. This is because bonds are rated by credit agencies, many of which have conflicts of interest.

The conflict looks something like this: The credit rating agency gets paid by a banker to give a bond a rating. The banker wants a certain rating so he can make money selling the bond to his clients. If the banker gets the right rating, he'll be happy and sell a lot of bonds (and get his bonus!). The analyst at the credit rating agency who is rating the bond wants more business from the banker in the future because they also get a year-end bonus and junkets to places like Las Vegas (courtesy of the banker). To the best of my knowledge, no one gets bonuses for creating the most accurate bond rating.

Look no further than all the bad debt that was purchased in the lead-up to the financial crisis, much of it stamped AAA, the highest possible rating available, and most of it was worthless at one point. If you really want an insight into the players in the bond market, read Michael Lewis's epic retelling of the 2008 financial crisis, *The Big Short*. It's blindingly intelligent, raucously funny and will provide a peek behind the curtain of how debt is created, bought and sold worldwide.

Let's go back to Betty and Veronica. Each of them is asking for a loan to start her own business. Who would you expect to pay you back on time? Who would be rated AAA? Probably Veronica. And because more people would choose to lend to Veronica, she would be in a position to negotiate a lower payment to the lenders. As a lender, you might make less income but you would be assured that Veronica would pay you back.

Betty, on the other hand, is trickier. You might be paid on time, you might not be. She might even party away your loan. Without doubt, fewer people would want to loan to Betty so she would have to pay more interest to get access to any money. This is why Betty uses credit cards.

THE PROS AND CONS OF OWNING BONDS

The advantages of investing in bonds are as follows:

- Bonds generally provide safe, steady income.
- You can get fixed payments with a bond.

- You can pre-determine your income and return on your bond investment if you hold your bond to maturity.

- Investing in short-term US treasury bonds have, thus far, proved to be a safe haven during significant financial turmoil.

The disadvantages of investing in bonds are:

- Their value is sensitive to interest rates. Generally, the value of a bond goes down when interest rates go up, so you can incur capital loss if you are selling bonds as opposed to holding them until maturity.

- You can get stuck with a low fixed payment if inflation soars during the time you are holding your bond.

- The credit rating agencies can have conflicts of interest. *See* "Bond Buyer Beware" above.

- In Asia, it is often difficult to buy individual bonds with small amounts of capital.

A WORD ON GOLD

Ever since we left the gold standard behind in the 1970s, gold has gone through its own love-hate cycles. The "gold love" is brought on when interest rates are low and investors fear hyperinflation. Imagine a day when $1,000 can't buy you a bag of rice—that is the hyperinflationary mindset. If an extreme hyperinflationary scenario comes to pass, I suspect it won't be easy, safe or even feasible to take your gold coins to the store and buy food with them.

Asian investors have a unique attachment to investing in gold because historically speaking—over the last 100 years—many countries in Asia have experienced significant turmoil in their banking systems and governments. Therefore, gold has been seen as a safe store of wealth in countries where people do not trust their banking system, their currency or their government. In addition, some investors like that gold is transportable (you can flee the country with it), and in countries such as Vietnam you can actually use gold as a means of exchange for large investments (i.e. to buy a house or a car).

If you live in a country with a fundamentally sound government and banking system however, you need to remember the goal of the empowered investor. The goal is to find long-term and sustainable income-producing assets, not just assets that may gain in actual price over time. That's why I shy away from gold and prefer to buy stock in companies that pay dividends and/ or corporate bonds or invest in property and farmland as all of these are productive, income-earning assets.

If you still want to invest in precious metals or investment grade diamonds, buy real gold bars, gold coins and the like and avoid "paper gold" or funds that invest in gold. You will need to buy your gold investments from a reputable dealer and store them in a home safe, at a managed bank vault or via a professionally managed gold vault. For the record, the only gold ever bought in my family was kept in a vault ... in the World Trade Center in New York City. It wasn't recovered post 9/11.

CONCLUSION

Throughout the centuries, people have made sound investments across a wide variety of assets, some of which have been covered in this chapter. There is no right or wrong investment by which to build financial stability or wealth. After reading this primer, one type of asset may appeal more to you than another. The best way to approach investments, and risk and return which I cover next, is to understand that it is best to become comfortable diversifying across more than one asset class as this will allow you to spread your risk and avoid putting all your eggs in one investment basket.

CHAPTER 8

THE RIGHT HABITS AND DIY ASSET ALLOCATION

Your ideas of what is success must truly be
your own.
—*Alain de Botton*

In Chapter 6, we came to terms with why investing money for any return is a good idea while Chapter 7 explained what types of things you can invest in and why investing in different assets has both upsides and downsides. The next two chapters will cover the basic steps of "how to" if you want to invest on you own (DIY) in financial assets.

In a world awash with financial advisers, you might wonder why anyone would choose to DIY. The most empowered individuals learn the habits of good investors and how to DIY or, at the very least, learn enough to manage the people who are managing their investments. The first rung on the ladder to DIY is to understand why women can make great investors. Once you have done this, you then need to understand how much risk you can take on board given your individual situation.

WITH THE RIGHT HABITS WOMEN CAN MAKE GREAT INVESTORS

In general, because of the way we are wired, we humans do not make great investors. If you remember back to Chapter 1, the fastest part of our brain is not the analytical "scientific" brain but the monkey and lizard brains (which helps to explain why we tend to panic or overreact or experience the urge to climb a tree and hide). Consequently, we sell our investments when we shouldn't and we chase investment trends skywards because, like lemmings, we do not want to be left behind.

That said, all things being equal, most women *are more suited* to mastering the art of investing than most men. In the little tome called *Warren Buffett Invests Like a Girl and Why You Should, Too*, author LouAnn Lofton outlines that science has shown women investors have an advantage over their male counterparts for several reasons:

- Women trade less than men.
- Women do not exhibit overconfidence; they know what they do not know!
- Women are more realistic.
- Women will spend more time researching and understanding the details of an investment.
- Women are less influenced by peer pressure.
- Women learn from their mistakes faster.
- Men are actually the hormonal ones—their testosterone often leads them to take greater risks (than are necessary).

I will add two more observations. **First, women know a good sale when they see one and, second, women are better risk managers in general than men.** So in many ways, most women are imbued with the characteristics and the temperament to be competent investors. The problem I've noticed with women and investing is that, more than men, we are prone to defer all our financial decisions to other people, whether they be parents, husbands or financial advisers.

I would also add that the male-dominated financial industry has made investing seem very complex and very un-user-friendly. Therefore, I think the reason why women feel insecure around the idea of investing in financial assets, other than the obvious risk of losing money, is that we are out of practice.

Investing should be less about the great asset chase and more about merging the right habits with enough knowledge to find opportunities while, at the same time, understanding the risks involved and knowing how to manage them. In a way it's not that different from going to the same shopping centre all the time and knowing when something worth buying is on sale, except in this case the shopping centre is your local stock exchange or bond market.

This has led me to create the following 10 Golden Rules on planning and investing, which mirror the habits of a confident investor seeking long-term financial security. The first five were covered in the first half of the book while the latter five rules will be covered in these final chapters.

Golden Rule One: Conquer the Zoo in You

As stated earlier, if you do not control your mind, it is nearly impossible to control your money decisions in a way that will most benefit you in the long run. Conquer impulsive animal instincts or destructive thought patterns by engaging your analytical mind to realise your entitlement to long-term financial security.

Golden Rule Two: Savings Nirvana

It is impossible to invest what you do not save. Own your cash flow and your day-to-day budget decisions in order to create a healthy monthly savings surplus.

Golden Rule Three: Excess Debt Is for Dummies

Having multiple credit cards is finance poison much in the same way that borrowing off your assets can be. **Do not let anyone talk you into leveraging your solid investments with debt so that you can take on even more risk.** This can be a sure-fire way of losing a fortune. I've seen entire investment accounts wiped out this way, and in one case it was a divorced woman's retirement savings.

Golden Rule Four: Real Returns for the Real World

In all good planning, particularly retirement planning, you must be aware of inflation and how inflation affects your returns. Real returns (aka inflation adjusted returns) are the returns you will have to live off in the real world.

Golden Rule Five: Tailored Plans Not Hand-me Downs
Simplistic rules of thumb are for simplistic situations. There is a direct relationship between your available resources, your time horizon, your current assets, your cash flow, your income needs, the level of risk that you are comfortable with and how much money you can accumulate. Tailor an investment plan *and* your expectations accordingly.

Golden Rule Six: Buy the Sale!
The price you pay for an asset matters to your overall return. Chasing prices upwards as they peak is a bad habit; buying when there's a sale on assets is a good habit but not always easy to do when the people around you are in a panic. Rebalancing, which can be applied to index investing or dividend investing, can help instil emotion-free discipline to your investment portfolio.

Golden Rule Seven: KISS—**Keep Investing Simple Sister!**
The more complicated the asset, the greater the risk and the greater chance of regret. Look no further than all the complex investments (structured products) at the heart of the 2008 financial crisis or at the dismal returns over the last few years of costly hedge funds that promised outsized returns. For beginner investors, stick to property, stocks, bonds, time deposits or money market funds and KISS!

Golden Rule Eight: Keep Investing Expenses Low

Any money that is paid out of your pocket is money that you are not investing or compounding. Such costs include trading fees, advisory fees, commission paid to salespeople, fund management fees and so on. The best-managed portfolios maximise value and minimise expenses.

Golden Rule Nine: Commit to a Strategy

All assets rise *and* fall in value over time. Investing is about taking a calculated risk in the face of rising and falling asset prices with a long-term investment horizon. It is not about living in fear, gambling or impulsively following the herd. If you are doing it right, you will need a manicure more often than you'll need to look at your portfolio.

Golden Rule Ten: Slow and Steady Wins the Race

Turn off CNBC, ignore get-rich quick tips and talking heads. The media is entertainment so the more polemic the opinion, the more airtime it receives. This manic-depressive, play-by-play approach to delivering news will only make you feel euphoric one moment and miserable the next. If you need a rush, take up skydiving. Investing is not a sport for adrenaline junkies.

Now that you know why you should be able to be a good investor and you have an idea of the habits that are necessary to DIY, you need to understand how much risk you are comfortable taking on given your personal situation and needs.

Asset Allocation and Understanding Your Risk Tolerance

As noted in previous chapters, most beginner investors think tactically—i.e. "I want to invest in stocks" or "I want to invest in Asia"—whereas a long-term strategic plan will cover the answers to the following questions:

- What is your investment objective?
- What return do you need?
- What is your time horizon?
- What income do you need?

In Chapter 6, using the scenarios of Maria's and Alicia's retirement planning, we were able to set aside a certain amount of money given an interest rate or return and chart out retirement plans for both women. Here you can take a similar approach to determine how you can decide for yourself the amount of risk you want to take on to reflect your long-term needs and your investor psychology.

Asset allocation is how you divvy up, or allocate, your money to different asset classes—stocks, bonds and so on—because different weightings of different assets can greatly alter your long-term expected returns. After your tailored plan, **asset allocation is the second most important part of investment planning because it will determine your long-term expected returns.**

Your asset allocation should answer this type of question: "If I invest HK$7,500 every month for the next 15 years to build a retirement portfolio and I do not need much income now, but want at least a return of 5% per year, should I invest in stocks, bonds or what?!"

Think of asset allocation as finding the right mix of ingredients to make a recipe. With the right balance of ingredients, the recipe will turn out well in the end. If you add too much or too little of an ingredient though, the dish (in this case your returns) may not turn out as expected. Your asset allocation has to align with the returns you want or need but it must also align with the amount of risk that you can psychologically handle.

Finding Alignment: Long-term Returns versus Short-term Churns

The challenge most new investors face when thinking about risk and return is that their ability to stomach seeing the market go down for a period of time is at odds with being patient enough to achieve the long-term returns that they want. This is particularly true for anyone who has just gone through a divorce because you may feel more risk-averse than you might otherwise be. As noted earlier, the mechanics of investing are easy; it's our psychology that makes investing challenging.

Long-term investors have to look at annualised returns. This means the returns you get over a period of time. In other words, stocks may give you an annualised return of 7 to 9% over 20 years but there will be years when you can lose 14% and other years when you may gain 22%. And there may be years when the gains and losses are smaller (or larger). Bonds also have good and bad years but the volatility, or the extremes in gain and loss, is usually more muted.

Let's say you need to have returns of 8% to meet your long-term goals but you only want to buy bonds because bonds seem "safer" than stocks. At the time of writing, bonds are returning 1 to 3% for relatively safe corporate or government bonds, and they will not likely return 8% over the long run. Here, your long-term goal of 8% return is out of alignment with an asset allocation weighted heavily towards bonds.

In this scenario, you will have to either revisit how much risk you are willing to take on or accept the likelihood of lower returns and adjust your spending plans accordingly. Let's talk further about both of these approaches, namely how you can determine how much risk you can take on and how you can adjust your portfolio and expectations to match your risk tolerance.

So How Much Risk Can *I* Take?

Only you can answer this question. The following table provides a simple measure by which you can decide how large your allocation to stocks should be. (The table appears in its original format in *The Four Pillars of Investing* by William J. Bernstein but I have tweaked it here so that it is more reflective of the severity of recent crashes.) It is important to note that the "risk" in this type of table is seen as representing stocks, and not bonds. This is because most stocks have a history of being more volatile and swing up and down faster and to greater extremes than most bonds. It's not because bonds only post gains and have no risk.

I can tolerate losing ___% of my portfolio in the short term (six months) in the course of achieving long-term investment gains.	% Allocation to Stocks	Typical Investor Profile
60% or more	80% or more	Aggressive
50%	60–70%	Moderate
40%	40–60%	Balanced
30%	30–40%	Balanced–Conservative
20%	20–30%	Conservative
10%	10–20%	Defensive
0%	0%	Fixed

Using this simple table as reference, most divorcees, like most retirees, would most likely prefer to be "fixed" investors in that they would prefer to take on no risk whatsoever in order to preserve the money they currently have. We have already covered the big problem with this strategy, namely the threat of inflation destroying your savings.

So, in any ultra low-risk scenario, the challenge becomes how to stretch your money, if it is not invested at all, over 30 to 40 years. Yes, you can keep your money in the bank. However, as interest rates are very low, you will most likely need to prepare how you will manage inflation. This then becomes a budgeting, and not really an investment, issue, as shown in Chapter 6.

Also, if you want to invest for only a few years, financial markets are not for you unless you want to buy individual short-term bonds. There is simply too much volatility and no one can predict what will happen tomorrow. For the rest of this chapter, I am assuming that you want to invest at least some of your money for the long term (over 10 years) in order to earn some return.

Asset Allocation in Practice: The Ying and Yang of Stocks and Bonds

Do you remember what you learnt in Chapter 7? People invest in different asset classes to diversify and not have all their eggs in one basket. Investors buy stocks to achieve growth (greed) and keep pace with inflation, and they buy bonds to earn income and protect against losses when the stock market turns sour (fear). This ying and yang of stocks and bonds has both psychological and practical benefits.

If you invest $10,000 and lose 20% in your portfolio, you need to actually gain 25% to come back to your original figure of $10,000 (10,000x0.80=8,000; 8,000x1.25=10,000). If you lose 40%, you will need to gain 67% to break even at $10,000. So the larger the loss, the greater the gain and the more time it will take to make back your initial investment if you do not add any new money to your investments and buy at market lows.

This fear and greed approach is referred to as a "Balanced" approach to investing, and a mix of 60% stocks and 40% bonds has been the bedrock allocation of many investment portfolios because of the long-term return it has historically delivered.[1] Therefore, the attraction of holding some bonds in most portfolios is that they earn steady income and have traditionally served as a cushion to protect a portfolio against equity market volatility. As noted previously, US treasury bonds and the US dollar, in particular, have been thus far the safest of safe havens during crises like the one we had in 2008.

Psychologically speaking, it's also easier to look at a 20% loss than a 40% loss, even if you are invested for the long term. This is particularly true when a divorcee may have been granted a lump sum settlement and is not earning any income or receiving any maintenance. She may very well want to invest that lump sum but is not in a position to buy more when markets go down so therefore buffers her stock investments with bonds to cushion any market fall.

Asset Allocation and Total Return: How It Works

Let's take an investor who likes the idea of creating a portfolio, and she wants to know how much she should invest in stocks, cash and bonds. Let's start with $0 money having been invested, with a retirement goal of $1,000,000 to be reached in 20 years'

---

1   A paper published by Vanguard, an American investment management company, called "Recessions and Balanced Portfolio Returns" looked at the benefits of a simple 50/50 portfolio. The paper studied the hypothetical returns of a mix of 50% high-quality US bonds and 50% US stocks, going all the way back to 1926. It shouldn't be surprising that the overall performance would have been excellent: the average nominal return was 8.3%.

time. Inflation has already been taken into account given that we have decided on the amount of $1,000,000 for retirement. So if the time horizon is 20 years, the ability to meet these goals is based on only two things: First, how much can be saved? And second, what asset allocation is the investor comfortable with?

Assume that the expected returns are as follows: 7% for stocks, 4% for bonds and 1% for cash. We will have to make assumptions using past data because, unfortunately, no one knows what the returns will be in the future. So we will need to use past information to project future returns. Let's look at two scenarios of investing in stocks, bonds and cash.

The first scenario is when the investor is terrified of investing and only wants to hold safe government bonds and cash.

Scenario 1: FIXED PORTFOLIO—50% bonds, 50% cash

	Column A	Column B	Columns AxB
Asset	**Weighting (% of portfolio invested in this asset)**	**Projected Return**	**Expected Return**
Stocks	0	7%	0
Bonds	0.50	4%	2%
Cash	0.50	1%	0.5%
Total Expected Return			2.5%

Under the Fixed Scenario, the investor is projected to achieve 2.5% return per annum and will need to set aside $39,147 each year, over 20 years, to meet her goal.

The second scenario shows what happens when the investor is willing to diversify her investments and take on risk.

Scenario 2: BALANCED PORTFOLIO—60% stocks, 30% bonds, 10% cash

Asset	Column A Weighting (% of portfolio invested in this asset)	Column B Projected Return	Columns AxB Expected Return
Stocks	0.60	7%	4.2%
Bonds	0.30	4%	1.2%
Cash	0.10	1%	0.1%
Total Expected Return			5.5%

Under the Balanced Scenario, the investor would have to set aside much less per year—$28,679—to meet the same goal.

A logical follow-on question to this analysis of expected returns might be, "I don't want to take on as much risk as that under the Balanced Scenario but I still want to save the same amount. What are my options?" The answer to this is simple. You need to do one or both of the following:

1. Save more.

2. Invest for longer than 20 years to allow returns to compound longer.

You can also adjust the retirement goal so that it is less than $1,000,000. The point is to be realistic and aligned in terms of what risk you can take on and what you can achieve given the expected returns of different investments.

Let's see how $1,000,000 would turn out for a woman who was granted a lump sum in her divorce settlement if we were to invest this money today given the two above scenarios. Under the Fixed Scenario, she would be able to generate a compounded return of around $1,638,616 in 20 years. Under the Balanced Scenario, she would generate a compounded return of $2,917,757, more than double the other amount!

These scenarios are only meant to illustrate the dramatic difference in compounded return over time simply by shifting the asset allocation from Fixed to Balanced investing allocations.

Having said this, **you should never reach too far beyond the risk you feel comfortable taking** given your time horizon and other material considerations. Sometimes, a safer strategy is to manage your spending better and save more along the way in lieu of chasing higher returns than you are comfortable with.

Asset Allocation: When Rules of Thumb Are Kind of Dumb

There are a lot of rules of thumb around asset allocation, many of which are just too simple and cannot be applied to complicated situations. For example, the idea that your bond allocation should be equal to your age is one of my pet peeves. It makes sense that you should invest more conservatively with a shorter time horizon and adopt a capital preservation approach that focuses on keeping your initial investment and earning some income. But piling 70% of a woman's life savings into any old bond fund just because she is 70 years old is insanity. Interest rates only need to go up 1% to inflict severe pain on parts of the bond market, turning capital preservation into capital destruction, particularly if you are invested in bond funds and not holding individual bonds to maturity.

Much ado is made regarding your time horizon with asset allocation, and rightly so, because as you near retirement it takes longer to make up for large investment mistakes. This is why more investors closing in on retirement, even those with ample income and resources, look to safer assets and steadier income. But always keep in mind that what is considered safe is relative to everyone's unique situation *and* long-term market trends. If bonds are at "all-time highs", then the long-term trend for bonds is that they will likely fall in price going forward and bondholders can lose a lot depending on their investment choices. In fact, we are beginning to see exactly this at the time of writing as interest rates turn upward and investors flee bond funds.

In addition to long-term trends and time horizon, there are other variables to take into account when it comes to deciding your asset allocation, such as your ability to earn an income or draw down on a pension and any dependent's needs. Therefore, looking at all of these factors, including where you are in your life cycle, will ultimately help you to decide on a more accurate asset allocation than simply going by your age.

Meant for illustrative purposes only, here are some general personal risk profiles that an adviser may refer to when allocating your portfolio based on life cycle stage and investor-profile characteristics:

Profile	Asset Allocation	Stage in Life Cycle	Goals	Risks
Fixed	Cash and time deposits	Does not like market turmoil. Is willing to decrease living expenses to compensate for the effect of inflation.	Capital preservation	Inflation
Conservative	20% stocks, 50% bonds, 30% cash	Someone living on a reliable fixed income. Is willing to decrease expenses if necessary to compensate for inflation.	Capital preservation and income through bonds and dividend stocks or index funds	Income earned does not keep pace with inflation. Bond funds sell off and you face larger than expected capital loss.

Balanced	50% stocks, 40% bonds, 10% cash	40–60 years of age with a reliable income stream outside of their financial investments	Keep pace with inflation, reinvest income and dividends, steady wealth creation	Stock and bond funds fall together and you incur losses on both.
Moderately Aggressive	70% stocks, 30% bonds	A steady, reliable and growing income stream aside from their investment portfolio	Wealth creation, capital gains, dividend reinvestment	Short-term losses of 50% or more in a few months. May take years to regain losses if they do not invest at the lows.
Aggressive	70% or higher stock allocation	Can ride out market turmoil, however long or severe. Willing and able to "double down" and invest more during market turmoil.	Wealth creation, capital gains, dividend reinvestment	Short-term losses of 50% or more in a few months. May take years to regain losses if they do not invest at the lows.

So how would the logic of this table apply to someone who has gone through a divorce? Most divorcees, like most people, will fall on the continuum between fixed and balanced investors. Some divorcees still work and may have steady and growing income for the foreseeable future aside from their settlements. Other divorcees are living a lifestyle closer to that of a retiree. Take the following two examples for illustrative purposes only.

Kathleen is Singaporean and has been granted a lump sum payment as part of her settlement of S$750,000. She has a home paid off that she lives in alone. She is in her mid-sixties, does not work, receives money from her children and has a small government pension that covers basic expenses.

Her goal is capital preservation, i.e. to preserve that S$750,000, and not incur any loss of that capital. Therefore, she sets aside S$350,000 in short-term time deposits and uses S$400,000 to buy short-term Singapore government bonds. This would give her a projected additional income stream of S$5,000 a year (S$400,000x1.25%).[2]

Kathleen has the investment characteristics of a fixed or a conservative investor. What if Kathleen needed or wanted growth from her investments to keep up with inflation? She could buy a few dividend stocks or REITs instead of only holding short-term time deposits. She would be taking on more risk with some of her capital but she would be willing to do so to earn more income.

At the other end of the spectrum is Suguna who is in her mid-forties and still working in a stable career. She received a smaller lump sum of $450,000 in her divorce settlement and receives child support. Suguna's goals are to keep pace with inflation and build a retirement portfolio.

---

2   This is an illustration only and the interest represents an average rate of interest on two- to five-year Singapore Government Securities (SGS) bonds.

As she wants to preserve her lump sum payment, but doesn't want to buy bonds, she has been investing in time deposits or money market funds. However, given regular monthly savings from working, Suguna can invest this portion of her savings more aggressively as she has 20 years until retirement.

So Suguna takes $2,500 in surplus cash flow from her monthly salary and invests in a mix of small company growth-oriented stocks and large dividend-paying companies. Suguna realises that her investment portfolio will post both gains and losses in the short term but she believes that over the long term she will make more total return than if she were to leave her money in the bank. With this mix of cash reserves and stocks, Suguna invests more like a balanced investor.

The charts and rules of thumb here are meant to provide food for thought. Obviously, it makes sense that you change your asset allocation as your time horizon and life cycle status change because your needs change. Your asset allocation is not set in stone, it's just a way for you to measure how much risk you are willing to take on for an expected return given a certain point in time.

Most investor risk profiling in Asia is done purely through fairly simplistic Investor Risk Profile Surveys that highlight what losses you can bear. Go to the website at www.bmo.com/advisor/canada/internet/us/files/Investor%20Profile%20Questionnaire%20-%20358E.pdf for an example of such a survey.

In addition to doing investor profiles and creating full financial plans, I also ask the following question to anyone I work with, "What did you do during the 2008 crisis?"

If the answer is "I completely and utterly freaked out, had no idea what to do and considered selling (or did sell) and going into cash", then you are probably a conservative investor at most, unless you can come to terms with the reality that stocks and bonds *both* rise and fall in price, and that these are often buying opportunities to embrace.

If the answer is "I was nervous, and not thrilled of course to see significant losses in stocks (and bonds in some cases), but I figured I would just sit tight and ride it out", then you are probably a balanced investor who should seek out more dividend income and possibly short-term individual bonds or bond index funds to offset the unease of a dramatic market fall. Holding a bit more cash might also be an option.

If the answer is "It was the greatest six months of my life. I'd been waiting for a crash and could not wait to buy more equity", then you are in the moderately aggressive to aggressive camp. That said, you need a large safety net to fall back on and enough cash on hand to invest more during large, dramatic sell-offs.

If you had no investment at the time but have seen the fallout from such a crash, how do you believe you would have felt *IF* you had seen your investments go down 50%?

I have met few moderately aggressive or aggressive investors—people are braver in hindsight. The truly aggressive investors that I know have trust funds or other significant sources of income to keep them going beyond their investment portfolios, and they have cash to double down on their losses. In fact, in general, the wealthier the client, the more conservative they tend to be. I have yet to encounter a divorcee who is a moderately aggressive or aggressive investor, with good reason!

Writing Your Own Personal Investment Policy Statement

At this point, you will most likely have an idea of how you might allocate your assets based on your personality and your need for return. This means that you are now ready to write your own Investment Policy Statement, or IPS.

This is something that a competent adviser would do for you to clarify objectives, goals, investment horizon and returns. However, as you are your own adviser, you will need to write this down for yourself. Your personal IPS should read something like: "In order to create a retirement portfolio over the next 20 years, I will contribute $2,000 a month into a portfolio that is an even mix of stock and bond index funds to achieve a 5% real return. My goal is to keep pace with inflation and yield 2.5 to 3% off my investments per annum."

An IPS serves as a means to create the rules and the boundaries for your investment portfolio, whether you are managing it or someone else is. The reason you write it down is to make a commitment to your own long-term financial well-being, and it also serves as a reminder to stay strong through difficult financial times.

Get Your Shopping Bag Ready: Opening a Brokerage Account

Other than knowing your asset allocation and writing your IPS, you will need to open some type of brokerage account if you intend to buy anything other than individual bonds and hold cash. Ideally this should be an online brokerage account as opposed to an offline account which requires you to go through a real live person (your broker) to execute your orders.

Online brokerages generally have lower fees per trade than offline brokers. In Hong Kong, all the large banks, many small independent brokers as well as Charles Schwab out of the United States provide this service.

If you plan to go online in Singapore, you could consider using Phillip Securities, which is an independent online broker, as the big bank brokers have become too expensive. Better yet, skip all the local platforms with their excessive fees and sign up with Interactive Brokers as this company allows you to trade in multiple currencies and across international exchanges at low costs.

Personally, I use Charles Schwab and Interactive Brokers. Up until recently, Schwab was only available in Hong Kong in Asia but it has rolled out its global platform and residents of Hong

Kong and Australia, among other countries, can now trade on this platform but, unfortunately, residents in Singapore can't trade local stocks. Schwab is 100% independent of banks and other potential conflicts, and I have found its user interface, low fees, well-trained staff, personalised service and independent research to be top-notch.

Singapore Rules: Accredited Investor versus the Mere Mortal

Unlike Hong Kong, Bangkok and many other cities that allow investors to buy whatever investment products or services they like, Singapore has identified a class of investor termed the accredited investor (AI). This is an investor who makes S$300,000 a year and has more than S$2 million in investable assets. The accredited investor has far more options in terms of how to invest (they are also at the mercy of being sold far more questionable investments than someone who is not an AI).

This system protects the small investor to some degree because financial intermediaries are forbidden by law to sell anything but the most basic investment products to residents of Singapore. Unfortunately, this has limited the investment options of Singapore residents who use Singapore investment platforms because, for example, only accredited investors can buy ETFs on Singapore platforms. As a result, many Singapore resident investors who are not accredited investors are herded into actively managed funds because there are limited options otherwise.

At S$25 per trade, Singapore platforms are expensive compared to other countries. Adventurous individual investors in Singapore have got around this "no ETF" rule by going offshore and opening up accounts with brokers who charge 60% less per trade. Generally speaking, these are US dollar, US domiciled accounts, and investors are protected through federal investment insurance up to $500,000 per account if the firm fails (up to $100,000 in cash). Individual investors who choose to remain on Singapore platforms with mainly Singapore investments can buy individual stocks, REITs or bonds instead of being left with actively managed funds as the only alternative.

Analysing Your Legacy Policies: Investors' Prison

If you are in Asia, you may well be dealing with some legacy investment policies, pensions or portfolios as part of your divorce settlement. This book cannot possibly cover every possible scenario but I will address the most prevalent (and egregious) plan. This is the "forced savings/investment plan" that was most likely sold to you by the person who opened your savings account at the bank, an independent financial adviser (IFA) or a life insurance representative in Asia.

If you are holding or have been investing into a plan that is really a life insurance plan[3] and the plan demands monthly

---

3 If you are holding a policy that is written or underwritten by an insurance company, it is a type of life insurance plan, regardless of who sold it to you or what they call it.

contributions or premiums, locks you in for five or more years and has severe penalties for early withdrawals, then this part of your assets is in what I refer to as "Investors' Prison". I call it Investors' Prison because such a plan confiscates your money and charges often usurious fees for the pleasure, thus violating Golden Rule Eight: Keep Investing Expenses Low.

This type of plan is usually sold to people who do not have large minimum investments with which to start an investment portfolio. It is also sold to "keep you brave and investing through hard times", thus you must keep investing the money every month so that you stay on track. As a result, it is often sold as a pension plan.

It is likely that whoever sold this to your family has made a small fortune in commissions, and these commissions are being slowly bled out of your account over time in fees. You may or may not have been told about these fees and commissions. In addition, you may also be paying an annual management fee to your adviser in addition to the commissions they have already pocketed.[4]

Whether you have one of these plans or a put-together portfolio of investments that does not make sense to you, this is what you can do:

---

4 For example, a 25-year savings plan with a HK$35,000 (US$4,500) monthly premium generates an initial commission of HK$441,000 (US$56,903) and total renewal commissions of almost HK$200,000 (US$25,806). Not bad for a couple of hours' work. Sources: *Standard*, "Guided by Greed", 4 July 2005; www.tannerdewitt.com/media/publications/guided-by-greed.php

1. Ask your adviser what the *annualised real returns* have been to date. This means, on average, what has your return been for every year that you have been invested after inflation has been accounted for? Your account may have grown due to your monthly contributions, but have there been returns based on the actual investments?

2. Ask your adviser for a list of all the fees that have come out of your plan since its inception. Get them to write down the actual cash fees, charges and commissions, not the percentages or basis points.

3. Ask your adviser what commission they and the firm made (or continue to make) off your plan when it was sold to you.

4. If you were not involved when this policy was bought, find out why the policy was initiated. Was it meant to be a pension or a savings plan with a purpose and does it act as a tax shelter?

5. Ask your adviser what the base currency of the plan is. This means that if you intend to use the proceeds of this plan in Singapore, the returns in your account should be reflected in Singapore dollars and not US dollars. You should be able to see this in your statements. If your statements do not reflect your home currency, ask why this is so.

There is a chance that your adviser will not want to respond to these five questions, or even know what some of these things mean, even though by law they are often required to respond. There is also a really good chance that your adviser will get defensive. If this is the case and it is clear that your adviser does not want to help you, tell them that you are taking a holiday from your plan immediately and will no longer be contributing to it until you get the answers you need.

If you are unhappy with your returns and the fees involved, consider whether you want to continue working with this adviser. You may not be able to leave the plan, but you certainly can choose to manage your own account or have your account managed by someone else. There are hundreds of people managing money so you can pick and choose!

If, on the other hand, your adviser is open with you, then based on all the expenses incurred and the returns thus far, you need to decide if you want to continue contributing to this plan or portfolio. There may be some tax sheltering advantages and/or for someone who lacks the self-control to invest through downturns, these plans might pay off in the end. But more often than not, these policies can amount to just a huge waste of your money.

CONCLUSION

Very few investors regret long-term investment decisions but developing a dispassionate approach to long-term investing takes time. It takes time to develop the right habits and follow the Golden Rules. It takes time to find the discipline and self-control necessary to understand the psychology of markets. And because the psychological part of investing is the ultimate challenge here, it will help you to be realistic if you are in a financially stable place when assessing your risk tolerance and charting out your asset allocation and expected future returns.

CHAPTER 9

DIPPING YOUR TOE IN—
TIME TO GO SHOPPING!

The challenges with investing for most people are not the mechanics of opening an account and buying into the markets but rather mastering their own money habits, emotional responses and psychology. This is why, particularly for the divorcee, it matters that you are consistently cash-flow positive, free of heavy debt burdens and feel emotionally in control when you begin on the road to long-term investing in financial assets.

Always remember that there is no perfect way to invest money and there is no investing silver bullet. As we covered in the previous chapter, what to invest in has everything to do with your risk tolerance, where you are in your life cycle and how much you are willing and able to adjust your spending in the face of inflation.

There are hundreds of investment strategies. This chapter will cover two basic strategies for individual investors: Index Investing for a balanced return and Dividend/Dividend Growth Investing. These two strategies are presented as food for thought, as one may have greater appeal to you than the other. I will present each strategy separately to clearly communicate the advantages and disadvantages but they can also be mixed and matched to great effect.

UNDERSTANDING MARKET MELTDOWNS

As you are on the verge of investing, I want to address two issues that are most likely on your mind: investment bubbles and the financial crisis of 2008. These types of events can be psychologically scarring for a good many investors, so let's talk about bubbles and why they happen.

Many people act as if the 2008 financial crisis was a "once-in-a-lifetime" occurrence that will never happen again. This is patently false. There have been financial bubbles and panics ever since there has been money. There were also charlatans pushing bad investments on unsuspecting buyers long before there were credit default swaps or any Wall Street firm was established.

Modern bubbles form during times of economic expansion, much like we have now in many of the world's major economies such as the United States and Japan. Governments have been spending money to kick-start a new business and economic expansion cycle on the back of the 2008 financial crisis. They are also keeping lending rates low to make it easy for companies to borrow money. The idea is that governments use banks to push money out to businesses at low interest rates which, in turn, create jobs. This then makes people feel confident so they spend money and a normal economic cycle begins again.

Here's the thing though, just because a government injects money into a bank in the United States or Japan, it doesn't mean that the money will stay in the United States or Japan for investment. You may think it should but it doesn't. Businesses, banks, pension funds and other large pools of money search the world over for investments with a good return. Inevitably, some of that money sloshing around the financial system gets funnelled, sometimes very rapidly, into select assets, then bubbles form. This happened in the 1990s in Asian property and equities, and in the US property market more recently.

Eventually, governments try to curtail a bubble and raise interest rates, restrain lending or use other means, such as the new rounds of stamp duties introduced in Singapore's and Hong Kong's property markets. Very often, that fast flow of "hot money" can reverse suddenly, causing bubbles to deflate rapidly and often painfully for investors caught up in the mania of the moment. These reversals of money flow can feel particularly acute in smaller, open economies like those of Singapore and Hong Kong.

These bubbles follow patterns, and it's the long-term patterns that you need to get a feel for because these are the ones that can help or harm your investment decisions. You need to avoid being greedy and buying when everyone else is in a buying frenzy, aka market tops, or being fearful and selling in a panic. In fact, the best investors do the opposite. Investors who bought equities or property in the first half of 2009, a time of maximum fear, will have realised significant returns a few years later.

For the reader who is seeking simple economic security, it is not enough to be fearful when others are greedy and greedy when others are fearful, as Warren Buffett is so often quoted as saying. Sitting around waiting for a crash is one way to invest but not ideal for someone needing regular income. You need to figure out what to do when many people are fearful and many people are greedy all at the same time!

INDEX INVESTING FOR A BALANCED RETURN: HOW TO IN A WORLD THAT IS HALF FEARFUL AND HALF GREEDY

In Chapter 7, we covered Index Investing and why people buy passive funds or ETFs to do Index Investing, which essentially enables you to diversify through one fund, pay very low fees and track the index. In Chapter 8, we discussed total return, which is the idea of investing in a portfolio of assets, usually stocks and bonds, that provides an expected return depending on your allocation. Now let's put these two concepts together.

Remember the fear (buying bonds to earn income and protect losses) and greed (buying stocks to achieve growth) approach? That is why stocks and bonds generally make up the majority weighting in most Balanced portfolios. There are many stock and bond index funds as well as other investments such as REITs, gold and so on that you can buy into but let's get started here by following Golden Rule Seven: KISS (Keep Investing Simple Sister!) to create a portfolio.

To begin with, let's create a portfolio with $100,000 to invest. You then decide that you want to invest 40% of your money in stocks, 40% in bonds and 20% in cash. So you would need to buy $40,000 of a stock index fund, $40,000 of a bond index fund and leave $20,000 in cash. By investing in this blend of assets, you would ideally achieve your expected return over a specified time horizon.

Your expected return will be estimated based on this asset allocation. As in Chapter 8, let's say we expect a 7% return for stocks, 4% for bonds and just 1% for cash. From this, you can estimate the return of this portfolio when annualised over many years to be as follows:

$100,000 DIY PORTFOLIO—40% stocks, 40% bonds, 20% cash

Asset	Column A	Column B	Columns AxB
	Weighting (% of portfolio invested in this asset)	Projected Return	Expected Return
Stocks	0.40	7%	2.8%
Bonds	0.40	4%	1.6%
Cash	0.20	1%	0.2%
Total Expected Return			4.6%

Singapore

If you are living in Singapore and you need to use the returns of your portfolio in Singapore, then your local stock and bond markets should be represented in your portfolio. So you should buy the SPDR Straits Times Index ETF (ticker symbol: ES3) as this tracks the Straits Times Index for stocks while, for bonds, investment should be made into the ABF Singapore Bond Index Fund (ticker symbol: A35).

If you like the idea of Index Investing but you cannot invest in ETFs because you are not an accredited investor in Singapore, you have two options: go offshore and buy ETFs or stay onshore and buy actively managed funds.

If you decide to go offshore, you can try to open an account in Hong Kong or go through a US online broker to enable you to buy the Singapore Equity Index (ticker symbol: EWS), which closely tracks the Straits Times Index. Then look into buying individual government bonds, which you can do through your local brokerages or banks here, for relatively small denominations.

If you stay onshore, look at combining funds like Aberdeen Singapore Equity Fund and LionGlobal Short Duration Bond Fund (nearly 50% of Lion Global's holdings are Singapore corporate bonds). Keep in mind you will be paying higher expenses for actively managed funds, and such bond funds are higher risk than a Singapore government bond fund. The two actively managed funds mentioned here have fees of 1.5% and 1% respectively, but each also has a loading fee of 3%, which you are charged on your initial investment.

Hong Kong

If you are in Hong Kong, you should look at the HSBC ABF Hong Kong Bond Index Fund (ticker symbol: 2819), which invests in debt backed by the Hong Kong government. For stocks, you can follow the Hang Seng Tracker Index ETF (ticker symbol: 2800), which tracks the Hang Seng Index. (Note that as the Hang Seng Index is heavily weighted towards property developers and the finance sector, it would pay to diversify further. (*See* "Go International for More Diversification" below.) Both these funds pay a regular dividend and they charge well under 0.20% per annum, which is peanuts compared to most actively managed funds.

If you feel that the HSBC Bond Fund is rather paltry, you can invest in something like the ABF Pan Asia Bond Index Fund (ticker symbol: 2821), which holds Pan Asian government debt. It currently yields around 3.9% and its top-country holdings are China, South Korea, Singapore and Hong Kong. There is no initial charge and the annual fee is just 0.13% but the risk is higher than just holding local government bonds. Oddly, this fund is domiciled and managed in Singapore but only listed in Hong Kong.

Go International for More Diversification

Singapore and Hong Kong are uniquely small markets so most equity investors should include some geographical diversification in their portfolios to get exposure to large multinational companies with global reach. They also could include some safe haven government debt such as US treasuries in their portfolios. Doing this can lower your risk to some degree as you are not dependent only on your home market for all your returns. Also, most global equity index funds track big brand name companies that have a lot of cash, pay good dividends and can strategically manage through challenging economic times.[1]

For a 40% allocation to stocks, consider putting 20% in your local index and 20% in an international index, with the remainder of your portfolio being a mix of bonds and cash. Based on the model DIY portfolio of $100,000, this is how you would invest using Hong Kong as an example:

Asset	Column A **Weighting (% of portfolio invested in this asset)**	Column B **Projected Return**	Columns AxB **Expected Return**
Hong Kong Stock Index	0.20	7%	1.4%
International Stock Index	0.20	7%	1.4%
Bond Index Fund	0.40	4%	1.6%
Cash	0.20	1%	0.2%
Total Expected Return			4.6%
Expected $ Return in 20 Years			$245,829

---

1 In Singapore, you can buy many index funds and ETFs if you are an accredited investor. Similarly in Hong Kong, you can invest in a potpourri of ETFs through its exchange as well as many large US multinationals. I have listed some of your options for each of these exchanges in "Resources" in on pages 369–376.

There are literally hundreds of different types of passive index funds and ETFs that you can invest in across geographies (emerging markets, Global Index, Europe, the United States, etc.) and sectors (IT, consumer discretionary, industrials and so on). Here's an example of a more diverse selection of index funds and ETFs and the respective tickers offshore. Some of these funds can most likely be purchased onshore depending on where you live.

Sector	Ticker Symbol
Vanguard Total Market (US) ETF	VTI
Vanguard Global ex-US Real Estate ETF	VNQI
Vanguard MSCI EAFE ETF (non-US markets)	VEA
Vanguard Total Bond Market ETF	BND
PowerShares International Corporate Bond (PICB)	PICB
Vanguard FTSE Emerging Markets ETF (VWO)	VWO

Easing into Indexing

You can invest in any number of index funds. To start with, however, pick two to three funds and KISS! until you get the hang of it. The price you pay for your investment matters—index funds can become grossly overpriced, just like any asset. So, slowly invest your money as per your asset allocation over six months to ensure you do not buy at all-time high prices.

Once you get a feel for indexing, you can expand your portfolio as you see fit, and as your confidence grows.

Rebalancing Your Asset Allocation—Watering the Cactus

Index Investing is like taking care of a cactus. You don't need to do a lot to a cactus to make it grow; you just need to water it every so often. "Watering the cactus" in indexing is known as rebalancing. By rebalancing your portfolio occasionally, you enforce the concept of "selling high and buying low". If you do Index Investing as described here, rebalancing will instil a discipline on the portfolio that you may not otherwise develop as an investor.

Let's look at a portfolio of $250,000 invested in low-cost index funds, with it being a balanced portfolio of 50% stocks and 50% bonds. Through your online broker, you would buy $125,000 in a stock fund and $125,000 in a bond fund.

What will happen when stocks rise significantly? Say your stock index has risen 20% and your bond index has gone down 10%. Then you would have $150,000 ($125,000x1.2) in your stock fund and $112,500 ($125,000x0.90) in your bond fund. Your total account would be up $262,500–250,000=$12,500, but the asset allocation would have shifted from a 50/50 ratio to a ratio of 60% stocks and 40% bonds.

This is where rebalancing comes in handy. Rebalancing forces you to do one of two things in this scenario: You can either put new money into the lagging index fund—in this case the bond index fund—in order to bring it back up to 50% of your total portfolio or you can sell off part of the stock fund and buy more bonds to bring the portfolio back to the designated allocation. Since stocks are high as they have run up 20%, you can sell around $15,000 to $20,000 (more or less) worth of stocks to buy low, in this case more of your bond index. Remember Golden Rule Six: Buy the Sale!

Leading on from this, the logical question to ask is this: "How do I know when to sell? How much does my fund need to appreciate before I rebalance?" There is a lot of opinionating around rebalancing. If you are adding new money to your portfolio regularly, add to the funds in such a way that you bring your allocation back into balance in order to meet your asset allocation.

If you are not adding new money to your portfolio, check in on it every six months. If there are no major movements, because the index funds are moving sideways, leave your cactus alone for a while. If, however, an index starts to breach a change of 15 to 20% upwards or downwards, it's time to start thinking about rebalancing. Ideally, this should not be done more than once a year or so.

Do I Have to Rebalance at all?

No, you do not *have to* rebalance, especially if you believe that there will be more and more money in the world and that "the high tide of printed money will lift all boats". But if you do not rebalance, expect much more volatility (bigger paper gains and losses) along the way.

Take a portfolio with an allocation of 70% bonds and 30% stocks. After a year or so, the portfolio balance shifts to 50/50 stocks and bonds because your stock index has appreciated. If the stock index "reverts to mean", which is finance speak for "sells off to the level where it normally trades", your portfolio will likely register larger losses than if you had rebalanced. Keep in mind that most of the time stocks and bonds don't just revert to mean, they fall far past the mean because people panic.

The Index Investing methodology mantra revolves around keeping your asset allocation in check with the amount of risk you feel comfortable taking. Rebalancing, by its very nature, forces you to not stray too far from where your asset allocation should be. By rebalancing, you buy low and sell high—and that's a good thing. It feels good to lock in gains or take some profit off the table. In equal measure, it is wise to shop around and buy what is on sale or lagging in price.

If you like the idea of Index Investing but do not want the responsibility of rebalancing, you can go offshore and invest in index funds that are a mix of stocks and bonds such as the Vanguard Wellesley Income Fund (VWINX). This fund mixes high-quality bonds and dividend-paying stocks. It pays a 4.33% dividend (at the time of writing) and only charges 0.22% in management fees.

Who Benefits the Most from Index Investing for a Balanced Return

Remember the book *Battle Hymn of the Tiger Mother*? Then imagine there were a book titled *Battle Hymn of the Tiger Investor*. Okay, now think of the exact opposite. Perhaps *Battle Hymn of the Manatee Investor*? Index Investing is for people who want hands-on involvement with their money but in a minimalist way—minimal fees, minimal investments and minimal portfolio minding.

- For portfolios under $50,000, you can diversify with just a couple of index fund investments.
- It is more suited to wealth creation, where new money is being added regularly, than for managing a fixed retirement portfolio.
- It is better for investors who believe that their money should be invested at all times and do not want to sit on much cash.
- It's psychologically easier to execute this strategy if you are adding new money regularly to the portfolio. This is because you can always divert those new funds to the lagging index fund (or funds) and bring the asset allocation back into balance, as opposed to selling the winning index fund.

Index Investing is relatively simple conceptually, but it's not always easy to do. It is hard to always think long term, particularly if those around you are panicking. It is also hard to sell your winning index and buy what looks like it is going down and "losing money". And it's impossible to know the absolute market tops and bottoms for your index funds. But the longer you do this type of investing, as with anything, the easier it will become to get a feel for the market and rebalance accordingly.

The Downsides to Index Investing for a Balanced Return

As mentioned, there is no sure-fire investment strategy that guarantees your returns at all times. Index Investing is no different.

- Index Investing to achieve a balanced return, as described above, did not hold up like the Holy Grail of Investing that it is meant to be during the 2008 crash for many portfolios because most asset prices fell, including most bonds. So the "bond as a cushion" concept did not work as well as prescribed. Select US treasury index funds performed well because in a crisis everyone rushes to the safe haven of US treasury bonds and the US dollar. But, if you had an Asia-centric portfolio with 60% Asian equity and 40% Asian bond fund or index exposure, the fall was fast and hard for both.[2, 3, 4] All of these "fallen" index funds and ETFs have come back with a vengeance since 2008, posting outsized returns. So, if a systemic crash is what

---

2   www.trustnetoffshore.com/Factsheets/Factsheet.aspx?fundCode=FDFY9&univ=E

3   http://sg.finance.yahoo.com/echarts?s=XSB. TO#symbol=xsb.o;range=my;compare=; indicator=volume;charttype=line;crosshair=on;ohlcvalues=0;logscale=off;source= undefined;

4   www.nikkoam.com.sg/files/documents/funds/fact_sheet/abf2_fs.pdf

you fear most, consider diversifying outside of just Asian markets. You can also consider keeping some cash on hand and be brave when others are fearful and buy low.

- Index Investing can be preached with such dogma that it belies the reality that index funds, like any asset, can become grossly mispriced. Be wary of buying too much of anything that is priced at or near an all-time high.

- It is less ideal for investors who are income focused. Index funds often pay dividends or other income, but the yield can be much lower than the individual stocks or bonds that the index funds track. (Index funds that pay very high yields are probably tracking very high-risk investments.)

- Countries like Singapore, with tiny bond markets, may have only one passive index fund or ETF with little volume (relatively few investors), so expect a Singapore government bond fund to behave more like a stagnant puddle than an ocean wave. It might be easier to go to the bank and buy individual Singapore government bonds and skip small market bond index funds altogether.

Do these shortcomings tell us that we should not use Index Investing to achieve a balanced return? No, it simply means that you have to understand that every investing strategy has its limitations, and this type of investing is no different. This is particularly true if you fear systemic crashes and/or need a lot of exposure to your local bond market but it is small and inaccessible.

Can Someone Else Do This for Me?

Index Investing for a balanced return, as described here, is the skinny latte version of a theory that has been applied in finance by advisers worldwide for over 50 years. This theory is referred to as the Modern Portfolio Theory (MPT), and it's used to create a portfolio that maximises your absolute return for a certain amount of risk. Mind you, it's the only thing I know that's 50 years old and still called modern.

This theory was initially developed for a US-centric portfolio and did not take into consideration the highly interconnected global financial markets and the risks that we have today. The theory also depends on the assumption that past returns in stocks and bonds will be the same in the future—a questionable assumption indeed given how the world has changed since this theory was put into practice.

Much of MPT's credibility also rests on the assumption that stocks and bonds, among other asset classes such as precious metals, other commodities and REITs tend to move in opposite directions. In other words, when one asset class rises, another falls. This assumes that if you have a loss in one asset class, you can be protected by a gain in another and thus achieve the absolute return of all your investments based on your asset allocation. Most of the time, this holds true, but the obvious risk, as it was in 2008, is that multiple asset classes can reverse together reaching all-time lows again.

DIVIDEND AND DIVIDEND GROWTH INVESTING—SHOW ME THE MONEY!

While Index Investing may be the easiest approach for the beginner investor, it does not suit every investor's needs. To combat inflation and create income streams, dividend payments from stocks are another source of income. Solid dividend portfolios not only bring in quarterly, semi-annual and annual revenue streams, but with the right investments, the dividend payments grow over time to keep pace with inflation.[5]

Income from dividend portfolios can also withstand crashes like we saw in 2008 relatively well. In fact during 2008, the majority of the companies on the S&P 500 continued to pay dividends right through the meltdown. Some even increased their dividend payments.[6] The main losers were the banks and other financials, many of which were forced to suspend dividend payments to receive a financial bailout from the US government.

Revisiting the Dividend

There was a time when almost all companies paid dividends; it was almost unheard of not to do so. In the last 30 years, however, too many investors have turned to stocks purely for

---

5 REITs for the sake of this explanation can be considered a dividend-like payment. They are investments in property trusts, as covered in Chapter 7, and traded on stock exchanges.

6 S&P tracks dividend payments from stocks on the S&P 500. Here is the history for 2008 dividend payments:
- Q1 2008: 93 increases, 7 dividend cuts, 4 suspensions
- Q2 2008: 65 increases, 9 decreases, no suspensions
- Q3 2008: 45 increases, 6 decreases, 8 suspensions
- Q4 2008: 32 increases, 17 dividend cuts, 10 dividend suspensions

capital gain, and now only 19% of all companies listed on the US stock exchange pay dividends. That percentage is smaller in most other markets.

Dividend payments are cash payments to the shareholders that come from corporate profits. So when a company makes its profit, some of the profit is put back into the company and reinvested so the company can grow, and other profit is paid out as dividends to shareholders. While many people associate dividend-paying stocks with companies that have little or no growth, such as utilities, this is a misperception.

Within the world of dividend-paying stocks, there is a huge amount of diversity. There are companies that are considered more stable dividend payers with higher yields such as many utilities or REITs. There are many large multinational companies that are growing their businesses globally and, as a result, they grow their dividend payments annually. There are also many medium-sized companies in growing fields, such as medicine and IT, which generate enough profit for both reinvestment and small dividends.

Dividend Yield

As mentioned in Chapter 7, yield is basically measured by any regular payment you receive for any asset that you hold. For property, your yield is based on the rental income. For bonds, it is the interest payment on the loan. For stocks, the yield is based on the dividend payment. For example, if the annual dividend is $1.25 a share and the stock trades at $25, your dividend yield is $1.25÷$25=5%. As the price of the stock rises, the yield will go down (unless the company raises its dividend). As the stock price goes down, the yield will rise.

For companies that pay dividends, as a shareholder, you will receive a dividend payment for every share of stock that you own. Let's say you own 1,000 shares, and the annual dividend is $1.25 per share, you will receive $1,250 (1,000x1.25) in income for just holding those shares. You may receive that payment once a year, but many dividend stocks pay out their dividend distributions quarterly or semi-annually. Remember the Time Value of Money concept that was covered in Chapter 6? The sooner and more frequently you can receive your dividend payment, the better!

Investors who seek *steady income streams* lean towards "widow-and-orphan" stocks. These types of investment are often held in trusts because they have a history of paying out a reliable income stream to their beneficiaries. These stocks generally are utility companies or blue-chip companies.

However, for investors seeking *growing income streams*, dividend growth stocks are preferred. Dividend growth companies generally have a dividend policy oriented towards growing their dividend payment annually. So, the initial yield may be low, sometimes under 1%, but the yield is likely to climb by 3 to 8% per year. It is often the combination of reliable dividends and growing dividends that make up a dividend portfolio for many investors.

Dividend Growth—How It Works

The difference between a dividend payment and a bond interest payment is that a bond is a fixed payment—that's why it is called "fixed income". So is the rental income from a condo, at least for the term of the lease. If inflation picks up over the next few years, you will be stuck with whatever your bond and lease contracts state regarding payment.

What can be great about individual stocks, as I mentioned above, is that **many large international companies grow their dividends annually by 3 to 8% or more** to keep pace with inflation. This is how it works: If you buy stock in a company that paid an annual dividend of $1.25 per share this year, but every year thereafter increases its dividend payout by 3%, their payments to you based on 1,000 shares will look like this over eight years:

Time Frame	Annual Dividend	Amount Earned
Year 1	1.28	1,287.50
Year 2	1.32	1,326.12
Year 3	1.36	1,365.90
Year 4	1.40	1,406.88
Year 5	1.44	1,449
Year 6	1.49	1,492.56
Year 7	1.53	1,537
Year 8	1.58	1,583

So, regardless of the stock price, or market fluctuations, your dividend payment is growing.

Some companies have grown their dividends over the last 25 years, earning them the title Dividend Aristocrats. They are all US-based multinationals[7] and some of them, such as Emerson, have been paying dividend increases for over 50 years. There are also international stocks called Dividend Achievers that are in a slightly less illustrious category, having increased dividends only for the last 10 years.[8]

These growing dividend streams are attractive to managers of some of the world's large trusts and pension funds. These managers are looking for stable and growing income streams to keep pace with inflation, and so an entire category of companies has oriented their dividend policy towards keeping these investors happy.

It is important to note that investors who look for growing dividends are not necessarily looking for the highest-yielding dividend payment. This is an important difference between any old dividend and a growing dividend. Dividend growth companies tend to pay lower dividends than utility companies or higher-yield dividend payers.

Many of the world's Dividend Aristocrats can be bought over stock exchanges in Singapore and Hong Kong. Asian-based companies also pay dividends but they do not yet pay *growing dividends* with the same commitment or reliability as companies from the United States, Canada, the United Kingdom and

---

7 www.buyupside.com/dividendaristocrats/displayalldividendaristocrats.php
8 www.buyupside.com/dividendachievers/achieversintmainaz.php

Australia do. Therefore, if you go down this route of dividend investing, or even just try experimenting with it, you will need to do some research online and see which companies have the best dividend payment histories.

There are very active dividend investors in Asia who worry about inflation and are attracted to the idea of a growing dividend. Here is a useful website that tracks the dividend history of Asian companies—http://sg.dividendinvestor.com/ (there is a separate page for each country). The most useful website that I've found by far and wide is www.buyupside.com/dividends/dividendchampionsaz.php for US and other international stocks

Reinvested Dividends—Sleeping Beauty Returns

If you do not need the income generated by the dividends and are able instead to reinvest these dividends, you will create compounded returns like money manna from heaven. By reinvesting, you are essentially using the payments the company gives to you in dividends to buy more of its shares. This allows you to systematically grow a portfolio position in a stock over time without ever investing another dollar.

So, if you do not need to draw down on your dividend income, you can accumulate many additional shares by just buying and holding dividend and growing dividend stocks. This is the Sleeping Beauty approach to investing as you are Making Money While You Sleep. Below is a conservative estimation of your hypothetical investment of 1,000 shares with a dividend payment of $1.25. I have conservatively estimated only 2% appreciation in the value of the stock and 3% annual growth in the dividend payment over 10 years.

	Without Dividend Reinvestment	With Dividend Reinvestment
Total Value	$45,234.61	$50,968.41
Number of Shares	1,000	1,672.47
Dividends Paid	$14,759.75	$18,963.01
Annualised Return	6.11%	7.38%

Do You Ever Sell with Your Dividend Portfolio?

Although the goal of this portfolio is oriented towards buying, holding and earning income, price still matters, even with dividend growth assets. So there can be a right time to buy and a right time to consider selling. However, the lags between buying and selling tend to be years (or decades!). Dividend and dividend growth investors sell for the following reasons: They believe the dividend may not continue to grow or could be suspended for some reason and/or they have found a better opportunity than the one in which they are invested.

In addition, many people who hold dividend portfolios rebalance occasionally. They sell a portion of their "winning" stocks, which have climbed significantly over the years, to buy more of their portfolio's lagging stocks or even take new positions, or shares, in undervalued stocks. This is done so that there is not too much risk in one stock position in the portfolio. By rebalancing, you can buy more of a lagging stock position that is less in favour and take a bit of money off the table with your winning investment.

How To—It's Like Running a 7-Eleven

Owning a portfolio of income-focused assets like dividend stocks is a bit like owning a 7-Eleven. If you owned a 7-Eleven, you would stock it with products like soda, cigarettes, aspirin, magazines, deodorant, toothpaste and canned soup to create many income streams. A 7-Eleven owner chooses the most reliable and suitable items to create sustainable and growing income streams. Once it's set up, a 7-Eleven can pretty much run itself.

Whereas the work involved in Index Investing is in getting your asset allocation right and then watching your portfolio for optimal times to rebalance, the work involved in Dividend Investing comes upfront in setting up a portfolio. You need to do much more upfront work in order to be able to forget your portfolio for a few years.

Most dividend portfolios have between 20 and 30 stocks in them across sectors, i.e. energy, industrials, consumer staples etc., and geographies (the United States, Canada, Asia, Australia, etc.). Therefore, you need to get comfortable with both Yahoo!

Finance and other online resources like the ones mentioned throughout this book. If you do go down this route, you must also read books about Dividend Investing, a couple of which I list in "Resources" on pages 369–376.

Here are just a few tips on what to look out for when considering a portfolio of dividend or dividend growth stocks:

- Dividends generally get paid with cash. You need to make sure that whichever company you are looking at has cash and is generating cash from its business. You do not want to consider a company that can only pay or grow its dividend using debt.

- In the same respect, if a company seems to be posting gains in earnings but the dividend is not growing, this is a red flag and the stock should be avoided.

- Some dividend payers are more reliable than others. If you need a consistent income stream, then you need to consider the company's dividend payment history and the probability that it can maintain its dividend payments to you based on its business prospects. Do some research and find at least 15 to 20 investments that are a mix of local and international companies you can live with and forget about for a couple of years. Bloomberg lists dividend growth in each stock's Key Statistics such as for BHP below (shown in grey):[9]

---

9 This is for illustrative purposes only.

Key Statistics for BHP

Market Cap (M USD)	160,053.97
Shares Outstanding (M)	1,605.85
30-Day Average Volume	2,674,277
Dividend Indicated Gross Yield	3.56%
Cash Dividend (USD)	1.1400
Last Dividend	03/06/2013
5-Year Dividend Growth	**15.28%**

- Growing dividends are generally the domain of individual stock portfolios. However if you do not want to pick individual stocks, you can choose index funds that track dividend companies and dividend growth companies, such as the Vanguard Dividend Growth Fund (VDIGX) or the SPDR S&P Dividend ETF (SDY), the latter of which seems to track more closely the Dividend Aristocrats. Vanguard Dividend Appreciation ETF (VIG) and Vanguard High Dividend Yield ETF (VYM) are two others. Expect a lower yield and less income than if you were buying individual stocks.

- Choose financially stable companies instead of "hot stocks". In Singapore, the most stable companies will most likely be Temasek-linked. In Hong Kong, people may gravitate towards the finance or property sectors but you will not be diversified during a downturn if you do. Look at everyday needs, i.e. food, transportation, electricity, gas, etc. Many of these companies have monopoly-like advantages (i.e. no competition!) which should allow them to continue to pay dividends in hard times.

- Find companies that pay dividends monthly, quarterly or at the very least semi-annually. REITs pay monthly or quarterly while US stocks tend to pay quarterly. Many Asia-based companies pay their dividends semi-annually or annually. Going back to the rules of compounding in Chapter 6, the sooner you get your money, the better!

- Find companies that are not trading at, or near, all-time high prices. Some people won't even buy near 52-week highs (highs for the year). This is particularly important because dividend stocks have become a trend again as people have woken up to their own needs for income. So always look for good solid dividend payers that are out of favour with the market.

- Find companies that keep creating cash flow from their businesses. This is particularly important if you are worried about systemic crashes and the ability for a company to sustain its growth and its dividend through hard times.

- Find companies that have a payout ratio of 60% or less, with the exception of REITs and some utility stocks. The payout ratio is listed on sites like Bloomberg and Yahoo! Finance under Key Statistics. The payout ratio for Starbucks is shown below in grey:[10]

---

10 This is for illustrative purposes only.

Dividends & Splits	
Forward Annual Dividend Rate[4]:	0.84
Forward Annual Dividend Yield[4]:	1.50%
Trailing Annual Dividend Yield[3]:	0.76
Trailing Annual Dividend Yield[3]:	1.30%
5 Year Average Dividend Yield[4]:	N/A
Payout Ratio[4]:	**39.00%**
Dividend Date[3]:	Feb 21, 2013
Ex-Dividend Date[4]:	Feb 5, 2013
Last Split Factor (new per old)[2]:	2:1
Last Split Date[3]:	Oct 24, 2005

- If you don't need the income, reinvest your dividends. It's the Sleeping Beauty approach to investing, i.e. making money while you sleep.

- Many high-yielding stocks pay out unsustainable dividends. It is extremely important to understand the difference between a sustainable dividend-paying company and a company that slashes its dividend and then it crashes. Nokia was a dividend darling until it started to rapidly lose market share as well as its cash hoard, then the company suspended its dividend indefinitely!

- As a final piece of advice, do not believe that any investment is a keeper and absolutely must be held until death do you part. Keep your emotional and psychological attachments to people, pets and hobbies, not to any company (unless you are the CEO of it).

What Does a Dividend Portfolio Look Like?

Here, I'm going to share a portfolio that was put together by a couple of individual investors. Their particular time horizon is 10 years and their mandate was simple—find up to 10 stocks, half being reliable utility-like stocks and half being big brand names that are global companies. One of these stocks could be a speculative investment. All but the speculative investment had to pay dividends but not all had to be dividend growth stocks.

Half of the stocks had to be in their home country while the remainder had to be outside of their home country, and they could keep 10% in cash. (For the record, the average dividend portfolio should comprise 20 investments and no more than 5% per position, i.e. not own more than 5% of your total investment in any one stock.) They had to choose companies they knew and used. They also had to have an idea of why they were actually interested in investing in those companies so they could "own it".

Many dividend portfolios do not have a time horizon. This one does because while the investors want to keep the portfolio past the 10-year mark, they want to specifically learn how to invest for income. I also advised them that during volatile times with very low interest rates, it makes sense to be in dividend stocks as long as they keep showing you the money.

Stock	Region	Number of Shares	% of Portfolio	Dividend Income	YTD Gain/ Loss %	Annualised Return	Initial Investment in $	YTD Gain in $
Core								
Wendy's	N. America	505	10.00%	80.81	12.37%	0.0601	2,500.00	2,809.25
Microsoft	N. America	100	10.00%	158.00	16.50%	0.0777	2,500.00	2,912.50
Costco	N. America	33	10.00%	67.41	55.46%	0.2436	2,500.00	3,886.50
Starbucks	N. America	70	10.00%	95.05	63.55%	0.2789	2,500.00	4,088.75
SingTel	Singapore	103	10.00%	335.93	19.34%	0.0849	2,500.00	2,983.50
Royal Dutch Shell	UK	33	10.00%	226.61	1.03%	0.0084	2,500.00	2,525.75
BCE	Canada	67	10.00%	290.77	29.78%	0.128	2,500.00	3,244.50
HK Electric	Hong Kong	371	10.00%	185.10	41.32%	0.1776	2,500.00	3,533.00
Speculation: Short-term Investments (under 2 years)								
Apple			10.00%		87.46%	0.376	2,500.00	4,686.50
Total Invested Portfolio			90.00%				2,500.00	2,500.00
Cash			10.00%				25,000.00	33,170.25
Totals			100.00%	1,439.67				
Total Return (Dividends + Unrealised Capital Gain)								38%

This particular portfolio started with $25,000 and earned 38% in two years, between 5 April 2011 and 6 April 6 2013. The annualised total return was around 17%. After inflation, the rate of total return was around 15% per annum, depending on whose inflation numbers you believe. The investors reinvested their dividends, but I have broken down the income under the Dividend Income column to show the actual cash from investing this portfolio.

The income earned off this portfolio is roughly $715 a year, or 2.8% on their original investment. This is less than what the investors had hoped to achieve. Despite the nice year-on-year capital gains, the portfolio has not performed exactly as expected. So, the owners have a bit of work to do in order to derive more income or at least ensure that half their choices will pay growing dividends here on out.

When I show this portfolio to people, they are either surprised or say that the investors were lucky because their annualised return beat most professional money managers by a wide margin. I suspect there is a stroke of luck in here somewhere, but let's talk luck for a second. If they had chosen McDonald's over Wendy's, ExxonMobil over Royal Dutch Shell and Walmart over Costco, they would have been perceived as much luckier with larger income and bigger capital gains.

If you had looked at this portfolio in the summer of 2011, three months after they had invested, they were down around 15 to 20% due to the ongoing crisis in Europe. You probably would have said they were unlucky. On the other hand, had they bought in the summer of 2011, they would have posted larger returns—and been even luckier. Imagine if they had bought in 2009! In other words, luck is a relative thing!

You have to be careful about feeling lucky or unlucky with investing. It is much better to judge a portfolio based on what it was set up to do. It could be down 50% by the summer or up 50% by next year. Who knows? Who cares? For these two particular investors, they are trying to invest for income anyway.

What Next?

Two years have passed since the portfolio was set up, which means the investors' time horizon is now down to eight years. This is a fixed portfolio, in that no new money is being added, so the two investors have started to think more conservatively. On 10 April 2013, they took some profit in Starbucks and Costco and bought more out-of-favour shares in Microsoft, Wendy's and Royal Dutch Shell because they like the outsized dividends (over 3%).

The rest of their money will remain in cash while they look for another investment. There is nothing wrong with holding some cash if you are not sure where to invest. It's better to lose a dividend payment here or there than invest in something just because you think you should be invested.

If you would like to continue following this story, you can follow these two investors on a website called TeenInvest (www.teenvesting.weebly.com). These two amateur investors are my children and, at the time of writing, they are 11 and 13 years old. They chose the portfolio positions at ages 9 and 11 when I gave them part of their college savings to invest at their request.

They used the parameters I provided above and this portfolio was chosen after about 2 hours of discussion and research. The only stock I picked was the Canadian stock (I tried to steer them to Walmart and McDonald's to no avail!). They basically chose what they knew and used. While I would not only buy what you know, it's one way of starting to understand companies and their growth prospects.

They are going to use this portfolio to draw down some income at college in eight years' time, so if they can build a portfolio with quality stocks that maintain decent or growing yields, it will give them a bit of pocket money. If they keep the portfolio over the long term, they have a very, very long investment horizon, which means they can recover from a big screw up, which inevitably everyone makes.

The lesson here is that most portfolio management is about tweaking, not giving your portfolio a lobotomy by buying and selling like a day trader. What this exercise taught them, and I hope you, is that you have to start small and you have to start slowly but you have to start somewhere.

Downsides to Dividend and Dividend Growth Portfolios

The risk for dividend investors is not what other investors normally associate with risk, i.e. that the asset price goes down temporarily, or even sharply. In fact, most dividend investors call a pullback a "sale". If they are reinvesting their dividends, they are accumulating more stock at cheaper prices! Dividend investors love a sale.

Anything, even extraneous things, can make markets crash (a hedge fund going bankrupt, terrorism, market glitches, panics, etc.). As long as you are able to earn your income, then price fluctuations do not matter. The risk with Dividend and Dividend Growth Investing is less market specific and more company specific:

- The major risk with picking individual stocks is that you can lose your entire investment if the company you choose to invest in goes bankrupt. While the probability of this happening is fairly low if you invest in a Dividend Aristocrat, there are no guarantees. Many nervous equity investors during the 2008 crisis saw enormous losses in financial stocks and indefinite dividend suspensions. The same was true for BP during the Gulf of Mexico disaster, which was far more unpredictable. Most of these companies recovered and started paying dividends again, but the suspension of income is exactly what the dividend investor wants to avoid.

- Companies can cut or stop growing their dividends for other reasons. Old reliable Kraft stopped raising its dividend because it needed cash for the acquisition of Cadbury in 2010. Companies that grow dividends tend to grow organically or through strategic acquisitions, not by buying companies of equal or larger size.

- Companies can dilute your shares, meaning that they issue more and more shares. This is not a sign that a company is on a path of paying sustainable dividends. Better-managed companies buy back their shares, and take shares out of the market, thus increasing the value of your shares.

- An income-first approach is hard for many investors, particularly investors who have a history of looking at only capital gains as the investment "feel good factor".

- Even a portfolio of high-quality dividend stocks can get to a point of being mispriced and sell off for a period of time, with the result that you can incur paper losses over years. Alternatively, the portfolio can take a hit in a stock market meltdown. This does not mean that companies will stop paying dividends at all but the capital loss on paper can look ugly for a while.

Do these risks mean that you should not buy dividend stocks? No, just like Indexing Investing, you need to understand this strategy's limitations and risks. I would say the biggest risk in dividend investing is you—the investor. As you are the one who chooses the stocks, you need to do your homework on your investments. And you have to be prepared to watch your portfolio sink if dividend stocks sell off or take a hit in a systemic crisis. The take-away is this: Do not build a portfolio for income one year, then fret over absolute return the next!

This type of investing is also not for you if you have to constantly check your portfolio and feel anger, regret and shame over short-term setbacks. Many inexperienced investors take any kind of capital loss on paper very hard and internalise these feelings in an unhealthy way. Dividend investors take a fairly Zen-like approach to investing, and learn to take some profits along the way and move on from setbacks very quickly.

Can Anything Protect this Portfolio?

Professional managers often try to use derivatives to protect these long equity portfolios. **Do not dabble in derivatives if you are a beginning investor.** Instead you can do one of two things. Revisit your asset allocation, and if you believe bonds can protect your stock losses, then hold dividend stocks for your stock allocation and individual bonds for your bond allocation. Otherwise, if bonds make you nervous or are inaccessible in your market, hold cash.

Who Benefits Most from Dividend and Dividend Growth Investing?

I would like to say it's as simple as "anyone who needs income" but this is only partly true. The greatest beneficiaries of dividend portfolios have a genuine interest in investing, they have methodical—not impulsive—habits, they understand the concept and they understand how to be patient. As with most things, there's a learning curve involved, so if you do not have the time or inclination to experience a bit of trial and error, then it's not for you.

Most individual stock portfolios are diversified across 20 to 25 individual stocks. Therefore, Dividend and Dividend Growth Investing is easier to tackle with amounts of $200,000 or more to "shop" with. Clearly the more money you can invest, the larger the revenue stream you will generate over time, especially if you can reinvest your dividends and let your investments compound for over 10 or more years. Then when you hit retirement, you can start to use the dividend income for your cash flow.

Can Someone Else Do This for Me?

I've had long tedious debates over which of the two approaches is better, and it's like comparing apples and small furry pets. Investment advisers in Asia who build predominantly Asia-centric portfolios tend to shun Dividend Investing, or an income-focused portfolio management approach, because it is riskier to invest in individual companies or bonds compared to funds. Also Asian companies do not have the dividend-paying history that US, UK, Australian and Canadian companies do, so for someone who only wants to invest in Asian stocks, this approach may not be ideal.

Investment advising is a business that has to mitigate its own risks. Most advisers, even in large banks, also do not have the experience or comfort level to advise you on anything other than funds. So many advisers are unfamiliar seeing quarterly dividends reinvest, grow and compound over years. It's also just more efficient to buy the broader markets and take the balanced return approach because it's easier to explain and the returns have been good enough over the long term.

PARTING THOUGHTS: INDEXING AND DIVIDEND PORTFOLIOS

While Index Investing uses index funds and ETFs to create the building blocks of your portfolio, dividend investors look at individual companies and their abilities to pay a sustainable or growing dividend income stream. These are two extremely different ways of investing for two very different purposes, thus you need to know your goals and limitations before you go down either path.

If you do not want to feel you are doing worse than your peers, then find other ways to earn more income because Index Investing is most likely more suited to you. Index Investing is also more suited to investors with a very specific time horizon. This finishing line is when you begin to draw down the portfolio to meet your needs.

If you use your index invested fund for retirement, then in most cases, you will normally need to draw down, or sell, 3 to 4% of your fund each year to meet your cash flow needs in retirement. Minimally then, once you reach retirement, you need to continue to make 3 to 4% per year in total real return in order to preserve the capital in this fund, if you factor in inflation, or you will deplete it over time. This is fine as long as you can juggle your needs for cash, your ability to get the return you need and your shrinking account balance.

For dividend or dividend growth investors, there is often no finishing line or goal. Dividend investors ideally draw down income from the dividends for their cash flow without selling any of the portfolio to fund their retirement. These portfolio owners intend to pass the 7-Eleven—their portfolio—on to their heirs and live off the income it generates in the meantime.

Risk management and returns are also perceived differently. Total return index investors believe bonds will always save them in a time of crisis whereas income investors just want their investments to keep showing them the money in good times and bad. Likewise, dividend growth investors believe growing dividend companies will ultimately provide the best total return in the end if the portfolio is diversified and held long enough compared to a portfolio of diverse asset classes that are rebalanced.

Risks to Both Index and Dividend Investing

There are some risks unique to both types of investing that you need to be aware of, namely tax risk and currency risk.

TAX RISK

For *any investment (index fund, stock, actively managed fund and so on)* that is domiciled, or stationed, outside of Singapore, Hong Kong, the United Kingdom and a handful of other jurisdictions expect to pay varying degrees of tax on any income, though not necessarily on your capital gains. The tax varies from 10 to over 30% on your income across different jurisdictions. There is generally not a tax on your capital gain when you sell financial assets, just your income.

CURRENCY RISK

Any investment that does not trade in your local home currency is subject to currency risk. For example, if you are buying a US dollar investment, you need to be concerned with the appreciation or depreciation of the US dollar versus your home currency. There is no point gaining 5% in the US stock market if the currency is falling 5% against your home currency in the same time period. However, if you can gain 5% in the US stock market while the US dollar is appreciating against your home currency by 5%, then you are up 10%!

I've seen people in Singapore buy homes in London and marvel at the price appreciation of 20%, only to see the British pound fall against the Singapore dollar by 20% in the same time frame. So no matter what the asset is, be it cash, stock, bond or property, you need to be aware of currency risk.

Currency swings can also benefit you. If you had bought dividend-paying US stocks before the financial crisis and then your currency depreciated against the US dollar by 25 to 40% (as most did), you would have received much more income when converted back to your home currency. Currency swings can either hurt you or benefit you. It's not a one-way street.

CONCLUSION

Ultimately, there is risk to all investing and in every investment strategy. Too often when people write about investing, or when you are being sold an investment idea, it can feel as though someone is putting forth an infallible strategy for your money. And while this sells investment books, and creates a lot of money for the financial industry as a whole, it belies the truth that much of modern finance is built on the past, i.e. "historical averages" and "historical returns", which promises no guarantees of future returns. There is really no better way to learn about investing than by practising it yourself.

CHAPTER 10

HOW TO USE
FINANCIAL ADVISERS

I walk my pug Clover to a dog park near my home every day. When she was just four months old, she met a massive Rottweiler, Daisy, who became her primary playmate. During that time, I got to know Daisy's owners, a lovely professional couple in their mid-forties who had lived in Singapore for about three years. After several weeks of dog-minding together, they asked me what I did for a living and I replied, "I am a financial planner."

It was as if I had told them that I had contracted the SARS virus. Their faces went white and they started to move away from me, mumbling under their breath, and even Daisy growled. Thank goodness they didn't take her muzzle off. Luckily, I was able to explain what financial planners do and got them to open up to answer a few questions. The conversation went something like this:

Me: I'm writing a book to help individual investors.
                 Can you tell me what happened?

Daisy Owner: When we first arrived in 2007, we wanted to invest in the markets out here (Asia) because the markets were doing so well. We lost so much money.

Me: So what kind of person did you work with? A financial adviser? A certified financial planner?

Daisy Owner: I don't know. Some kind of planner and investment adviser. I threw away the card but it was XYZ Group.

Me: How did you come to meet them?

Daisy Owner: A colleague of mine invests with them. As I was getting so many calls each week from one group or another, I went with a recommendation.

Me: May I ask if they put together a financial plan for you or did they create an investment policy statement with you?

Daisy Owner: I don't remember. But I do know that I am stuck with this plan that I pay into and we are down 60%. I can't even open the statements any more.

I'd say that 8 out of 10 people who have had a close encounter with the finance industry and who are unhappy with the outcome have told me similar stories. They wanted to invest so they took a friend's (or husband's!) advice and signed a bunch of papers, then lost a lot of money and still have no idea why. And worst of all, they are stuck in some plan that they cannot extricate themselves from to save their lives. You very well may be stuck with an adviser that your ex-spouse chose or was buddies with, and you have no idea why you are investing with this adviser or who actually is even managing the money.

ORPHAN POLICYHOLDERS

Research by Bluerock Consulting indicates that there are around 10 million "orphan" policyholders, holding investments sold by life and pension companies, who no longer have any relationship with the adviser that sold them the product. Yet these policyholders still pay commission to these advisers who are no longer looking after their investments. The size of these fees can be substantial. Most investment products pay around 0.5% of the money invested as a trail commission to the adviser each year (although this percentage fee can be higher).

Source: www.telegraph.co.uk/finance/personalfinance/investing/9232113/Investors-pay-IFAs-millions-for-doing-nothing.html

---

So whose fault is it? I'm not on anyone's side. I know advisers, bankers and brokers can take advantage of clients, and clients often do not ask enough questions and are not as self-aware as they should be when choosing advisers. That people are so uninformed is a fault of all societies that do not teach basic financial literacy and financial planning in secondary schools.

Let's go through the basics so that if you decide to use intermediaries, you have a clear overview of the finance sector and know which questions to ask.

THERE IS NO FREE LUNCH IN FINANCE

There is a continuum of expertise in all professions, from teaching history to dentistry to law, and the same is true in finance. I've met just as many complacent teachers and marginally competent lawyers as I have encountered questionable investment advisers. Personally, I find a bad teacher just as offensive as a bad adviser.

What has opened the finance industry to much of its deserved criticism is the sea change in how financial products are sold and how incentives have changed over the last few decades. At one time, financial institutions made money through simple transparent practices such as lending. Today however, banks, life insurance companies and financial advisers are incentivised to sell whichever investments, services and policies make *them and their firms* the most money, and not necessarily you.

People generally succeed in finance for the same reason they succeed in any profit-making businesses—they develop a large client base to whom they sell a suite of high margin products and services. This creates streams of income for their firms, namely banks, life insurance companies, brokers or independent advisory services. Many client-interfacing finance professionals are hired for their rolodexes, and they are given sales targets, just like representatives in any profit-making business.

So while you may have a long-term investment horizon of 20 years, your banker or adviser may be looking no further than meeting this month's sales goal or this year's bonus target. Does this mean that your private banker, investment adviser, account manager, wealth planner, wealth specialist— the titles are endless—has potential conflicts of interest? Yes, absolutely. Does this mean that every single person in finance is out to milk you? No, of course it doesn't. It does mean this though: There Is No Free Lunch.

If you engage advisers, they are providing a service and you will pay one way or another, either in the form of a fee or commission, and sometimes both. While I believe people generally understand this, the reign of disappointment in Asian markets seems to arise from the following issues:

Investors' Prison. People are sold contractual insurance "investment" or "savings" plans that restrict their ability to escape and get their money out by imposing heavy penalties. When the client experiences heavy losses, they want to change the policy but, alas, they are stuck paying into these plans for years, if not decades. (Refer to "Analysing Your Legacy Policies: Investors' Prison" in Chapter 8 to see how to handle this issue.)

Sixty Shades of Grey. The lack of transparency around the fees and commissions increases the opportunity for conflicts of interest.

Who Is Watching the Portfolio? It is not always clear whose "expertise" you are paying for, and how much value you gain from that expertise.

Nickel and Dimed. The hidden fees and commissions can be so excessive that the gains in your portfolio are marginal at best given that we are looking at real return.

The industry is slowly changing in Asia as regulators have woken up to these conflicts. And Asia's wealthiest families are starting to ditch their private bankers altogether and instead are building family offices, essentially hiring and paying for their own team of investment professionals who just bat for the home team.

For the rest of us, we need to know what we want and what our goals are in order to use financial professionals effectively. No one needs open heart surgery for an ingrown toenail. So why get locked into a 15-year savings plan rife with penalties for early withdrawals if you just need someone to write a financial plan? Why hand all of your money over to a life insurance company to buy an annuity if you just need a few income streams from your investment portfolio? That is why it is so important to know what you really want and need.

HOW IT IS DONE IN OTHER REGULATORY ENVIRONMENTS

In many countries, there are laws that separate the job of a fiduciary, someone legally responsible for giving you unbiased advice, and a salesperson who is just brokering sales of financial products. Countries like the United States and the United Kingdom also require anyone selling financial products to disclose commissions. And if any of them don't, they can lose their licence. In an environment where there is a clear separation between a fiduciary and a sales rep, it's easy to cherry-pick and find the best people to meet your financial needs.

ASIA IS STILL COMMISSION-CENTRIC, AND FEE-HEAVY

In Asia however, using investment professionals tactically is far more difficult. There are few truly independent investment managers due to licencing restrictions, and even less pure financial planning—although it does exist. The Asian consumer is also much less attuned to the concept of "paying for advice", as you would a lawyer or accountant. That is why most finance practitioners have no choice but to work for a firm or a large institution, such as a bank or life insurance company, where they are judged by their ability to build assets under management (AUM) that incur regular fees or high commissions.

There are highly ethical financial practitioners in Asia who understand these conflicts. And there are many financial advisers who studiously avoid conflicts of interest; in fact it's often their competitive advantage! But alas, we do not live in a perfect world. So be prepared to do some shopping around for the right adviser in Asia. Let's first look at the client acquisition process as it exists today in most cities around the region.

How Advisers Hook You

Using an independent financial adviser (IFA) just as an example, you will most likely be cold-called by someone who wants you to come in and talk to "their people" or you will visit an IFA based on a recommendation. At the first meeting, someone will ask you about your needs and, at some point, the adviser will have you fill in an informal balance sheet and cash flow statement. These will tell the adviser how much you make and how much you have free to invest. If the adviser thinks you are a viable client, at some stage, you will be asked to fill in an investor risk profile survey to assess your risk tolerance.

Then at a separate meeting, or possibly during the same meeting, you will be pitched an investment idea, a portfolio strategy or an investment methodology based, at least in theory, on how they think they can best invest your money. Or this is how it will be presented. At this stage, you are happy; you have not spent any money, you've had a few cups of coffee and all seems well, right? You are through the first barrier to investing and have had some basic analysis and asset allocation done, and it was "all for free!"

Once you decide to invest, depending on which city you are in, your adviser will probably have to do some due diligence on you, mainly to make sure you are not a terrorist or smuggling drugs or arms. You may also be provided with some analysis of your current financial situation based on the information you gave to them. This analysis may be very detailed or very simplistic; it depends entirely on the adviser. If you agree to invest, you will have to sign a bunch of papers confirming your investment. And it is *after* signing on the dotted line that you have to start paying.

Depending on what you have invested in, you might feel like you are paying nothing but then be hit with commissions throughout the life of the plan or investment agreement. This is common with "Investors' Prison" plans. If you can escape the commission trap, there will most likely be a set-up fee between 0.5 and 1% of your initial investment up to a specific amount ($500,000 to $1 million is the norm).

The set-up fee can mean a lot of things depending on who you are investing with. It can mean the effort it takes the staff to set up your portfolio. It might be a commission. It might be that the IFA actually does some analysis and you get something that resembles a mini-financial plan. It might even be a combination of all these things.

If you have not bought an Investor's Prison plan, then you will also be charged an annual management fund fee, usually around 1%, spread out over four quarters. This is in addition to the fund fees that I mentioned in Chapter 7. All of these fees add up and are deducted from your portfolio and are often referred to as your **total expense ratio**.

Most advisers will not tell you about their total expense ratios unless you ask them, and others may not even know these ratios. Some advisers will work harder and be more transparent about their practices than others when trying to win your business. The more questions you ask, the more you will understand where all the effort is going, why you are paying and for what, and the more likely you will be happy with your adviser. The murkier it is, the more likely you will misunderstand what is being said or they will misrepresent what they can truly do for you.

So that is the process, more or less, as it works with most financial advisers today, whether they are IFAs, banks, insurance companies and so on. There's nothing wrong with it per se, except that the process of "free" analysis and asset allocation are too often treated as a means to an end—to get the client to sign on the dotted line. Far too often, there's no real discussion about expense ratios. So many issues can get glossed over when the process moves in a way that benefits the adviser first and the client second.

HOW TO INTERVIEW PROFESSIONALS—FROM 30,000 FEET

If we were in the United States or Australia, I would say this: Have an independent, fee-based certified financial planner (CFP) put together a financial plan. Then get that same planner, or find a fee-based adviser, to use a low-cost custodian to invest in either passive index funds or, if you need income, help you build an income generating portfolio using dividend stocks, bonds and other investments. And then this chapter would be done.

Unfortunately, different countries in Asia have different rules so here's the skinny: You only need to pass three to four multiple choice tests to be licensed to start selling financial products and services in Asia, if that. So be prepared to wade through a buffet of euphemistic titles—relationship manager, wealth planner, broker, private banker, wealth specialist, etc.— which may mean everything or nothing at all.

The licencing is easy; a 21-year-old with no investment experience can get licensed. It's the experience that you need. You need to know what the adviser's *experience* is and what their role will be in the hands-on management of your portfolio. In other words, you need to know if you are talking to a salesperson or the actual portfolio manager. **You also need to be assured that the advice is objective** and that you will not be herded into any fund purely because it makes the adviser the highest commissions.

But They Said They Were in Banking ...

Even if someone says, "I've been in banking for 20 years", it may sound credible and/or reassuring, but what exactly did they do in banking? Were they in sales or did they manage portfolios? If they were managing money, what was their investment mandate? Did they specialise in retirement portfolios? And how does what they did apply to what you need?

You are looking for hard skill sets such as: certified financial planner, qualified asset manager and certified financial analyst. In addition, you also want to **find someone with a history of investing their own money**. Ask them how they made money. If it was from anything other than investing in financial assets based on the same methodology that they are selling, this should give you pause for thought. That old saying about people eating their own cooking has never been as true as it is in finance.

Even with some relevant accreditation and hands-on experience, you want an adviser who can empathise with your situation, and who will explain investing in simple terms if that is what you need. If you sense you are on the end of a sales pitch, if they don't like you asking a lot of questions, if they are patronising or cannot explain how to invest in language that an 11-year-old can understand, move on to someone who can. There's nothing clever about making complex ideas more complicated.

Ratios, Relatives, Religion and Returns

Don't choose the path of wilful ignorance; it's your money. Ask your adviser how much or what per cent they make in commission and which fees you will incur if you invest through them. In fact, get them to write down all the fees—

administrative fees, annual management fund fees, fund load fees, switching fees, trailing fees and other costs—that will impact your overall return. Then have the most senior person in the office sign it. The total expense ratio can be as low as 1% all in or it can reach as high as 3% and beyond. Refer back to Golden Rule Eight: Keep Investing Expenses Low. It goes without saying the lower the ratio, the better.

Another issue prevalent in Asia is the habit of investing only with someone of the same religion, community, political party, nationality and ethnicity. This approach has never guaranteed anyone higher returns and can be limiting in terms of perspective. In fact, fraudsters often prey on their own communities (this is known as affinity fraud) because it's the easiest and quickest way to establish "credibility".

On this point, do not let ANYONE, even a relative, take custody of your money in order to manage and invest it. You must never write cheques payable to your adviser or asset manager. Your money first has to be deposited into a custodial account, such as a bank or brokerage, and then only with your permission should you allow anyone to trade or invest your money. This is called non-discretionary asset management, and it's the best way for you to keep abreast of your own investments.

The wrong reasons for hiring professionals are because you can't find the willpower and/or because you think it's glamorous to do so. Empowered investors use advisers tactically until they are sure of what an adviser can and cannot do for them, and they are prepared to shop around for some time to find an adviser most suited to their needs.

HOW TO HIRE FINANCIAL PROFESSIONALS: THE DETAILS

Different professionals can be used to meet different stages of your investment needs. Although most people will want all your business and consequently present themselves as one-stop shops, few firms truly deliver great value at every stage from financial planning and analysis through to hands-on investment management. In fact, you'd be surprised how many advisers are actually just sales representatives who will sell you on an idea with the result that your money is managed half a world away.

Here, I will present a way of turning the process around so that you are actually asking for things from financial intermediaries. This may be easier to do in some cities around Asia than in others, given regulatory constraints, but it outlines the steps in a way that *will benefit you*. Good consumers shop around to figure out how best to meet their own needs, and this instance is no different.

Step 1: Situational Analysis and Goal Setting

For situational analysis, goal setting, strategy and long-term planning, the most rigorous analysis will be given by a professional who is a CFP. You pay a CFP a specific project fee and, in return, you'll end up with a 10- to 20-page financial plan that clearly outlines balance sheet and cash flow analysis, financial ratio analysis, projected returns for any investment goal, an analysis of past investment choices and an opinion on asset allocation and also an investment recommendation if you ask for this. This whole process will take at least two, if not three, meetings, follow-up calls and a barrage of detailed questions.

Who Does It? CFPs are professionals who are certified only after going through a fairly extensive set of exams that cover taxation, insurance, estate planning and investments. A good certified professional accountant (CPA) with some background in financial planning may also be suitable but I think CPAs are not always as fluent on the investment side. There are also lawyers working with estates who are CFPs. These professionals are used to being paid just to understand your specific situation and long-term goals, and are tasked with creating a plan of unbiased, conflict-free advice.

Who Doesn't Do It Well? A thorough, unbiased financial plan is one of the most important documents you can have, however, most IFAs, bankers, wealth planners, etc. won't bother with these, even if they are accredited CFPs. It depends entirely on what their firm's mandate is. Financial planning is seen to be a lot of work for a small return so it's considered "small potatoes".

THE ADVANTAGES OF PAYING FOR A FINANCIAL PLAN

- For a fee of around US$2,000 (HK$15,000) on up depending on the complexity of your situation, you will get what you pay for and eliminate any potential conflicts of interest.
- You are paying for an objective perspective and a plan that specifically caters to your needs and long-term goals.
- Find a seasoned planner who has managed client money through a crisis or two or who has worked with someone going through a divorce or some life-changing event. By doing so, the planner will have experience in helping people who have been in similar situations to your own and may be more in tune to your specific needs.

THINGS TO WATCH OUT FOR

- CFPs can have obvious conflicts of interest. As already mentioned, in Asia some CFPs work for the same firms that want to sell you financial products on commission. If your CFP thinks it's strange that you want to pay for a financial plan, or if they only want to sell you life insurance products or put your money in high cost funds, you have the wrong financial planner.
- All planners are dependent on you being forthcoming with information and telling them what you want out of a plan. If you only give them half the information, then they'll only be able to produce a half-baked plan.

- As noted, some firms give you a free financial plan if you commit to using their investment services over the long term. Before you agree to anything, ask to see a sample plan and do the maths. If their minimum investment amount is $250,000 and there is an initial set-up fee of 1%, that's $2,500 right there. Do you want a plan or a long-term commitment?

Step 2: Investment Policy Statements and Asset Allocation

The single biggest source of unhappiness among investors is that their returns are not what they thought they would be. These investors generally have no investment policy statement that answers the following questions: (1) "Why am I investing (objective)?" (2) "For how long (investment horizon)?" (3) "What return or income do I need (risk, return and income)?" and (4) "What rules and restrictions should there be on my account?" The answers define what you want, what you expect, your asset allocation and how your account will be managed. These same investors also do not clearly understand the fees involved pertaining to their investments.

When there is no investment policy in place, you do not have a strategy for managing your portfolio and everyone is flying blind. So, in essence, you are giving your advisor carte blanche to buy, sell and pitch everything but the kitchen sink. As a result, you are likely to have an experience like my friend Jacqueline.

Jacqueline, a very busy marketing director with one of the world's top consumer brand companies, had her portfolio "managed" by one of the most prestigious investment banks in the world. To the best of Jacqueline's knowledge, she had been investing well because her wealth manager called her regularly with investment ideas.

She trusted the bank and by extension her wealth manager, so even when she wasn't sure about the investment, she'd say, "Why not? Go ahead and buy." Jacqueline felt good when she bought the ideas being pitched; she felt catered to and appreciated all the attention, and this made her feel very much in control of her financial destiny.

That said, Jacqueline never really read her investment statements or thought much about her returns, assuming they were "good enough". When I opened up her account and saw the portfolio, my jaw literally dropped. She must have been invested in over 20 different actively managed funds, all with upfront commissions of 2 to 4%.

No one had ever done a financial plan. Jacqueline had a six-figure income and a seven-figure portfolio—"Why would I need a plan?" she asked. Nowhere was there an investment policy statement (IPS) to show how her funds were to be invested—"This is the most prestigious private bank in the world, it must have the best managers!" she proclaimed. No one had even communicated an asset allocation strategy—"What's that?" she asked. Her per annum return was 1.8% in nominal return, in real return it was -2%. She was actually paying this bank just to hold her account.

When Jacqueline called and asked her wealth manager for a plan or a strategy statement, he told her that he'd do one. A year later, Jacqueline was still waiting. Jacqueline could have accomplished more in 10 years with a simple investment strategy and three low-cost index funds.

These runaway portfolios get built out by advisers because there is no plan beyond the simple idea that "the client wants to invest". Therefore, only use advisers who will happily write down an investment strategy and make it part of the process to secure your business.

INVESTMENT POLICY STATEMENTS

An investment policy statement basically outlines general rules for the portfolio manager. It can state many things, the most important of which are:

- your objectives for your investment
- the frequency of your contributions if it's not a lump sum account
- how to divvy up your investment into stocks, bonds and cash to achieve the return you need (i.e. asset allocation)
- what types of fund or vehicles you are to be invested in, i.e. only passive funds or ETFs or only dividend growth stocks, etc.

- when the adviser will rebalance or take profits for the client
- how dividends will be handled, i.e. as income distributed to the client or reinvested

An IPS can be 20 pages long but it's better to keep it simple and in plain language, such as: "The objective is to build a retirement fund of HK$3,000,000 over 20 years, by adding HK$85,000 per year distributed in a balanced portfolio of 60% stock index funds, 30% short-term bond index funds and the remaining 10% in money market funds or short-term certificates of deposit (CDs). We intend to achieve 5.6% real return per annum, after fees. Over 90% of these investments must be held in low-cost, no-load passive index funds at all times. All dividends will be reinvested. The adviser must rebalance the account when there is a 15% rise in any asset class. No trade is to be done without my approval. We will revisit this statement in five years."

Asset Allocation

One of the most significant parts of your IPS is the asset allocation, which we covered in Chapter 8. As noted, in much of Asia, investor risk profile surveys will be used to derive your asset allocation, nothing more. In most major financial hubs, these surveys are required by law and are generally done as part of the initial interview and information collection process when you first meet your potential adviser.

These profiles address "what you are afraid to lose", and they usually dump an investor into Defensive, Conservative, Balanced, Moderate or Aggressive profiles. Defensive investors are put into more money market and bond funds while more aggressive profiles have a higher allocation to equities.

Investor risk profile surveys protect investors from being put into assets that are much riskier than they can take financially or emotionally. This is a very good thing. The downside is that the profiles are overly simplistic and may not take into account the current market risks we face. So work with your adviser on an investment policy statement and an asset allocation that factor in the following: long-term trends, your investment horizon, your investor profile results, the returns you need and any other material issues.

Many financial intermediaries do not do asset allocation in-house or even portfolio management. They basically act as sales offices that funnel their clients' money to professionally managed funds in the United Kingdom, the United States, South Africa and so on. There is nothing wrong with this per se, but it is important to note that your "adviser" may be mostly a salesperson with a point of view.

Who Does It? A proposed or recommended asset allocation strategy generally comes as part of a financial plan if you ask for it when you purchase one. If you are using an IFA, life insurance company or a bank, asset allocation is often given to you "for free" as part of the process to win your business in order to then sell you a product on commission or inflict a set-up fee on you. Investment policy statements are not that common in Asia. Ask for it anyway and find an adviser or planner who will draft one.

Things to Watch Out For

Once you begin down the road of strategy and planning, you are no longer "dating your adviser", you are getting close to engagement. It is often hard to extract yourself from your adviser once you travel down this path so understand the fees (*see* Step 3) upfront and choose wisely. Here are some things to keep in mind:

- Once you pay a set-up fee, you cannot get it refunded if you want to switch advisers. This means that you may have to pay another set-up fee unless the new adviser agrees to take your portfolio on just for the annual fee income stream.

- If you already have a full-blown financial plan, and the financial intermediary does not really do anything in-house, have any prospective adviser review your plan and ask for some minimisation of set-up fees if they charge them.

- I will repeat: Watch out for Investors' Prison aka forced savings plans with restrictive escape clauses. If you must be forced to save your money at a premium, you need to go through chapters 3 to 8 again and develop the habits of a methodical, emotion-free money manager.

- **Watch out for being herded into actively managed fund fees that compound just as fast as your returns as these can be devastating to your portfolio.**

Step 3: Execution-only Management

We are near the finishing line! By now, you know your time horizon and approximately how much risk you'll need to take to get the return you need, and you have a specific objective for your investment. You just need someone to build your portfolio, buy into the markets based on your asset allocation and monitor those investments for the long haul. It's like you've planned an entire trip and now you just need someone to buy the tickets and book the hotel.

Who Does It? Everyone but my pug Clover does investment management in Asia because it's where the ongoing income streams are for advisories, life insurance companies and financial institutions. Which intermediary you will work with is largely determined by how much you have to invest. IFAs generally service the mass affluent, or a client base that has between $100,000 and $1,000,000 of investable assets. Private banks look at client bases with over $1,000,000 or more of investable assets as High Net Worth (HNW) clients.

Private banks provide a much wider range of products and services than most IFAs by tapping into a network of specialists such as dedicated dealers in bonds, proprietary research and other investments not normally available to retail investors. Private banks generally offer lending, usually within a 24-hour time frame. They also have discretionary asset management, which means you entrust them to manage your money based on your investor profile (not always a good idea).

If you are an HNW client and use an IFA, this adviser will generally use a private bank as the custodian of your account, enabling you to then tap into all the benefits of the private bank. The point here is that High Net Worth investors have all kinds of options so shop around and find the best bank and the best adviser to suit your needs.

Having said this, private banks can be *more* biased than IFAs and push their proprietary actively managed funds. Private bankers can also go just as quiet when the product or plan they sold you doesn't pan out as expected. So your results in private banking may not be *that* much different than if you use an IFA, you'll just enjoy superior coffee, service and junkets.

Brokerage houses, retail banks and life insurance companies deal with small-scale investors through relationship managers and involve starter accounts of under $100,000. Relationship managers often manage relationships with hundreds of clients, they are heavily commission driven and their main product tends to be actively managed unit trusts and Investors' Prison contracts.

If you are starting from scratch with no money to invest upfront, it might be better to DIY by opening up an online brokerage account. You can also execute trades offline through a broker but keep in mind that they, just like a property agent, are working on commission and experience levels will vary greatly. Whomever you decide to invest with, please take note of these three aspects of execution: which investment platform you are on, expense ratio and who is minding the portfolio.

Investment Platform. When you use an intermediary, your money will be held "in custody" and invested through a bank or an online brokerage platform, depending on your minimum investment amount. The investment platform is used to invest in different financial assets such as stocks, bonds, etc. and custodial costs tend to be low, but ask anyway to make sure. Find an adviser who uses a platform(s) that offers a broad range of investments, **including low-cost passive index funds and ETFs as much as possible,** which allow you to get your money out as easily as it is to invest.

Again, you must invest through a custodial account and never write a cheque to your adviser directly. The biggest frauds happen when there is not a custodial involved who can provide independent confirmation of your account and trades. Google Bernie Madoff.

Expense Ratio—Keep an Eye on Costs. The fees you pay to an adviser to build, manage and monitor a portfolio of investments, regardless of whether they are an IFA or with a bank, tend to be around 1% for your set-up and 1% thereafter paid out quarterly based on your average balance. There are also custodial fees, trading fees, dealing fees, etc.

These fees are usually measured in basis points so a fee of 0.20% is 20 basis points, a fee of 1.5% is 150 basis points and so on. It can be annoying when advisers speak in basis points. Feel free to tell them to skip the finance speak and use percentages to show you the total percentage of all the costs when investing with them, including the fund fees. As mentioned earlier in this chapter, this total is your expense ratio (obviously the lower the better).

Here is a chart that you can use when you are with an adviser to understand their fee structure in addition to set-up and annual management fees:

Fee	What It Is	Fee Range
*Front-end Load	A one-time fee normally charged upfront for an investment	0.75–5%
*Back-end Load	Charged over the initial term, 3–7 years of an investment, common with Investors' Prison plans	0.75–5%
Set-up Fee	This is a fee to administratively set up your account but it is also used as a means to secure a commission. Try to get it waived or minimised as it is a front-loading fee on all your initial investments.	0.5–1%

*Annual Fund Fees	The annual fee you pay to invest in actively managed funds that are recommended by your adviser	0.5–2%
Annual Management Fee	The annual fee you are paying to have your portfolio managed and monitored	0.5–1%
Trailing Commissions	Fees that are paid by funds to the advisers who recommend them	Varies
Switching Fees	Fees that are paid when you switch from one fund to another fund	Varies

*A very simple way to not be charged many of these fees is as follows: Have the adviser write an IPS and state that you only want to be invested in passive index funds or ETFs where possible with no loads and no trailing commissions.

A transparent adviser should be able to tell you something like this: "The upfront fees are 1% in commission or set-up fees, then there are ongoing fees which will entail 1% management fees and 0.1% platform and custodial fees. For these specific funds that we are recommending, there will be 2 to 3% front-loading fees, and there is an early exit penalty of 10% the first year, 5% the second year and so on." Get the adviser to write this down with an illustration of what these fees would do to a $100,000 investment and ask them to sign it. This makes it easier to compare different expense ratios of different advisers.

I cannot emphasise enough how much this expense ratio—the costs you pay to invest in funds and have them managed—matters to your long-term return. The chart below shows you the impact of investing $100,000 over 30 years with an 8% nominal return. The three returns reflect three different total expense ratios, 1%, 2% and 3%. If your account is dealing with a 3% overall expense ratio, expect to make only around half the return you could if the expense ratio was 1%.

This would be the total of your annual management fee, your fund fees and your custodial costs. Once you are paying out more than 1.5% in these fees, the *compounding of fees* starts to seriously work against you.

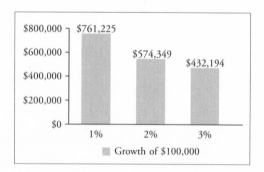

Management—Who Is Minding the Portfolio? Other than the fees, you need to have a good idea of how the adviser will handle your portfolio. Some advisers may want to trade, rebalance or shift around assets more often than others. Minimally, you want an adviser who:

- will rebalance your portfolio once a year, either as you add new funds or to take advantage of the market gains
- has a house view, i.e. an investment perspective on long-term trends that resonates with you
- understands your unique situation
- will look out for tactical opportunities which enable you to take advantage of short- to mid-term market movements with a small portion of your portfolio

The best investment advisers will happily write an investment policy statement, explain their investment philosophy and state as part of their investment contract that there are no conflicts of interest, i.e. "Neither our firm nor our financial planner will benefit from any commissions or trailer fees on client purchases of insurance or investment products. Our portfolio management clients pay us management fees based solely on the value of the investment assets we manage for them."

Sometimes, investors are unhappy when they end up with an adviser who spends all their time looking for new business instead of monitoring the portfolios under their care. The more you can talk to your adviser upfront, the better idea you will have of what to expect of them.

On this point, I often hear advisers tell their clients that they are being paid to "keep the client from doing something stupid". Well, ask your prospective adviser how they handled the 2008 crash. That should tell you something about how clever or stupid *they are*. Many advisers, like many investors, were in all-out panic mode.

What Your Adviser Cannot Do for You

You are not paying your adviser to be a mind reader or a market prophet because those skills do not exist in the real world. You should not be calling them once a day, once a week or every time the market wobbles. It is unlikely that every year will show the returns you need because you are investing for the long run and it's annualised returns that count. If this is hard for you to take on board, then you should not be investing in financial markets at all, with or without an adviser.

You are paying someone a 1% annual management fund fee for something though. So if your adviser expects you to add to your investments all the time without any real value add-on at their end, then you may as well get a financial plan done and manage your own portfolio.

In the end, the best way to keep your adviser on track is by devising an IPS and making sure the rules are clearly defined from the outset. You may find that you manage your adviser a bit through the first year but, like any good relationship, it should evolve into one of mutual respect. If you are not in a relationship of mutual respect with your adviser, then do not be afraid to part ways and find someone who can put your best interests before theirs.

THINGS TO WATCH OUT FOR

- Much investing is done through the restrictive insurance platforms that I have mentioned. Although this varies from country to country, it seems that the more you can invest, usually over $250,000, the fewer the restrictions, and you can leave the platform any time penalty free. So ask (or demand) to be able to leave the platform penalty free if you so choose.

- Private banks were as much at the heart of the 2008 scandals as any other institution, having sold unwitting clients fatally flawed products. Do not be fooled by the plush appearance of these banks; their mahogany panelled walls do not make them immune to hubris and greed where they can focus more on their bottom lines than yours.

- Private banks may offer you free custodial services if you are an HNW client, then nickel and dime you by charging premiums for a variety of other services. Get print-outs of all their trading fees, foreign exchange fees and so on upfront in order to judge the best overall option before committing. Much can be negotiated once you are a private banking client so use it to your advantage.

- While IFAs and banks may charge annual advisory fees, they are also likely to retain product commissions from the products or funds that they sell. Find an IFA or bank that doesn't if possible (and include this point in your signed IPS) and instead reinvests any commissions back into your portfolio. The best advisers try to return most commissions back to you.

- Many investors find themselves in a spot that I would call "over-diversified". They are in too many funds and they are often not sure why. If your adviser wants you to be in more than five to six funds, ask why it is necessary, and to be shown how much better the returns would be if you followed this strategy. I often wonder if over-diversification protects the adviser or the client.

Step 4: Insurance and Wills—One-off Purchases

If you want to have control over your financial future, insurance should be relegated to one-off purchases that cover the risk you are most concerned with (i.e. health, life, etc.). In some cases, insurance is used to protect the assets of very large estates, but other than that, insurance should never be used as your primary investment vehicle because of the excess and hidden fees involved.

The insurance industry trains sales reps extremely well, and these sales reps know a susceptible client when they see one. In other words, the second I tell someone that I am a certified financial planner, I am not bothered any further because the sales rep knows I'm not going to buy whatever they are selling.

The people most vulnerable to the life insurance industry are beginner investors looking for sure-fire deals such as a fixed income stream that products like annuities provide. People often get taken in by teaser rates and then realise far too late that they have no escape route when the product doesn't perform as they were told it might.

Beware the Hidden Flaws

Annuities have countless, hidden flaws that all too often remain undisclosed until it's too late: excessive commissions, lower returns, payout delays, surrender fees and long lock-ins. Still annuity sales climb. As *Business Week* puts it: "Potential buyers can ignore the sales fluff and dig into the fine print to figure out if an annuity is right for them. But that can be a real slog." Some prospectuses can run "over 500 pages, so you know why most buyers wind up relying on a sales spiel." The main reason why annuities sell so well is simple: Sales commissions are so lucrative for annuity salesmen, some as high as 14%. As a result, the industry attracts aggressive hustlers with questionable ethics preying on vulnerable customers, especially the elderly, a pattern that gives the rest of the industry a bad name. In short: Greed breeds ethical compromises tainting marketing tactics, and that's why annuities sell well!

Source: http://wallstreetwarzone.com/annuities-brokers-love-%E2%80%98em-press-hates-%E2%80%98em/

Here's some simple advice on the insurance front. Insurance is a means to mitigate or control risk. Buy insurance to cover the risks you face or are most concerned about, not as a long-term investment plan. The main types of insurance I recommend buying are as follows:

Term life insurance and disability insurance. Term life insurance, which generally includes disability, has no cash value, meaning that you get nothing but coverage in the event of the death or disability of the insured. That's fine. It's cheap to buy and that's all you will likely need. If you are dependent on your ex-husband for income, **you need to buy an irrevocable life insurance policy on his life with you as the policy owner. This should be part of your settlement if you remain dependent on him for maintenance and child support.**

Buy term life insurance that is either level term or renewable every year. **As the policy owner, you need to pay the premiums to make sure the insurance policy does not lapse.** This should be set up before your divorce comes through and/or be part and parcel of a settlement in any case you are dependent on his income.

If *you* currently earn an income and have financial dependents, you can purchase term life and disability insurance to ensure your dependents are provided for in the event of your death or disability. You will be the owner of the policy and the policy will be on your life. You will need to identify the beneficiaries and if they are minors, you must consider setting up a trust for them upon your death (written in the form of a will, which has to be written or re-written now that you are divorced). This way, your children will benefit directly and no one can access your life insurance payout but your beneficiaries.

Health insurance. If you are no longer on a health plan due to your divorce, it is imperative that you invest in one unless you are in a country that has a full-blown nationalised healthcare system, such as in Canada or parts of Europe. It is important that whatever healthcare system you are under, or health policy you buy, that you understand fully what you are and are not covered for.

Some health insurance policies do not fully cover critical illnesses in countries like Singapore. If you have a history of cancer in your family, this is another piece of insurance that you may consider purchasing, though I would do so sparingly. Two to three years' worth of coverage is generally enough.

Even if you have health insurance, you may have to buy travel insurance when you travel outside of your country, especially if you travel to the United States. Many health insurance policies do not cover care in the United States any more due to the excessive costs of care there.

Endowment policies. In some divorce cases, you may decide with your spouse to buy endowment policies for your children's education. By doing so, money is set aside and "kept" by a third party, and is only paid out at a specific time in the future. Personally, I'd rather keep any education money actively invested in an investment portfolio as you are more likely to get higher returns but this really depends on the trust levels of the two parties involved.

THINGS TO WATCH OUT FOR

The insurance industry is fiercely commission driven. If you are buying insurance products, you need to know what the fees and commissions are, and it pays to shop around. Any product that traps your money with restrictive clauses is the product that makes the most money for the insurance company, and most likely the least for you.

- Be wary of any "all-in-one" whole life type of insurance policy that promotes the great "cash value" you are building. This is a forced savings plan. Why not just build an investment portfolio and buy your term life insurance separately? Term life is easier to cancel or modify than whole life policies.

- Women love annuities but you really have to buy the right product because there is rarely any recourse (i.e. no escape!) if you don't. When you buy an annuity, you hand over a large lump sum to an insurance company and it pays you a stream of income back every month. So, in effect, you are being "kept" by your insurance company. I only recommend annuities if the person receiving the payments is incapacitated and unable to manage her own finances, a minor without a fiscally reliable guardian or a person with a drug or a gambling problem. Annuities may be one option for income but don't have them as the only option.

- One particular insurance agency was at the absolute heart of the crash in 2008. Hundreds of annuitants queued up outside its insurance offices in Singapore for fear that their annuity contracts would not be honoured. The lesson here is to read your insurance contracts closely and ask what provisions there are to ensure the company will keep its end of the bargain in the event of another crisis.

- **Above all else, write a will, especially if you are divorced and intend to leave your assets to your children. And for any individual with property or significant investment assets, consider forming a trust to protect minors. A trust can bypass cumbersome processes, such as probate, and protect your assets from other parties until your children are mature enough to manage those assets themselves.**

CONCLUSION

The only way to really interact with anyone trying to sell you anything is to know why you are investing to start with. So know your needs, goals and desires first. Then turn the tables and start telling your banker, broker or adviser what you want done for you. Knowing what you need also makes it very easy to escape sales pitches by saying, "Thanks for the product/service idea but I'm really not interested because it does not fit into my long-term plan in any meaningful way."

Most of all, if you are not happy with your adviser, do not think twice about changing to another adviser. It is always better to find someone that you not only trust your money with but who respects you and your personal situation. If you are unable to find an adviser who is in tune with your needs, you will need to go down the alternative route and invest your own money.

CHAPTER 11

INVESTING IN YOURSELF

*And the day came when the risk to remain
tight in a bud was more painful than the risk
it took to blossom.*
—Anaïs Nin

Now that we have learnt about traditional investments, let's talk about one of the best investments you will ever make—an investment in yourself. For the record, I am not talking about a new wardrobe, cosmetic surgery or a long holiday overseas. All such investments have a time and place. I am talking about an investment that will provide you with a sustainable return, the kind of return that can grow and compound over time, much like a good dividend stock.

RE-ENTERING THE WORKFORCE

If you have been out of the workplace for any length of time, re-entering the workforce to establish yourself can feel daunting. You may feel you have lost skills, not kept up with the latest buzzwords and/or watched your professional network erode over time, particularly if your previous work required business development and manic networking.

Alternatively, you may be at the point where you are considering an entirely new type of career or employment opportunity. Perhaps you are not able to go back to work full-time because you may still have young children to take care of at home. Regardless of where you are now, if you cannot be employed at the moment, **stay employable**.

Some of the best ways to re-enter the workforce if you want to remain in your previous field are to upgrade your skills and start networking again. If you are not sure what you want to do, try developing an interest in an entirely new career. Have a good long think about what genuinely interests you, where you see opportunities in the market and where the possibilities to develop a new career are. A number of women I have met in my own industry did exactly this, studying finance both out of need and out of interest and then parlayed their studies into successful finance careers. I've personally experienced no age discrimination; in fact my age has worked to my benefit more often than not as a certified financial planner.

Many other women I have known who have re-entered the workforce in their forties and fifties are involved in careers as diverse as counselling and teaching to running REITs and restaurants. Some industries tend to be more age aware than others, such as advertising or event planning, but there are many professions out there that are "ageless" and will enable you to build your credibility primarily with age and experience.

Deciding what to retrain yourself in is a personal decision. You should understand how much time you will need to retrain yourself, the costs and time commitment involved and what real job prospects exist. You may have to make peace with starting at the bottom of your profession and be willing to work your way up again. Clever, hardworking people do not stay at the bottom rung of any profession for very long.

That said, I realise starting over again can be difficult for some people to come to terms with, so I would recommend that you find an area of genuine intellectual interest. This way you will benefit beyond just the ability to generate future income. You will feel more genuinely fulfilled and hopefully be surrounded by like-minded peers and future colleagues.

The great thing about Asia is that everyone is into learning, retraining and upgrading their skills. I have sat in classes with people of all nationalities who ranged from 20 to 65 years of age, and it was genuinely enjoyable going back to school. There are also many ways to become certified through online learning if there aren't courses available for your particular area of interest.

ENTREPRENEURSHIP OVERVIEW

Probably nothing can seem as fulfilling as being your own boss and the master of your own employment destiny, but starting a business has to be done for the right reasons. Starting a business involves serious time commitments, serious focus and often serious money. So start a business because you have the energy and a passionate desire to create a business, not just to give yourself a job.

Starting Business Reality Check

No surveys have been done on divorcee business start-up successes and failures in Asia, or at least none that I can find, so I am going to share some of my observations with you.

Over the years I have lived in Asia, it seems the majority of businesses started by women are retail-oriented businesses (usually clothing, accessories or restaurants). The women who are not knee-deep into retailing are generally acting as agents or representatives (in property, wine, etc.), providing a professional service such as law or financial planning, teaching or doing niche consulting work. Many of this latter group of women started their businesses from home. While these women are not always successful, their success rate is infinitely higher than the retail group. So let's explore some of the reasons why this is the case.

1. The most obvious reason is that start-up costs are significantly lower if you are a sole proprietor of a home-based business when compared to opening a retail business, which involves renting a public space, hiring staff and having inventory. The more successful retail-oriented entrepreneurs, if they can, start from home as a means to test the market before creating a retail presence. They do this specifically to keep costs low and manage their own expectations in terms of demand.

2. People who can work from home or who run home-based businesses generally have identified a market need and provide a service that responds to that need whereas the retail and restaurant group, by and large, start a business to provide a service that they (and their friends) want. A lot of successful retail businesses grow from the idea of what someone wants, but you need to do your market research before you launch that cupcake outlet or designer swimwear collection. Just because a particular idea appeals to you and your closest friends, it doesn't mean that it will be a viable business venture.

3. Of the retail and/or restaurant group that is successful, the success appears to come from the entrepreneur's ability to establish a niche concept that caters to a very specific audience and being able to charge a premium for their product. They also generally have the right location to attract this audience. So they are immediately identified as an "expert" or the "go to store/restaurant" for something unique, and the location is convenient for their target market.

HOW TO START THINKING LIKE A BUSINESS OWNER-TO-BE

There are so many informal businesses being run by women across Asia that it renders statistics meaningless most of the time. According to surveys compiled by MasterCard across

Asia in 2010, female entrepreneurship is growing steadily across much of the region.[1]

Women can and do make great entrepreneurs and make huge contributions to their country's economy. In the United States alone, women own 10.6 million businesses and employ 19.1 million workers—that's one in every seven employees. In addition, their businesses account for US$2.5 trillion in sales.[2]

For the very same reasons why they can make great investors, women make great entrepreneurs because, by and large, they are practical consumers and are cautious with their cash flow. Here are some statistics that represent all US small businesses (owned by men and women):[3]

- 93% have revenues below $250,000.
- 57% make revenue under $25,000.
- 51% are based at home.
- 63% are sole proprietorships (they have no other employees).
- 85% of these businesses fail in the first year (this figure decreases the longer you can remain in business).

What these statistics show is that starting a business is easy; having it be successful over the long run is not as easy. Here are some tips on how to begin envisaging your new venture and some pitfalls to avoid.

1 www.masterintelligence.com/asset/upload/252/179/MC84-WomenSME-S.pdf
2 www.entrepreneur.com/sbe/women/index.html
3 www.census.gov/

Put Your Own House in Order First

Honestly, even if your divorce has left you with hundreds of millions of dollars, sit down and create a financial plan for yourself based on how you think you would like to live for the rest of your life. It is even more important to do this if you have never had to dabble in your own finances until now and/or you have dependents for whom you need to provide.

I have seen women with eight-figure settlements (that's at least $10,000,000) who somehow managed to spend most of it on failed business endeavours. Now they are stuck trying to understand exactly how to manage the amount that they have left. Make your financial well-being as a family your first priority.

No Two Businesses Look Alike

There are millions of businesses that may not fit your impression of what a business should be. The lady who walks dogs for absentee pet owners has a business. So does the woman teaching art out of her condo, the freelance yoga teacher and the piano teacher who works out of her tiny flat and is paid under the table by her students. These are all businesses and they are all run by women who needed to create cash flow for themselves.

If you need to be at home more often than not because you have young children or other commitments, find a business that will allow you flexibility in time and schedule. There are no rules as to what a business should look like. As long as you are making money consistently every month, you have a business!

Humble Starts Can Make for Fabulous Finishes

Many a great business started from a humble idea. It's often the simple desire to offer a better product or service than what is currently on the market. Look no further than Mrs. Fields Cookies, Liquid Paper, Post-it Notes and many popular retail brands such as The Body Shop, Crocs and Nike. Most of the entrepreneurs behind these concepts started at home, and they created either an entirely unique product or a product with a distinctive value proposition and a competitive advantage.

It Takes 1,000 Days

Most businesses take around 1,000 days from the day you are "open for business" to knowing whether you have a financially viable business or not. Plan your money for 1,000 days at a minimum and be patient while you are impatient!

Think Big but Start Small

Many entrepreneurs have other jobs or start working from home to keep expenses low. Starting small, i.e. working from home and making a positive cash flow, is better than renting retail or office space and having a consistently negative cash flow. Once you understand the demand for your product or service, you can always expand. It's much easier to start small and expand a business than to start big, commit to leases and employees, then find that you need to lay off employees or downsize to a smaller space. Having to contract your operations hurts morale, is harder psychologically and can damage your brand.

Whatever Amount You Think You Need to Start, Double It

The best advice I was given when starting my business was to plan on spending about twice as much as I had budgeted for in order to get it off the ground. Undercapitalisation (not having enough money) is the number one reason why many businesses fail. Just like there is no shame in starting your business from your home, there is no shame in starting on a shoestring budget. I'm not inferring that you need a lot of money, just that you generally will need more than you might think to launch a business.

Define Success in Financially Relevant Terms

I've seen people talk about the many parameters in their mind which they use to measure the success of their business: a successful launch, really positive feedback, a great product, a great logo, good advertising, etc. Ultimately though, you need to ask, "Does this make more money than I spend in the course of doing this business?" and "Does this make enough money to be a viable way to make a living for myself?"

In the same way that I told you in Chapter 9 to invest in businesses with good cash flow prospects, for you to succeed in your own business, you need to consistently generate positive cash flow. Eventually this cash flow will become large enough to enable you to create a healthy salary for yourself, and then employ others if you need to. You may be able to achieve this in a few months or it may take 1,000 days or more. The point is that a business is about creating positive cash flow—it's quantitative, not qualitative.

Create a Business Plan and Have It Vetted by Business People, Not Friends

I love my friends but they would be the last group of people I'd ask to vet my business plan, unless they were business owners and had experience running a business in my chosen field. Friends will always be supportive, and good friends may point out one or two problems with whatever idea you have. However, you really need to seek the advice of a neutral party when putting together a serious business plan for a serious idea. You may get feedback that you do not want to hear or that you do not want to take on board but at least you know the feedback came from a neutral third party.

Create a Product or Service for a Market, Not Just Your Social Circle

Many retail businesses fail because people create products and services for themselves or their social circle. This generally means that the market was not researched well enough, and the market size and market reach projections were too ambitious or too optimistic. If you think the potential market is 100,000 people, there's a good chance that you may reach only 5% of this market at first, or much less.

Some cities such as Hong Kong and Singapore make it very easy to start a small business and encourage individuals to do so. Great resources to tap into are professional women's organisations, such as the Singapore Association of Professional Women and the Business and Professional Women's Association of Hong Kong, as these will help you network with other women entrepreneurs. At the end of the day, however, the motivation, inspiration and leadership to run your business has to come from you.

A Settled Mother Means Settled Children

No matter which route you choose to take in terms of education or a new business venture, if you have children, don't dive into anything new until they are back into a routine. School-age children in general need a lot of attention and reassurance from their primary caregiver and this is especially true before, during and after divorce.

As far as possible, it is better to wait until your children are settled emotionally and back in some sort of routine at school and with homework before you start anything as you will then have more time and energy to focus on your studies or your business. Remember to explain to your children why you have chosen to go back to school or start a business, and how it will help the family as a whole. Being on time and being fully present for children is a necessity. If you are only available certain hours of the day to help them or spend quality time with them, they will know they can count on you during these periods and they will understand when you need to focus on your own work.

CONCLUSION

I've never underestimated the strengths and resourcefulness of women who know what they are entitled to, own their decisions and have a desire to control their financial future. I would like to end this chapter, and by extension the book, with a story that illustrates the strength and resourcefulness of one such person.

A friend of mine took time off from a well-established career to marry and follow her husband to another country so he could advance his career. Months of early retirement turned to years, and then she became a mother. She gave birth to a beautiful daughter who was born with special needs. A few years later, my friend divorced. She was very much left to fend for herself and her daughter in a country that was not her own.

Amid the shock of divorce and in the absence of any safety net, she was left to meander through byzantine systems of healthcare and education options to find people to help her daughter develop physically and intellectually. In her quest for clarity, she compiled a directory of healthcare and education resources and read everything she possibly could about children with special needs, becoming more knowledgeable than many of the professionals she met working in this field. She logged hundreds of hours reading, reviewing, observing and challenging a lot of what she was told were the best practices for special needs children.

She came to realise over the years of caring for her own special needs child that this was something she had become excellent at doing and that she should retrain herself and develop a career in this field. This was a brilliant life move. Not only did she decide to use her first-hand experience, but she also tapped into a situation where there was a growing demand for trained, qualified and certified professionals to work with special needs children in Asia. She re-educated herself and became an entrepreneur. Today, she is not only surviving but thriving!

Her story reminds me of this saying: "Sometimes the wrong choices bring us to the right places."

APPENDIX 1

Divorce— The Legal Procedure

The following was drafted by a lawyer but is for information purposes only and is not a substitute for legal advice.

Regardless of the circumstances surrounding your divorce, the divorce process itself is often one of the most stressful times in your life and it is common for women to feel varying—sometimes extreme—emotions at different times throughout the proceedings. As much as possible though, you should put any such emotions to one side. Although many divorces are neither quick nor smooth sailing, it is best to realise that reaching a divorce settlement is more like a business deal than anything else. The best divorce is quick and fair, allowing you to get on with your life and minimise your legal costs. In order to get a divorce, an application must be made to court. This is basically a document stating you are divorcing and lists all the issues it involves. There will be different filings, or applications, for child custody, finances and so on. In the end, you get a settlement through a court order. This court order is a legally binding decision as to who gets what and it can be legally enforced.

It is important to remember that it is your lawyer's responsibility to navigate you to the best settlement possible. However, in order to understand how to live on the money you receive in your settlement, you will need to look beyond your legal team. The chapters in the main part of this book will serve as a practical step-by-step guide as how to do this.

Here, I aim to let you know broadly what happens in the course of a divorce settlement and will cover some of the key issues related to your rights regarding what you are entitled to during the divorce. The information given here is based on the law in Hong Kong as it follows British common law which, in general, is the foundation for the laws of many jurisdictions in Asia.

THE STEPS OF DIVORCE

The steps of divorce, or the procedure, depend on which jurisdiction you are in but broadly fall into three main categories: the divorce suit (the actual divorce), the children (if any) and the finances. In short, you are required to make an application for everything you need in the divorce suit but you cannot get your divorce settlement until the arrangements pertaining to the children and the finances are sorted.

Therefore, the divorce normally proceeds in this order:

1. File for divorce
2. Sort out child custody
3. Sort out the finances
4. Get your divorce settlement

It is important to point out that you are unlikely to get a financial settlement until the judge is happy about the arrangements for the children, if there are children.

The above applications and the procedures they trigger happen concurrently but for the sake of simplicity each is addressed separately here.

PRELIMINARY MATTERS

There are a number of preliminary matters that are important to understand. These include questions as to forum, or where you file for your divorce, how to finance your case and which divorce option best suits you.

Forum—Where to File

It is outside the scope of this book to look at all the different jurisdictions and compare them. However, here are the rules of thumb as to where you can file for divorce:

- In most jurisdictions, you can file for divorce if you are resident in that country or, in the case of Hong Kong, you have a substantial connection to that country. For example, an English woman living in Hong Kong can choose to file in either England or Hong Kong.

- If you live, work and own property in more than one jurisdiction, you will have a valid question as to where to file.

- Just getting married in a country is generally not enough to file for divorce there.

Differing Forums

Here are some examples of how forums differ as at the time of writing:

- England has earned a reputation as the "divorce capital of the world" due to its starting point of 50% for the distribution of capital (this means "whatever is in the matrimonial pot less any debts"). Hong Kong follows this approach. Therefore, Hong Kong, England and, by extension, Wales are seen to be more favourable to the non-breadwinner.

- In Australia, the concept of contribution (or who has contributed what to the household) is very important, more so than the concept of equality, and all property will be taken into account.

- In Singapore, pre-marital property, unless it is the matrimonial home, will not normally be taken into account. In addition, there is the Women's Charter which can benefit or curtail your settlement depending on the length of time you have been married.

- In China, there is a distinction between property owned jointly and separately. The court there will consider the parties' contributions, each party's needs and conduct.

- In the United States, divorce is governed by each individual state. Very broadly, the states are divided between "community property" states, which follow the principle of a 50% division of all marital property, and "equitable law or common law" states, which provide that, in the absence of agreement, the courts follow a fair but not necessarily equal distribution.

Financing Your Divorce

Lawyers charge by the hour and do not work for a cut of the winnings (known as contingency). You will have to pay a retention fee once you have chosen your lawyer. Then you will be given monthly bills, which will be itemised, so you can see what has been spent.

At the end of the case, you normally agree how your fees (the total amount of all the monthly bills) will be paid with the other party as part of the settlement. Either you each pay your own fees out of your division of assets or your spouse may be ordered to pay your costs or you may be ordered to pay his, whichever is appropriate.

LEGAL AID

Most countries will offer some sort of legal aid. As this varies from one country to another, it is best to check the rules applicable in your country. Some legal aid offices are listed in "Resources" on pages 369–376.

Not all law firms will do legal aid work so check beforehand with the firm that you want to represent you or have already chosen if you are going to rely on legal aid. Be prepared to be rejected for legal aid if you have any property, including joint property. Lastly, legal aid is not free in most cases so be prepared to pay a contribution towards the costs of the work done to the legal aid office once your settlement has been reached.

Borrow

You can get a loan from the bank or from a friend, which can be declared and recognised as one of your liabilities. If you borrow from a friend, make sure that the terms of your loan are formal and you are paying proper interest. This is to avoid your loan being mistaken for a gift, as it will then become an asset in the matrimonial pot.

Create a Fighting Fund

Putting aside a "fighting fund" from the matrimonial assets is allowed, and the judge may even make provision for it if you make an application for interim maintenance (support). This is likely in a case where the husband has complete control over the bank accounts.

Your Divorce Options

There are a number of ways as to how you proceed with your divorce. You can:

- attend mediation
- represent yourself
- instruct a lawyer
- engage in collaborative law practice

However you decide to proceed with divorce, there is no way a party can avoid the court process altogether. There are ways to minimise your costs and make the process less drawn out (but this will require some cooperation from your soon-to-be ex!).

MEDIATION

Mediation is where both parties attend sessions with an independent mediator jointly appointed by you and your husband. The mediator cannot give legal advice and must be impartial. Their duty is to assist the parties in finding an amicable settlement.

Mediation is becoming increasingly popular as a way to resolve family disputes and is used prior to divorce to help parties settle issues relating to the finances and the children if the parties have separated. Mediation allows for much more detail in the agreement, such as a whole parenting plan, which is unusual in a court order.

Mediation is confidential (so you cannot use what has been said in a court of law later if ultimately mediation breaks down and you end up going to court) so this generally allows the parties to be less guarded and talk more freely. Also, as attendance must be voluntary, both parties have to buy into the process and agree that they will try to settle in this way.

The process normally consists of a joint session during which both parties set out their respective cases, followed by individual sessions with the mediator and then another joint session. Depending on how complicated it all is, this could take a few sessions or last weeks.

It is generally accepted that the mediation process is less expensive than a full-blown court case, although it is fairly common too for both parties to engage and take their respective lawyers into the mediation sessions. This can give them a feeling of comfort knowing they have their legal advisers on hand.

A word of warning: If you go for this option, choose someone who has a track record for being a good mediator, especially if there is a difficult husband involved who has a history of not fulfilling promises. I have come across several women deeply disappointed with their mediators and the final outcome.

Represent Yourself

It is always an option to represent yourself and file for a divorce without any legal representation. If everything is very straightforward, if you have a settlement ready to go which you sorted out through mediation and if you are comfortable with the arrangements, then this is an example of when you can represent yourself.

However, if your husband has a lawyer or there is any degree of complexity, in terms of financial or child arrangements, you are better off getting an agreement checked over by a lawyer. It is very difficult to change a court order once it is handed down.

Instruct a Lawyer

This is still the way divorce is handled in the majority of cases. The costs vary enormously from case to case. If you and your spouse can come to a quick agreement and your case is simple, your lawyers will help you negotiate a settlement early in the process and this will keep down the costs. However, if there is much acrimony and disagreement and there are many applications that must be made—to protect assets (injunctions, undertakings, etc.), award custody and so on—the costs will rise.

As already mentioned, most lawyers charge by the hour, and good law firms will send you an interim bill every month so that you can keep track of the charges. In addition, the court insists on seeing a cost estimate before each court hearing so you will not only see your costs but also your husband's. This can be an eye-opener. There is nothing like seeing both sets of costs to focus the mind on settlement. Choose a lawyer who treats you with dignity and with whom you can discuss the issues in this chapter. Make sure too that you get a feel for not only the overall costs but also insist these costs be itemised to enable you to scrutinise them.

COLLABORATIVE LAW PRACTICE

This concept is relatively new, especially in Asia, but it is worth finding out if your lawyer is qualified to conduct a collaborative law case. In this scenario, the lawyers agree to help their respective clients reach an amicable settlement, and they may get other professionals, such as psychologists and child specialists, to join the collaborative "team".

Like mediation, it is all about finding an amicable solution in a non-adversarial environment. Taking this route can be better for everyone in the long run, especially the children. As with mediation, if you find an early settlement, it will be cheaper than litigation through the courts.

THE DIVORCE PROCEDURE—THE BASICS

Now that we have gone through the options of where and how to divorce, we can move on to the actual divorce procedure. In other words, the basics of the Divorce Suit and issues around reaching a settlement regarding the children and the finances.

THE DIVORCE SUIT

In many jurisdictions, there are a number of facts on which you can rely for a divorce—fault-based facts, such as adultery, unreasonable behaviour and desertion, and no fault-based facts, such as separation with or without consent. In these cases, there is one ground for divorce—that of irretrievable breakdown of the marriage.

As difficult as it may be to hear, particularly if you are on the receiving end of the divorce, it is really not worth fighting over the divorce itself. You can attempt to delay the proceedings if this works in your favour financially speaking, but it's tricky to change someone's heart. So, you can either agree to a separation or agree to go ahead with the divorce. By agreeing to go ahead, it rarely affects what happens with the children or the finances.

If you are not disputing the divorce itself—i.e. both you and your husband agree that divorce is inevitable—you can both choose to make an application for divorce. This is known as a joint application. By doing this, it gets around the question of who is, and who is not, the petitioner (the one who files for divorce) and requires one year's separation by consent.

If you do not want to get divorced, you can skip filing for divorce and settle matters with a Deed of Separation. Of course, if one party still wants to divorce, they can get a divorce after a certain period of being separated, whether or not the other party concurs.

Finally, you can make an application to the court to nullify your marriage if you think, for some reason, you are not legally married or that the marriage should be declared void. This is only common in the Philippines because it means that you must allege some unusual event, such as your husband is already married, you were under age at the time of marriage or your marriage has not been consummated.

The Paper Chase

Below is an example of a normal, step-by-step process in a divorce suit. This example is based on a divorce suit in Hong Kong.

1. DRAFT AND FILE THE PETITION OR WRIT

Divorces in jurisdictions such as England and Hong Kong are brought by filing petitions. In Singapore, it is a Writ of Divorce and the parties are called the plaintiff and defendant. In Hong Kong, they are called the petitioner and the respondent respectively unless a joint application has been made, in which case, they are the applicants.

Depending on the jurisdiction, the grounds for the divorce will vary, as will the papers that need to be filed with it. In Hong Kong and England, the divorce must be filed in court with other documents that explain what is happening and what you hope will happen to the children. Your petition should also include an application for all the financial relief you are seeking, as well as your application for custody of the children.

2. SERVE THE PETITION

The papers, once filed at court, then get served on your spouse, which means that someone has to hand them to him. It is not okay to give your husband divorce papers in person; the papers need to be served by a third party. If you have been served divorce papers, it's best to contact a lawyer to understand your options in terms of representation.

3. REPLYING TO THE PAPERS

Once you have served your spouse, he has 14 days to reply and tell the court (and you) that he does or does not intend to defend the divorce case itself. He can also say if he plans to contest the application for the finances and the children.

If you are on the receiving end and it's not amicable, you need to see a lawyer as soon as possible. If you do not reply within 14 days, the court may assume that the divorce is not contested and set a date for the decree nisi (or interim judgment in Singapore).

4. THE DECREE NISI

The decree nisi is the first stage of the divorce process. This hearing only deals with the divorce itself, and you need not attend. In the least acrimonious cases, the parties file what has been agreed at the same time as the divorce papers. In such cases, there will be no preliminary hearing date set by the court.

If there are any disputes over children or the finances, all parties are expected to turn up to the next hearing, which is the preliminary hearing, also called the First Appointment, or the Status Conference in Singapore.

Before you attend the preliminary hearing, you will need to go through the discovery process. "Discovery" is the word used for the gathering of documents that prove to the court and the other side what assets you have. The parties must file and exchange these financial statements nearly a month or more before the preliminary hearing. In Hong Kong, it's 28 days before the preliminary hearing. However, it can be 35 days or more in other jurisdictions.

Each party's financial statements are the main source of information for the judge to work out what is in the matrimonial pot. Each party must declare here what they own solely and jointly. This is a very important document, and it may well be that your husband has not disclosed everything he owns either jointly or solely (if applicable, it is more likely to be the latter). Refer to Chapter 2 for more on this.

5. THE PRELIMINARY HEARING

The preliminary hearing is designed to let the court know what the main issues are at stake, and for your lawyer to summarise these to the judge. Although the parties do not normally say anything, the idea is that everyone comes to court in an attempt to narrow down the issues at stake. It is even hoped that a settlement can be reached at court when all the parties are present.

If you feel that the financial information that has been exchanged during the discovery process is incomplete, i.e. there are hidden assets or properties that have not been accounted for, this is the time when you should ask the court for more information.

6. INTERIM CUSTODY

If the arrangements for the children are not settled, the judge will set a date for an interim custody hearing to sort out who the children will live with (known as custody in Hong Kong and Singapore) and who has the visiting rights (known as access in Hong Kong and Singapore).

THE CHILDREN

The court will not look in detail at your finances until the children's issues are settled. This is because who has the children will have a great financial burden on a day-to-day basis, and caring for young children will affect a person's ability to work.

DOS WITH CHILDREN DURING DIVORCE

- Do keep the children as your priority at all times. It is hard to see the forest from the trees sometimes but be sure that the court will be looking at their interests above yours—it is the judge's duty to do so.
- Do keep a record of your children's schedules, be organised and be aware of how much time you spend with them.
- Do make sure that the children's routines are not disrupted. Attendance at school, going to friends' houses, extracurricular activities and so on should go on as normal.
- Do be civil to the other party at all times in front of your children.
- Do draw up a comprehensive parenting plan, which includes time with the other parent. It's only in rare cases (where abuse is involved) when this isn't appropriate.
- Do consider the position of your soon-to-be-ex-spouse by keeping him informed.
- Do get the other party's written consent before holidaying outside the country.

DON'TS WITH CHILDREN DURING DIVORCE

- Don't discuss the case with your children; they are not your new best friends.
- Don't try to influence the children to stay with you.
- Don't denigrate the other parent in front of, or to, your children.

- Don't be selfish—the decision to divorce is not theirs.
- Don't spoil them either!
- Don't take your children to another country without first getting the other parent's consent. They can be brought back under the Hague Convention.
- Don't put your children through multiple interviews with child psychologists. Choose one and try to stick to that one expert if you opt to go down this road.

If Custody Is Contested

If custody is contested, you will need to prepare for a custody hearing that involves a few steps, namely a social welfare report, possibly the judge interviewing your children and then the hearing itself.

The social welfare report, which will be ordered by the court, is very important to the court, but the judge is not bound by it. This involves a visit to the social welfare office by each of the parties, and then a visit by the social welfare officer to each of your homes. The social welfare officer will interview you, the children and possibly teachers and the domestic helper if you have one.

In addition, your judge may want to interview the children but this varies from judge to judge. Increasingly, the voice of the child is seen to be of value but it may not be the deciding factor. To prepare for the hearing, if so advised, you can call witnesses, such as family members, friends and teachers, to give evidence on your behalf. Keep these to a minimum—they can be of limited usefulness and only prolong the hearing, which will increase the costs without much real advantage. You can also call experts, such as child psychologists, to give evidence.

At the child custody hearing, there will be examination and cross-examination of both parties as well as the experts. Preparing for a court hearing is very time-consuming and you may even find that instructing a barrister may be the most cost-effective way (although their fees make your eyes water) as they are experts in cross-examination.

THE FINANCES

With luck, you will have resolved your divorce and your children before the battle over finances begins.

DOS WITH FINANCES

- Do be aware of what your husband has in his sole name and follow the advice given in Chapter 2.
- Do keep track of your spending and keep receipts and bank statements.
- Do be prepared for legal advice to possibly change as you discover more about the family finances.
- Do keep working if you are employed.
- Do consider that if you have a new partner, his assets and income may be relevant, particularly if you are cohabiting.

- Do give your legal team what they need and what they ask for—nothing more.

Don'ts with Finances

- Don't be disorganised, it will ultimately increase your legal costs.
- Don't think you will "take him to the cleaners", even if you feel you are the victim of betrayal or worse. The courts are not generally that interested in your husband's uncouth or unfaithful behaviour unless it directly relates to the state of the family finances, i.e. he is a compulsive gambler who has frittered everything away or he has hidden assets.
- **Don't panic, it's a long process.**

The Procedure for Settling the Finances

Once each party exchanges financial information with the other side, go through your husband's financial disclosure to see if there is anything missing or otherwise worthy of note and tell your lawyer (or the mediator). You will have to attend the preliminary hearing and ask for further documents if anything is missing. It's a good idea to ask for a valuation of property and jointly instruct an agent to split the fee between you and your husband.

If you are content that everything has been disclosed, start settlement negotiations. Your lawyer should send your spouse a letter "without prejudice save as to costs" so you can show the court that you tried to settle early. This might result in your husband paying all your costs from the moment of that letter, so please do bear this in mind.

You will continue with this process at the settlement hearing at court. This hearing is like mediation but, instead of a mediator, you have a judge. If you fail to settle at the settlement hearing, you will proceed to trial. You will be given a different judge for the trial as the judge at the settlement hearing will have seen all the "without prejudice" settlement letters. Continue settlement negotiations all the time.

You may need to get a barrister for the trial. It is worthwhile pointing out here that the comments made regarding a child custody hearing also apply here. It is often the case that you have further incentive to settle when you get an idea of the barrister's brief fee. Think about the fact that this is double trouble—your husband will no doubt have a barrister too, so double the fee to get a minimum idea of the total costs coming out of your family assets.

If you go to trial, you will be cross-examined by your husband's lawyer about everything you are fighting over. During your cross-examination, you will not be able to talk to your legal advisers. Your lawyer will cross-examine your husband. Depending on the complexity of your case, cross-examination can take half a day or many days.

In the end, once the judgment has been given by the court, and all issues relating to the children have been settled, your lawyer will apply for decree absolute. The decree absolute is the legal document that ends your marriage. The application should be straightforward by this stage and will only take a short time. The person who filed for the divorce makes this application.

THE SETTLEMENT: KEEP YOUR EXPECTATIONS REAL

Once you have come to terms with the thought that life may be harder financially post-divorce, the big question is normally, How much will I get in the end?

Clients get frustrated with the vague answers that they get from their lawyers. There is never a straightforward answer because the final settlement decision depends on a number of factors and is up to the discretion of the judge. The seven factors listed below are what a judge in Hong Kong and England must look at in order to make a fair division of assets. Similar considerations exist in most jurisdictions.

How the Judge Views It

- Your family resources, including family income, the earning capacity of both parties and property solely and jointly owned now and in the foreseeable future (so next year's bonus, a big imminent inheritance, even damages in a court case will be taken into account)

- Your family needs, including obligations to all dependants (which could include elderly parents), as well as what you will need to maintain yourself
- Your family's standard of living
- Your ages and the length of the marriage
- If you or your children have any disability
- Contributions by both parties to the welfare of the family
- Any loss of benefit as a result of divorce, such as loss of pension rights

Do note that the judge, as already said, will rarely take into account bad conduct—unless it is "gross" (this is a technical term that refers to extensive physical abuse or criminal behaviour)—so it is wise not to get sidetracked with "who had the affair first" type of thinking. If your husband has been transferring assets out of the marriage and hiding them, and this is uncovered during the discovery process, the judge will most likely charge him with the costs of that particular discovery process. However, it does not mean you will be awarded all the assets that are discovered.

LENGTH OF MARRIAGE RULES OF THUMB

As stated above, the length of marriage has significant relevance to the judge's final ruling regarding the finances. Below is an indicator of what you may be awarded in the final settlement based on how long you have been married and whether you have children.

- A long marriage with children (over 30 years in Singapore but less in other jurisdictions): Your likely starting position is 50% of the capital (i.e. all your assets less debt) plus maintenance as well as maintenance for the children.

- A short childless marriage (less than 10 years): You will most likely be awarded a small percentage of the capital to re-establish yourself, with possibly very little or no maintenance.

- A very wealthy couple who has been married for some time: Although there is a starting point of 50%, in the end, it is likely that the spouse of a very wealthy breadwinner will not obtain an award of 50% of the matrimonial assets due to many considerations.

- A couple of modest means: It is likely that the wife in this situation may get more than 50% if that is what it takes to maintain her and the children with a comparable lifestyle, in particular if this involves her retaining the matrimonial home.

INTERPRETING CONTRIBUTION

In legal terms, "contribution" refers not only to what the breadwinner makes but specifically includes any contribution made by looking after the home or caring for the family. Therefore, the court recognises that being a homemaker, in most cases, is as valuable as being a breadwinner.

The compensation concept works on the principle that you have given up something of value, such as a career, for the greater good of the family during marriage. By raising this argument, you are asking the court to recognise and compensate this in the divorce settlement. This may be particularly relevant to a spouse who agreed to give up her job to follow her husband overseas. It is also relevant to career women who made a joint decision with their husbands to give up work to care for young children.

Contribution is at the heart of the other very important factors in divorce, namely age of the parties and length of the marriage. A couple nearing retirement will have very different priorities to a young couple. An older couple needs to take into account retirement issues and the cessation of income. In contrast, a young wife's priorities will normally be how she will survive if she has young children and how her earning capacity has been compromised.

As stated, the court generally will start from equality, i.e. a 50/50 split, but then make adjustments bearing in mind contribution, compensation, age of the parties, the length of the marriage, standard of living and needs. These adjustments could take you over or under the 50% mark. The judge will often try to achieve fairness by means of a mixed award of capital and income, i.e. a lump sum of money and/or transfer of a property to you as well as monthly maintenance, or alimony.

Settlements: Lump Sum or Maintenance?

If given the option, most wives do not relish the idea of being dependent on their ex-husbands for their ongoing financial survival, although some do not have a choice. Courts generally will encourage a clean break if there is enough money to ensure future financial security. It may be that agreeing to a clean break at a sum greater than 50% is achievable.

If you agree to a clean break with no monthly maintenance, you are banned from making any future claim. That's it. So, another option is to go for nominal maintenance, even $1 can be requested as nominal maintenance. This may be ordered by the court if the judge thinks that you do not need monthly maintenance but will allow you to make a future claim if necessary. If you opt for nominal maintenance, you can always apply to the court for an increase at any time.

Before you make a final decision, it is worth spending time with a certified financial planner to understand the financial ramifications of your decision, such as how to live off a lump sum payment. Too much time and money is spent on just reaching a settlement and not nearly enough time is spent on understanding how to live off your divorce settlement.

CHOOSING MAINTENANCE: WHAT TO EXPECT

In cases of maintenance, the judge will make two orders, one for the spouse and one for the children. This is because there are different rules that govern how long the orders last. Do note that the judge will look at the children's needs separately from yours.

In your case, the judge's starting point is equality. One party should not leave the marriage much poorer than the other. That said, if you can work, you are expected to do so—this goes for both parties. Husbands who threaten to stop work to avoid paying maintenance will be viewed unfavourably and will be deemed to have an income anyway.

The judge will look at your monthly expenses during the marriage (that's why you have to keep track of them when you are preparing for divorce) and balance these against what your husband says he can afford. The judge will not be impressed if one party's expenses are much higher than the other's or they look very high in the context of his income.

If you have a very high standard of living, and can show that this has been met comfortably over the years, you should expect a reasonable monthly maintenance. This is true even if the lifestyle has been met by a family business and it has been difficult to show where the income is coming from.

If you receive maintenance, it will last for your life or until you remarry. Maintenance will automatically terminate on remarriage.

CHILD SUPPORT

Orders for maintenance on behalf of a child normally last until a child is 18 or until they finish full-time education, whichever is later. There is no such thing as a clean break where children are involved. You can always make an application to court to maintain a grown-up child if necessary, especially if there is significant disability involved.

Child maintenance consists of the child's basic monthly needs in terms of their share of food, rent and utilities, medical and dental expenses and incidental school expenses and extracurricular activities. Other major expenses, such as school or university fees, are often dealt with by way of a separate agreement within the settlement agreement.

INFLATION AND INSURANCE: SAFEGUARDING YOUR PAYMENTS

It is advisable to get safeguards for maintenance included in a settlement. Get the maintenance payments linked to an inflation index so that, 10 years down the road, your monthly maintenance will not be worth substantially less than what was intended.

In addition, your maintenance will cease when you die (fair enough) but if your husband dies, you will still need money from somewhere in place of the maintenance you had been counting on receiving. To avoid making a claim against his estate (which can be expensive), think about getting your monthly payments protected with life insurance on his life. This should be an irrevocable life insurance policy, where you are the policyholder and make the payments (out of your maintenance) to ensure the policy remains in force. It is usually laid out in the final settlement that this type of policy is taken up or if one exists that it remains in force with you as the beneficiary and policyholder.

APPENDIX 2

A Word on Risk and Return

There is always the assumption that the more risk you take, the more return you will get. For example, stocks, which are thought to be riskier than bonds, will generally outperform bonds, smaller companies—perceived as riskier—will generally outperform larger companies and developing countries, like Indonesia, the Philippines and Brazil, will generally outperform developed countries, such as the United States, Europe and Japan.

To illustrate using one market, in Singapore over the last 10 years, the Straits Times Index has shown annualised price gains of 9.23%, including dividends, while property has only returned 6.04% over the same time frame.[1] Regional bond fund returns have averaged between 3 and 4%. Stocks have experienced more volatility (thus are perceived as a riskier investment) and, in fact, the return has been better compared to bonds and property in this time frame.

Given shorter time frames however, a very different picture can emerge with regard to risk and return. From 2008 to 2013,

---

1 *Straits Times*, "Property vs Stocks—It's a matter of timeframe", 9 July 2012.

the US stock market has outperformed emerging China, boring Walmart, SingTel and Power Assets Holdings have outperformed high-flying Facebook and, over the last 10 years, dull US treasury bonds have outperformed the US stock market as shown below:

Time Frame	Stocks	T-bills (3-month short-term bonds)	Treasury Bonds (10-year bonds)
1928–2011	9.23%	3.61%	5.14%
1962–2001	9.20%	5.19%	6.85%
2002–2011	2.88%	1.80%	6.49%

Source: http://people.stern.nyu.edu/adamodar/New_Home_Page/datafile/histret.html

Being at ease with risk and return is to recognise that even though much historical data is used to rationalise many investment decisions, what has happened historically may not hold true in the future. No one can predict the future prices of any asset because no one can accurately account for all the uncertainty that exists in the world. This means that the assumptions underpinning much of modern finance are just that—assumptions with a fairly good track record so far.

APPENDIX 3

Using a Financial Calculator

Although you can buy any financial calculator, the instructions given below are following the Texas Instrument BA II Plus Calculator, which I have found to be the easiest to use. Here are the meanings of the fields:

- N=time period (can be hourly to annually)
- I/Y=interest or inflation (depending on the calculation)
- PV=Present Value
- PMT=Payment
- FV=Future Value
- Yellow button tagged "2nd"—You need to use this button in conjunction with other inputs to make sure you are calculating if your payments are at the beginning or at the end of a time frame.

RETIREMENT PLANNING FROM CHAPTER 6
1. Real Return (or "Adjusted for Inflation" Return)
Nominal Return is 8%.
Inflation is 3%.

Enter 1.08

Divide by 1.03

Subtract by 1

Multiply by 100

Answer: 4.85

4.85% is the real return in this scenario.

2. Maria's Bali Retirement

Maria's current age: 40

Maria's retirement projected age: 62.

Maria has (62-40=22) 22 years until retirement.

Inflation will be estimated at 2% per year on average.

Maria's after inflation return in retirement is 2% per year on
average.

Step 1. Maria's monthly cost of living would be S$1,750 today
if she were in Bali. Next, we need to find out her monthly cost
of living in 22 years' time.

Enter 1,750 into PV

Enter 22 into N

Enter 0 into PMT

Enter 2 into I/Y (this accounts for inflation)

Hit CPT and then FV.

The answer is 2,705.

This means that in 22 years' time, Maria's cost of living
each month will have risen from S$1,750 to S$2,705 due to
the effect of inflation.

Step 2. Multiply 2,705 by 12 = 32,465. This is Maria's annual cost of living 22 years from now under the Bali scenario.

Step 3. Maria's life span is projected to be until 90 years of age so she needs a nest egg that will support her for (90-62=28) 28 years.

Step 4. Calculate the nest egg that Maria needs given her 2% real investment return after retirement.

Hit the Yellow 2nd button followed by the PMT button (which has BGN at the top of it). END may appear. If it does, you need to tap on the ENTER button on the top row. Then tap on the 2nd button again until you see BGN. This is necessary as your money is drawn at the beginning of the time period.

Enter -32,465 into PMT (it's negative because you are spending it)

Enter 28 into N

Enter 2 into I/Y (this now accounts for your returns on your nest egg after retirement)

Enter 0 into FV

Hit CPT and then PV.

The answer is 704,714.

This means that Maria will need a nest egg of S$704,714 to live off by the time she retires if she chooses to retire in Bali.

RESOURCES

DIVORCE, ABUSE AND FAMILY RESOURCES

Hong Kong

- **SoulTalk**

24-hour Hotline: 2659 9910 / 2659 9211

www.soultalk.org

- **Harmony House**

24-hour woman hotline: 2522 0434

Main hotline: 2295 1386

www.harmonyhousehk.org/eng/

- **Association Concerning Sexual Violence Against Women**

RainLily hotline: 2375 5322

Main line: 2392 2569

www.rapecrisiscentre.org.hk/

- **Hong Kong Family Welfare Society Mediation Centre**

Divorce mediation hotline: 2832 9700

www.mediationcentrehk.org/Eng_index.html

- **Hong Kong Single Parents Association**
Hotline: 2338 1303 / 2776 4113

Singapore
- **AWARE (Association of Women for Action and Research)**
Helpline: 1800 774 5935
www.aware.org.sg/

- **National Council of Social Service**
Main line: 6210 2500
Community Chest Hotline: 1800 210 2600
www.ncss.org.sg/social_service/family_services.asp

- **Samaritans of Singapore (SOS)**
24-hour hotline: 1800 221 4444
www.samaritans.org.sg/

LEGAL RESOURCES FOR DIVORCE
Hong Kong
- **The Judiciary of the Hong Kong Special Administrative Region**
www.judiciary.gov.hk/en/crt_services/pphlt/html/divorce.htm

Singapore
- **The Law Society of Singapore**
www.lawsociety.org.sg/forPublic/YoutheLaw/Divorce.aspx

LEGAL AID

Hong Kong

For more information, go to
www.gov.hk/en/residents/government/legal/advice/advice.htm

• **Hong Kong Federation of Women's Centres**
Women's helpline: 2386 6255
http://womencentre.org.hk/en

Singapore
• **Legal Aid Bureau**
Tel: 1800 325 1424
E-mail: Lab_enquiery@lab.gov.sg
www.lab.gov.sg

• **Singapore Association of Women Lawyers**
Tel: 6837 0611
www.sawl.org.sg/legal-clinics.html

• **The Law Society of Singapore**
Tel: 6536 0650
E-mail: ProBonoServices@lawsoc.org.sg
http://probono.lawsociety.org.sg/Help-for-Public/personal-legal-issue/CommunityLegalClinic/
* You can also register at any Family Service Centre

PSYCHOLOGICAL COUNSELLING RESOURCES

Hong Kong

• **Hong Kong Federation of Women's Centres**

Women's helpline: 2386 6255

http://womencentre.org.hk/en

• **The Mental Health Association of Hong Kong**

Tel: 2528 0196

www.mhahk.org.hk/chi/index.htm

Singapore

• **Singapore Association for Mental Health (SAMH)**

Helpline: 1800 283 7019

www.samhealth.org.sg/

CREDIT COUNSELLING RESOURCES

Hong Kong

• **Caritas Family Crisis Support Centre**

http://fcsc.caritas.org.hk

Singapore

• **Credit Counselling Singapore**

Hotline: 1800 225 5227

Main line: 6338 2663

www.ccs.org.sg/

FINANCIAL REGULATORY WEBSITES

Hong Kong

• **Securities and Futures Commission (SFC)**

www.sfc.hk/web/EN/index.html

Singapore

• **Monetary Authority of Singapore (MAS)**

www.mas.gov.sg/

• **Financial Planning Association of Singapore (FPAS)**

www.fpas.org.sg

NOTABLE LISTINGS OF ETFS ON HONG KONG AND SINGAPORE EXCHANGES

Hong Kong

- 2800.HK Tracker Fund of Hong Kong (TraHK)—tracks the Hang Seng Index
- 2801.HK iShares MSCI China Index ETF—tracks the MSCI China Index
- 2802.HK iShares MSCI Emerging Asia Index ETF— tracks the MSCI EM Asia Index
- 2816.HK db x-trackers CSI300 Real Estate Index ETF— tracks the CSI300 Real Estate Index
- 2819.HK ABF HK IDX ETF—tracks the iBoxx ABF Hong Kong Index

- 2821.HK ABF Pan Asia Bond Index Fund—tracks the iBoxx ABF Pan-Asia Index
- 2823.HK iShares FTSE A50 China Index ETF—tracks the FTSE/Xinhua China A50 Index
- 2825.HK W.I.S.E. – CSI HK 100 Tracker—tracks the CSI HK 100 Index
- 2827.HK W.I.S.E. – CSI 300 China Tracker— tracks the CSI 300 Index
- 2828.HK Hang Seng H-Share ETF—tracks the Hang Seng China Enterprises Index
- 2833.HK Hang Seng HSI ETF—tracks the Hang Seng Index
- 2836.HK SENSEXINDIA ETF—tracks the BSE Sensitivity Index
- 2838.HK Hang Seng FTSE/Xinhua China 25 Index ETF—tracks the FTSE/Xinhua China 25 Index
- 2839.HK W.I.S.E. – CSI HK Listed Mainland Real Estate Tracker—tracks the CSI Hong Kong Listed Tradable Mainland Real Estate Index
- 2840.HK SPDR GOLD TRUST—tracks the Gold Price
- 3000.HK HSBC MSCI Hong Kong ETF—tracks the MSCI Hong Kong Index
- 3002.HK Polaris Taiwan Top 50 Tracker Fund—tracks the FTSE TWSE Taiwan 50 Index
- 3024.HK W.I.S.E. – SSE 50 China Tracker—tracks the SSE 50 Index

- 3070.HK Ping An of China CSI HK Dividend ETF— tracks the CSI Hong Kong Dividend Index
- 3072.HK Ping An of China CSI HK Mid Cap Select ETF—tracks the CSI Hong Kong Mid Cap Select Index
- 3083.HK HSBC MSCI Taiwan ETF—tracks the MSCI Taiwan Index
- 3088.HK HSBC MSCI Golden Dragon ETF—tracks the MSCI Golden Dragon Index

Singapore

- CIMB FTSE ASEAN40 ETF
- iShares MSCI India ETF
- Daiwa FTSE Shariah Japan ETF
- Lyxor ETF China Enterprise (HSCEI)
- Lyxor ETF Hong Kong (HSI)
- Lyxor ETF India (S&P CNX Nifty)
- Lyxor ETF Japan (Topix)
- Lyxor ETF MSCI AC Asia-Pacific Ex Japan
- Lyxor ETF MSCI Asia APEX 50
- Lyxor ETF MSCI India
- Lyxor ETF MSCI Korea
- Lyxor ETF MSCI Malaysia
- Lyxor ETF MSCI Taiwan
- Lyxor ETF MSCI Thailand
- Lyxor ETF Reuters/Jefferies CRB Commodities
- Lyxor ETF Commodities Non-Energy

- Lyxor ETF Nasdaq-100
- Lyxor ETF MSCI Emering Markets
- Lyxor ETF MSCI Latin America
- Lyxor ETF Eastern Europe
- Lyxor ETF MSCI World
- streetTRACKS Straits Times Index Fund

Sources: Morningstar to Yahoo! Finance to Wikipedia

BOOKS ON DIVIDEND AND INCOME INVESTING

Peris, Daniel. *The Strategic Dividend Investor.* New York: McGraw-Hill, 2011.

Stooker, Richard. *Income Investing Secrets: How to Receive Ever-Growing Dividend and Interest Checks, Safeguard Your Portfolio and Retire Wealthy.* CreateSpace, 2010.

Thau, Annette. *The Bond Book.* 3rd ed. New York: McGraw-Hill, 2010.

GLOSSARY

annualised returns: the average amount of money earned annually on an investment, which includes the capital gain and income, when measured over time

annuity: a form of insurance or investment entitling the investor to a regular stream of fixed or variable payments

asset: anything you own that has economic value. Your assets can gain or lose value over time. They can also produce income for you.

blue-chip stock: stock in a corporation of long standing that is usually valued in the billions, has a reputation for quality and reliability and, as such, is often a leader in its sector

bond index: a method of tracking and measuring a selection of bond investments

capital gain: the increase in value of an asset less what you originally paid for it. If you sell an asset for more than what you paid for it, you have a "realised capital gain".

compounded returns: cumulative gains (or losses) over a period of time for an investment

consumer discretionary: a sector of the economy that consists of businesses that sell non-essential goods and services

derivative: a financial instrument like options that investors use to speculate on price movements in different assets as opposed to owning the asset itself

dividend: the income you make by holding shares of a company that pays a dividend. The dividend payment is decided by the board of directors and is normally paid quarterly, semi-annually or annually.

dividend aristocrat: a company that generally has a managed dividend growth policy and has increased its dividends for over 25 years in a row

equity or stock market index: a way of measuring a group of stocks that represent parts of a stock market, including the Straits Times Index, the S&P 500, the NASDAQ 100 and the Hang Seng Index. The Dow Jones Industrial Average is an index that follows 30 US blue-chip stocks.

exchange-traded fund (ETF): an ETF is a collective investment in which your money is pooled with others in a fund that tracks or mirrors an index such as a stock index. An ETF is usually passively managed and it does not try to outperform the index it tracks.

expense ratio: (1) the fee that is charged by any fund to its shareholder, including management fees, administrative fees, operating costs, etc. incurred by the fund. This is higher for actively managed fees compared to passive index funds and ETFs. (2) the total cost incurred by investing with an adviser, including their management fee in addition to custodial and fund fees

hedge fund: a private, actively managed investment fund that often requires significant upfront investment and is usually not sold to retail investors due to the advanced trading strategies and the high levels of risk involved

home currency: whatever currency you need to deploy your investments in

hyperinflation: when money is devalued to the point of literally becoming worthless

index investing: collective investments in which your money is pooled with others to track an index, either through a mutual fund (passive index fund) or an ETF. You are not investing in one company but parts of every company that comprises this index. You can also invest in bond index funds.

investment horizon: the length of time an investment is held to meet an investment goal

liquid asset: any asset that can usually be sold and converted to cash quickly

maturity: the end of a loan term

money market fund: a type of cash mutual fund that is generally not guaranteed by any government deposit insurance but earns higher rates of return than an ordinary savings account. These mutual funds generally invest in only the highest rated government debt and are usually highly liquid.

nominal return: a stated return before factoring in inflation

passive index fund: a collective investment in which your money is pooled with others in a fund to track a specific index or sector. Passive index funds are managed passively, with no active trading. Passive index funds are valued by their net asset value (NAV), which is computed once a day, based on the closing market prices of the holdings in the fund's portfolio.

personal balance sheet: a spreadsheet or list that shows a combination of your assets (things that you own) and your liabilities (anything that you owe in the form of debt) and is used to find your net worth

personal cash flow: your income minus your fixed and variable expenses. This can be measured, monthly, quarterly or annually.

personal net worth: your assets minus your liabilities

probate: the legal process of proving a will and administering the deceased's estate

real estate investment trust (REIT): a type of collective investment in which your money is pooled with others to invest, via a stock exchange, in different types of property and/or mortgage assets

real return: a stated return that factors in inflation; also called "inflation adjusted return"

rebalancing: the act of buying and/or selling assets to bring your portfolio back in line with its original allocation

savings ratio: the monthly income that is being saved every month or year as a percentage of your total income

speculation: often a short-term investment made for a large pay-off in capital gain

tax sheltering: a means of legally avoiding tax or minimising income to lower your taxable income

unrealised capital gain: when an asset appreciates in value "on paper" but you have not yet sold that asset for cash; also known as "paper gains"

yield: yield is measured by the cash or income you earn on an investment. There are many types of yield for a wide range of investments. A simple calculation of yield is the cash or income you expect to receive in a year divided by the price of the asset.

BIBLIOGRAPHY

Aubele, Teresa, Doug Freeman, Lee Hausner and Susan Reynolds. *Train Your Brain to Get Rich.* Advantage Quest Publications edition 2012 by arrangement with Adams Media: Avon, MA.

Bernstein, William J. *The Four Pillars of Investing.* New York: Mc-Graw Hill, 2010.

Fisher, Ken. *Debunkery.* New Jersey: John Wiley & Sons, 2011.

Fisher, Ken. *How to Smell a Rat.* New Jersey: John Wiley & Sons, 2009.

Goldie, Daniel C. and Gordon S. Murray. *The Investment Answer.* New York: Hachette Book Group, 2011.

Klontz, Brad and Ted Klontz. *Mind over Money: Overcoming the Money Disorders That Threaten Our Financial Health.* New York: Crown Publishing Group, 2010.

Lofton, LouAnn. *Warren Buffett Invests Like a Girl And Why You Should, Too.* New York: Harper Business, 2011.

Orman, Suze. *Women & Money: Owning the Power to Control Your Destiny.* New York: Spiegel & Grau, 2007.

Peris, Daniel. *The Strategic Dividend Investor.* New York: McGraw-Hill, 2011.

Prins, Nomi. *It Takes a Pillage.* New Jersey: John Wiley & Sons, 2011.

Stanley, Thomas J. and William D. Danko. *The Millionaire Next Door: The Surprising Secrets of America's Wealthy.* New York: Gallery Books, 1998.

Talbott, John R. *The 86 Biggest Lies on Wall Street.* New York: Seven Stories Press, 2009.

ABOUT THE AUTHOR

Currently the principal of Wiser Wealth (www.wiserwealth.net), Andrea Kennedy is an investment manager who has been providing coaching and consultation services to couples, families and professional women for the past decade in Hong Kong, Singapore and Shanghai. Andrea also runs a not-for-profit finance education website—Women on Money—and is frequently interviewed for her perspectives on financial planning and wealth creation for women.

Andrea has a bachelor degree in Psychology and a Master's degree in International Affairs and Economics and is a certified financial planner (CFP). Originally from Chicago, Andrea has lived in Asia for the last 20 years. *Own Your Financial Freedom: Money, Women, Marriage and Divorce* is her first book.